# The Good
# **Trustee Guide**

Published by NCVO
Regent's Wharf
8 All Saints Street
London N1 9RL

Published October 2008



Design by Steers McGillan Ltd
Printed by Short Run Press

British Library Cataloguing in Public Data
A catalogue record for this book is available from the British Library

ISBN 978 0 7199 1767 7

## Acknowledgements

This new edition of the Good Trustee Guide has been co-ordinated by Peter Dyer and has been made possible by the contributions of many people and organisations who have helped ensure the Guide reflects the many and complex changes in law and best practice in recent years.

Thanks go to Lindsay Driscoll, Bates Wells and Braithwaite and to James Sinclair Taylor of Russell-Cooke Solicitors for contributing to the legal aspects of the guide; Linda Laurance, governance consultant, for contributing to the sections on handling conflict and relations with staff and volunteers, as well as her general comments and feedback; Roger Chester, LionHeart for his contribution to the section on ICT; Tom Wilcox and Sarah Walsh, Whitechapel Gallery for their contributions to the sections on fundraising and contracting; Volunteering England for the use of their Good Practice Bank in the section on volunteer management; Simon Croft, Richmond Council for Voluntary Service, Neal Green, Charity Commission for England and Wales, Sue Pearlman,TP Consultants, Sue Thomas, Citizen's Advice and Eve Dyer for their general comments and feedback; Keith Smith, Compass Partnership for his reflections on the topic of governance reviews; at NCVO, the Campaigning Effectiveness, Strategy and Impact, Collaborative Working Unit and Workforce teams for their contributions to the sections on campaigning and political activities, strategic planning, user involvement, managing change, making a difference, skills and learning, managing volunteers and employment and workforce; and finally to Anne Moynihan and Michael Wright at NCVO for their work on project management of the Guide.

# Contents

## Part two: Good governance

## Part three: Developing the board

## Part four: Improving governance



## Part five: Further information and support

# Foreword

UBS is delighted to be the sponsor of this new edition of the NCVO *Good Trustee Guide.* Andrew Hind, Chief Executive of the Charity Commission, wrote in his book *The Governance and Management of Charities*, that one of the distinguishing features of charity governance which sets voluntary organisations apart from private and public sector organisations is the nature of its governance. Charity trusteeship is not found in dictatorships or communist societies. Volunteers, such as you, are the adhesive of a 'civil' society.

From an investment management perspective you are custodians charged with ensuring the stewardship of your charity's assets. Central to the UBS philosophy is the concept of "You and Us", which signifies an inclusive team and sense of accord, a sentiment that I believe also underpins effective charity trusteeship.

UBS has a long tradition of private banking, and as wealth managers our approach is to fully understand our clients and then construct an appropriate investment strategy that meets the personal needs of that client. An approach we apply equally with our charity clients.

In the past, I have often observed that the interaction between the investment manager and the charity is a passive one: the manager receives the funds, takes a view and the charity spends according to what it receives. This is not how UBS approaches its clients. We take a holistic view, ensuring we understand your plans and ambitions for your charity and then manage your investments appropriately. Again, I believe this mirrors the role of a charity trustee, actively engaging in the strategy of the charity to ensure its aims and mission is achieved.

I would like to thank the NCVO Trustees for allowing UBS to sponsor this essential publication. Please do not hesitate to contact the Charity team at UBS if we can assist you.

**Andrew Pitt**
Head Charities
UBS Wealth Management, UK

## Introduction

The Good Trustee Guide is aimed at trustees of charities. As a charity trustee, you can use the Guide as a 'reader' to find out more about your responsibilities, as a reference guide to check individual issues as they arise or as a guide to develop your board or review its effectiveness.

The Guide is also useful for individuals supporting trustees – chief executives, staff, advisors, trainers and consultants – as a tool to develop good governance practice in organisations.

### Who is a trustee and what is a trustee board?

In the Good Trustee Guide, a trustee is a member of a group of people – the board of trustees, management committee or governing body – who take ultimate responsibility for a charity.

In the Good Trustee Guide, these individuals are referred to as trustees or board members and the trustee group referred to as a trustee board or 'the board'. It is recognised that some charities use other terms to describe their trustees, such as management committee members.

### About the Good Trustee Guide

This fifth edition of the Good Trustee Guide has been completely revised and updated to reflect the many changes in law, regulation and best practice affecting trustees over recent years.

Updating the Guide has been no easy task. This edition has covered the many legal and regulatory changes arising from the Charities and Companies Acts 2006, as well as the very welcome and extensive range of best practice guidance arising from a range of sector support agencies and regulators – not least those arising from a major investment in governance via the Governance Hub and National Support Service in Governance and Leadership.

The Code of Governance and National Occupational Standards for Trustees are two sets of governance principles, or standards, that are set to shape the way in which support for trustees will develop over the years and the Guide, too, takes account of these useful frameworks.

The structure and format of the Guide have also been updated, following feedback from readers and colleagues in the sector.

### What is in the Good Trustee Guide?

Part One of the guide deals with the essentials. This introduces the role of the trustee and where they fit into the charity, including guidance on legal structures and charitable status.

Part Two of the guide, Good governance, aims to explore the many and varied issues that may come to a trustee's attention. This section of the guide aims to provide essential information on a range of topics along with guidance on the role of the board in relation to each issue – from planning to health and safety to relations with staff and volunteers. This large section necessarily contains a significant amount of detail on some technical issues and the resources section is intended to signpost to further reading and sources of support where required.

Parts three and four of the guide concentrate on the role of the board itself and how the board can be supported and developed. Part three, Developing the board, covers key aspects of board practice from recruitment to board composition. Part four, Improving governance, explores how trustees can undertake a review of their charity's governance and to reflect on their own individual role as trustees.

The Good Trustee Guide is comprehensive and wide-ranging, but it is not exhaustive. Over recent years many sources of information on trusteeship and good governance have been developed and a number of organisations provide support and information to trustees at national, regional and local level. Part five, Further information and support, aims to signpost you to these key resources and support bodies.

### Features of the Guide

Throughout the Guide you will find references to further sources of information, either within other parts of the Guide or from external sources.

Each chapter or section of the Guide ends with a checklist, to help you identify action points for your trustee board. You may wish to add your own notes after the checklists.

We hope you find the guide useful and welcome your comments. Your feedback and ideas are extremely valuable to help plan future editions.

# Part One:

# The Essentials

# 1

# Introducing the role

## 1.1

### What is trusteeship[1]?

The concept of trusteeship has evolved over many centuries and broadly means that a donor gives or settles property on the trustees for the benefit of a third party.

This basic concept is still valid today. Charity trustees are people who are entrusted to look after money (or other resources such as land or property) given to a charity by a person or group of people. As a charity trustee, you must ensure that these resources are used effectively to achieve the particular purpose for which they were given (e.g. money donated by the public to cure heart disease should be spent on this area of work).

Trustees act within charities that generally have a formal structure, a set of rules and often delegate many day-to-day tasks to staff or volunteers. This structure will vary depending on your charity, and will affect your responsibilities and eligibility as a trustee.

This relationship works as follows:

[1] In the Good Trustee Guide, the term trustee refers to a charity trustee – a member of the governing body of a charity that takes formal responsibility for the charity.

[2] The Good Trustee Guide is aimed at trustees of registered charities.

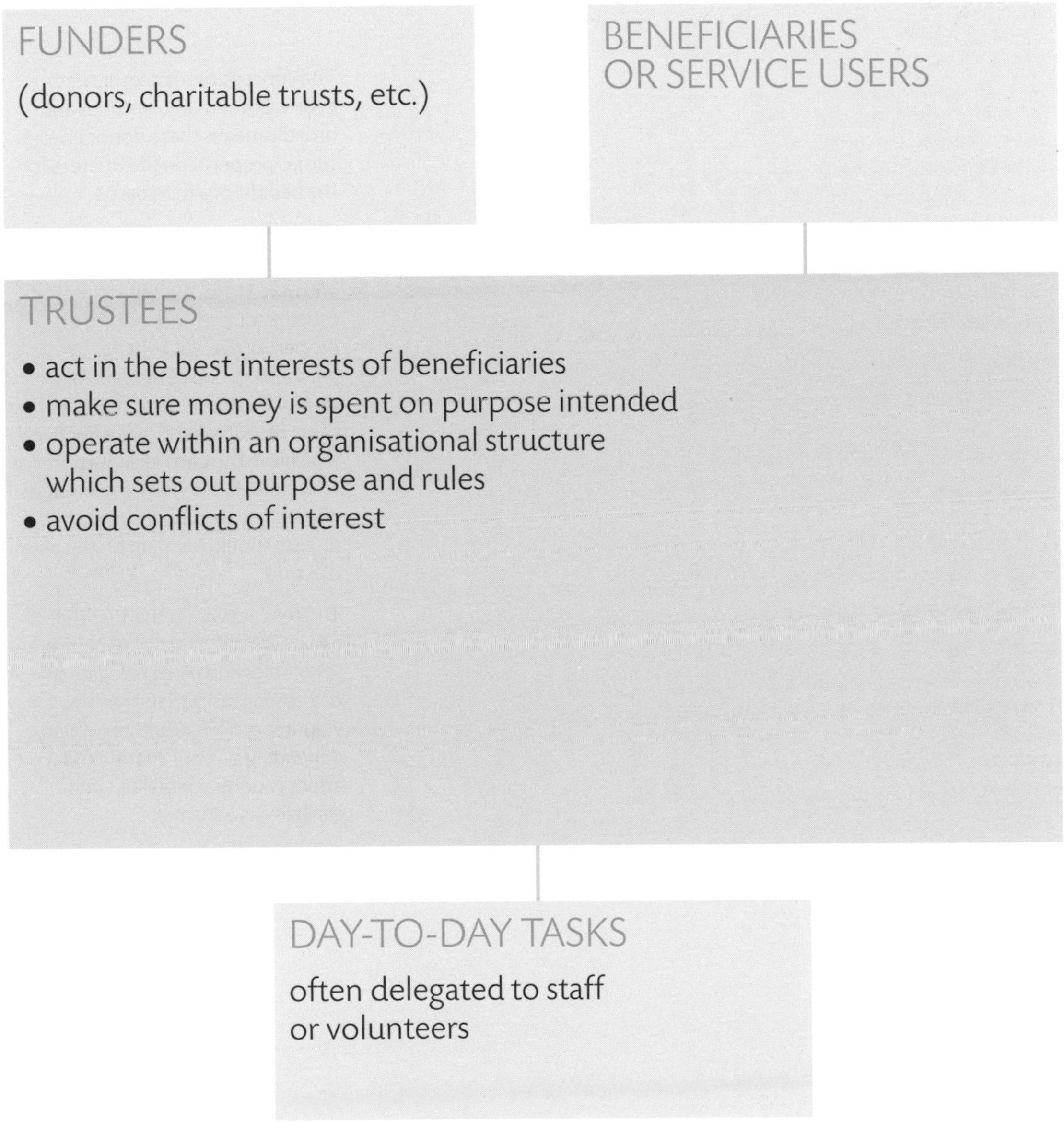

FUNDERS

(donors, charitable trusts, etc.)

BENEFICIARIES OR SERVICE USERS

TRUSTEES

- act in the best interests of beneficiaries
- make sure money is spent on purpose intended
- operate within an organisational structure which sets out purpose and rules
- avoid conflicts of interest

DAY-TO-DAY TASKS

often delegated to staff or volunteers

# 1.2

## Who are trustees (and who aren't)?

### Who are trustees?

Section 97 of the Charities Act 1993 defines charity trustees as: 'the persons having the general control and management of the administration of a charity'.

(Visit section 2.2 to find out more about charitable status.)

Trustees may also be called:

- members of the committee
- management committee members
- council members
- executive committee members
- governors.

No matter what title you are given, if you are a member of the governing body of a charity and you are entitled to take part in the decision-making process and vote at meetings, then you are a charity trustee.

NCVO recommends that charities call the people with the legal responsibility for trusteeship 'trustees' and refer to the committee or council on which they sit as the 'board of trustees'. These titles are used throughout The Good Trustee Guide.

### In a charitable company, are trustees and company directors the same?

Yes. Trustees are members of the governing body of the charity. If the charity is also a company then they will also be company directors (see section 2.2).

### Can I be a trustee even if another group in my organisation is known as 'the trustees'?

In some charities, those known as 'the trustees', and perhaps listed as such in the annual report, are actually patrons (see page 51) (or, in the case of unincorporated charities, merely hold the trust's property – see page 97). Those who take responsibility for controlling the management and administration of the charity may be known by some other term, such as 'the management committee'. It is the latter group who are the trustees in law.

### Can staff of charitable companies be 'shadow' directors?

Under the Companies Act 1985, a shadow director is someone in accordance with whose directions the directors of a company (in this instance the trustees of a charitable company) are accustomed to act. If someone is a shadow director, then he or she might be held to be a trustee for certain purposes, sharing the responsibilities and liabilities of trusteeship (for instance, in relation to liability for wrongful trading).

**Further Information:**
Guidance on the legal status of Charity Chief Executives (acevo, 2006)

Senior staff of charitable companies might be deemed to be shadow directors in circumstances where they dominate a passive board of trustees, e.g. where the management not only advises the trustees but tells them what to do. Trustees should ensure that they do not simply 'rubber stamp' decisions made by senior staff, but make independent decisions, albeit with the advice of senior staff.

### Am I a trustee if I am a member of the committee of a local branch?

Some national charities have groups or branches with local committees.

If the branch is constitutionally part of the national charity, then the members of the local committee are not trustees. The trustees are the members of the national governing body, and it is they who ultimately bear responsibility for the effective governance and conduct of the charity, including the work of the local branches. Some charities allocate places on their board of trustees for representatives of local groups.

If each local group is independent, with its own governing document, separately registered as charities but affiliated to a national charity, then the members of the local committees will be trustees of that local group. Age Concern is an example of a charity with this structure (see section 2.4 for more information on branches).

# 1.3

### Can a user of a charity's services be a trustee?

Yes. In most cases nothing prevents users from acting as trustees. Service users, or beneficiaries, can bring a vital perspective to the work of the board. Service user involvement can demonstrate that your charity takes an inclusive approach to involving users in decision making. It can give your charity greater credibility or legitimacy.

On the other hand, involving users at board level, if unplanned, can sometimes risk being tokenistic – that is, simplistic assumptions can be made that a user speaks for or represents all users (see section19.4). Also, some charities find that there may be more effective ways of bringing the voice of users as well as or instead of board membership, like advisory groups (see section 21.9). Finally, conflicts of interest can occur from time to time between the user's trustee role and service user role and these must be managed (see section 3.6).

## How do I become a trustee?

Trustees are elected or appointed in many different ways. These include:

| | |
|---|---|
| Election | Individuals may be elected at an Annual General Meeting and/or by post. Individuals may be elected by, for example:<br>• the entire membership<br>• an 'electoral college' where the right to appoint trustee(s) rests with a specific group of members or stakeholders, e.g. volunteers, interest groups, geographical areas |
| Co-option | A number of trustees may be appointed by the board of trustees themselves |
| Appointed from outside | One or more trustees may be appointed by an external organisation, e.g. a local authority |
| Ex-Officio | One or more trustees may be appointed by virtue of the office they hold, e.g. a mayor or vicar |

Check your governing document to see what it says about your charity's procedures for electing or appointing trustees (see section 2.3).

**Tip:** Visit Part Three to find out more about the practical ways you can improve your recruitment practices and more about governance arrangements for membership organisations.

### If a trustee is appointed by an outside organisation, do they have the same responsibilities as other trustees?

Yes. Some charities have a provision in their governing document that gives the right for another organisation to appoint a trustee or trustees. These trustees are sometimes known as representative or nominative trustees and may be appointed for a number of reasons:

- to ensure that vacancies on the trustee board can be easily filled
- to ensure that outside bodies which have an interest in the work of the charity can have an association with it
- to ensure that the charity has a well-balanced cross-section of either the community or service users

No matter how you are elected or appointed you have the same responsibilities as other trustees. If you are appointed by a nominating organisation, you are not there to represent that organisation; you are there to act in the best interests of the charity to which you have been appointed.

You should also note that, if you are appointed by a nominating organisation, you are personally responsible to fulfill your duty as a trustee – this means that, for example, the nominating organisation cannot send alternative people if you cannot attend a board meeting, nor will the responsibility as a trustee rest with them.

There may be occasions when your duty to act in the best interests of the charity is in conflict with the best interests of the organisation that appointed you as a trustee. If this happens, you should follow an agreed policy on how to deal with conflicts of interest. In the absence of an existing policy, you should remove yourself from discussion of the item concerned and your absence should be minuted. This may not, however, absolve you from being jointly responsible and liable for any decision made (see section 3.7).

**Note:**
there are certain circumstances when the governing document of a charity allows an organisation to be appointed as a 'corporate trustee'. However, this is a specific situation and will be clearly set out in your governing document.

See section 21.8 for further guidance on the role of trustee nominated by outside organisations.

### Can individuals attend a board meeting but not be a trustee?

Yes, it is quite common for individuals who are not trustees to attend all or part of board meetings, either occasionally or regularly – but it is very important to be clear about their role as distinct from the role of a trustee. These individuals are sometimes called observers or representatives or may be members of staff – for example:

- In charities that employ staff, it is usual for a chief executive to attend board meetings to report on day to day issues. Sometimes a member of staff may take the minutes of a meeting
- Some charities allow an individual to be elected by service users as a 'representative', to attend all or part of board meetings but not as a trustee (note that it is quite common for users also to act as trustees – see above)
- Sometimes, a member of an outside organisation – an officer or member of a local authority, for example – may regularly attend a board meeting in an advisory capacity, not as a trustee
- A person with particular expertise or experience may sometimes attend board meetings to provide advice, either on a one off or regular basis.

There can sometimes be confusion about whether individuals like these are trustees or not – for example in one charity a local authority member may be a trustee, but not in another. If individuals are attending board meetings but not as a trustee it should be made explicit that the individuals are not trustees and do not take part in decision-making, otherwise they may be found to be liable for decisions taken. You can make this clear in the meeting minutes (for example, by listing non trustees as 'in attendance', separate from the list of trustees present) or via a provision in the governing document.

## **Case study** – Whitstable Umbrella Community Support Centre

The Centre is a small charity with a small staff team (manager, finance officer and caretaker) supported by many volunteers. The trustees are elected by members at the Annual General Meeting. The centre manager attends every board meeting to report on day to day issues. A member of the local authority attends board meetings as an observer, and this is made clear in the minutes. A representative of service users, elected by service users but not a trustee, also attends part of every meeting to discuss user issues. Again, their role as 'in attendance' is made clear in the minutes. However, users are encouraged to join the board as full trustees and sometimes a service user has moved from being the 'representative' to being elected as a trustee.

# 1.4

## Who can and can't be a trustee?

The Charities Act 1993 sets out who is disqualified from acting as a charity trustee. This applies to all charities including excepted and exempt charities.

Company law sets out who is disqualified from acting as a company director. These provisions apply to charities formed as a company limited by guarantee (as well as all other companies).

### Who is disqualified from acting as a charity trustee?

Section 72 of the Charities Act 1993 disqualifies people who:

- have unspent convictions for offences involving deception or dishonesty (unless 'spent'), e.g. theft, fare evasion or falsely claiming benefit
- are undischarged bankrupts
- have been at any time removed from trusteeship of a charity by the Charity Commission or the court in England, Wales or Scotland, because of misconduct or mismanagement
- are disqualified from being company directors under the Company Directors Disqualification Act 1986
- have failed to make payments under county court administration orders
- have made compositions (i.e. come to an arrangement) with their creditors and have not been discharged.

As soon as someone comes within section 72 (e.g. the day they are convicted of an offence involving dishonesty) s/he is automatically disqualified from acting as a trustee. It is a criminal offence to act as a charity trustee while disqualified.

Charities can apply to the Charity Commission for a waiver of disqualification under section 72(4) of the Charities Act 1993, either generally or in relation to a charity or a specific class of charities. The Commission will consider what, if any, benefit is likely to result from an applicant acting as a trustee. Under the Charities Act 2006 if the ground for disqualification was removal from the trusteeship by the Charity Commission or the court in England, Wales or Scotland, and five years has passed, then the application for waiver must normally be granted unless there are special circumstances which would justify refusal.

**Further information:**
Charity Commission publication Finding new trustees – What charities need to know (CC30) and associated operational guidance on disqualification and waivers (OG41 & OG42)

### Who is disqualified from acting as a company director?

Under the Company Directors Disqualification Act 1986 the court may disqualify people:

- who have been convicted of criminal offences relating to the promotion, formation, management or liquidation of a company
- who have been persistently in default of company legislation for filing accounts and other documents
- who have been found guilty of fraudulent trading or fraud
- whose conduct as a director has made them unfit to be involved in the management of a company.

**Further information:**
Companies House Directors and Secretaries Guide (GBA1) – available from the Companies House website (see resources section).

### Are there any other factors affecting eligibility?

- Trustees of unincorporated charities cannot be under the age of 18. It is possible for a director of a charitable company to be under 18, but the Companies Act 2006 introduces a minimum age of 16. This is due to come into force in October 2008. In some circumstances parents can be liable for the actions of their children and parents of under 18s considering becoming directors of charitable companies should be made aware of the duties and responsibilities.

**Further information:**
Further advice on the appointment of under 18s can be found on the Charity Commission website (Statement from the Commission regarding young people under 18 years old as charity trustees, linked from Charity Commission publication CC30). Remember that there are other ways of involving people in a charity besides becoming a trustee.

- The governing document of a charity may include restrictions on who may become a trustee of that charity, for example requiring them to live in a certain area or to be of a particular religious denomination.
- The Charity Commission states that

*'It is important that anyone appointed as a trustee is made fully aware of his or her responsibilities and liabilities. It is unfair to impose on someone a range of duties that that person cannot properly understand and cannot, or does not want to, carry out.'* [3]

- The Criminal Justice and Court Services Act 2000 bans certain individuals from being a trustee of children's charities, e.g. anyone who commits one of a number of serious offences (generally against children) and who is subject to a disqualification order under the Act, made by the Court. Further information on this can be obtained from the Criminal Records Bureau (CRB).
- Some organisations working with children must check with CRB before employing individuals and this would include charity trustees. The Charity Commission also strongly recommends that trustees of charities working with children and vulnerable adults who are eligible to obtain disclosures from CRB should do. Further information on this can be found in the Charity Commission publication CC30 Finding New Trustees: What charities need to know
- All prospective charity trustees should sign a declaration of eligibility to act which should also cover CRB checks. See section 19.7 for a model declaration.

[3] Charity Commission publication *Users on board* (CC24) Crown Copyright.

## Checklist

Have you considered asking your board or committee to review the names it uses for the people and the committees, so that those who are the trustees in law understand their status?

Have you checked your governing document to see what it says about your charity's procedures for electing/appointing trustees?

Are any members of your trustee board appointed by outside organisations?

If so, are they clear that they must act in the best interests of your charity?

If individuals who are not trustees attend your board meetings do you make this clear in the minutes of the meeting?

Are you a trustee of a national charity with local branches?

Are the local branches separate legal entities?

If your charity has local branches, does your board need to review how it exercises its responsibilities for the activities of the local branches and how the local branches ensure their accountability to the national trustees?

Has your board checked that your trustees are eligible for trusteeship under the terms of your governing document, and that these disqualify only those you would wish to exclude?

Is there someone in your charity who is responsible for checking that trustees are not disqualified?

Do you ask new trustees to sign a declaration of commitment to the charity and eligibility to act as a charity trustee? (See the model declaration, section 19.7)

If your charity works with children, young people or vulnerable adults, have you obtained a CRB disclosure for trustees if required by law or if eligible to do so?

# 1.5

## What do trustees do?

Although in practice many day-to-day tasks can be delegated to staff (where they are employed) or to individual board members, volunteers or others, the central responsibilities of trustee boards are the same no matter the size of the board or the nature of the charity. These responsibilities are taken up in other parts of the guide in more detail but can be summarised into 12 essential areas (see box).

## The 12 essential board responsibilities at a glance:

**Set and maintain vision, mission and values**
The trustee board is responsible for establishing the essential purpose of the charity as set out in the objects of its governing document. They are also responsible for guarding the ethos and values of the charity.

**Develop strategy**
Together, the trustee board (and chief executive where employed) develop long-term strategy. Meeting agendas reflect the key points of the strategy to keep the organisation on track.

**Establish and monitor policies**
The trustee board creates policies to govern organisational activity. These cover guidance for staff and/or volunteers, systems for reporting and monitoring, an ethical framework for everyone connected with the organisation and the conduct of trustees and board business.

**Ensure compliance with the governing document**
The governing document is the rulebook for the charity. The trustees must ensure it is followed. In particular, the charity's activities must comply with the charitable objects in the governing document.

**Ensure accountability**
The trustees should ensure that the charity fulfils accountability as required by law to (including): The Charity Commission, HM Revenue and Customs and the Registrar of Companies (if it is a company limited by guarantee). This includes publishing annual reports and accounts. The charity should also be accountable to other groups who are sometimes known as stakeholders: donors, beneficiaries, staff, volunteers and the general public.

**Ensure compliance with the law**
Trustees are responsible for checking that all the charity's activities are legal.

**Maintain proper fiscal oversight**
The trustees are responsible for effectively managing the charity's resources and funding so it can meet its charitable objects. The trustee board: secures sufficient resources to fulfill the mission, monitors spending in the best interests of the charity, approves the annual financial statement and budget, protects the charity against liability by providing insurance, seeks to manage risk for the charity and ensures compliance with the law.

**Respect the role of staff / volunteers**
The trustee board recognises and respects the domain of staff and / or volunteer responsibility. At the same time, it creates policy to guide staff and/or volunteer activities and safeguard the interests of the charity.

**Maintain effective board performance**
The board keeps its own house in order. It engages in productive meetings, effective committees with adequate resources, development activities and regular reviews of its role. The board is also responsible for overseeing trustee board recruitment.

**Promote the organisation**
Through their own behaviour, their governance oversight and their activities on behalf of the charity trustees enhance and protect the reputation of their charity. They are good ambassadors for the charity.

Where staff are employed:

**Set up employment procedures**
The trustee board creates comprehensive, fair and legal personnel policies. These protect the charity and those who work for it. They cover recruitment, support, appraisal, remuneration and discipline.

**Select and support the chief executive**
If necessary, the trustee board creates policy covering the employment of a chief executive. They also select and support the chief executive and review their performance.

**Tip:** turn to Part Four to find out how you can use the list of responsibilities above to carry out a governance review.

What is governance?

Governance is about leadership and ensuring that an organisation is effectively and properly run. The twelve responsibilities above are based on principles of good governance.

Good governance is the board's responsibility, but governance covers more than the board's duties and responsibilities – governance takes in how the board is appointed and supported and how the board works to ensure decisions are taken properly and the work of the charity is effective and furthering its purposes.

Governance is distinct from day-to-day management and operations delegated to staff and volunteers. Sandy Adirondack wrote that 'governance is not necessarily about doing; it is about ensuring things are done'.[4]

Governance has been high on the agenda for charities in recent years. Since the publication of the previous edition of the Good Trustee Guide in 2002, two frameworks of good governance have been developed to help guide trustees and organisations. Both frameworks are used in the Good Trustee Guide to help trustees understand and carry out their roles and responsibilities:

[4] *The Good Governance Action Plan for Voluntary Organisations*, Sandy Adirondack (NCVO, 2002)

The Code of Governance was drawn up in 2005 by a founding group of support and membership bodies – the Association of Chief Executives of Voluntary Organisations (acevo), Charity Trustee Networks, the Institute of Chartered Secretaries and Administrators (ICSA) and the National Council for Voluntary Organisations – and endorsed by the Charity Commission. The Code sets out a statement of best practice in governance, designed around seven principles. The seven principles, explored in chapter 5, are useful in understanding more about what a well governed organisation should look like, and are good starting points to review the board and organisation's effectiveness and put in place good practice.

**Further information:**
Good Governance: A Code for the Voluntary and Community Sector is available from the NCVO website (see resources section).

The National Occupational Standards for Trustees and Management Committee Members were drawn up by the UK Workforce Hub in Conjunction with the Governance Hub in 2005 and set out the competencies that all trustees should develop to ensure that they are able to carry out their role effectively. The standards are particularly useful for individual trustees to help understand their duties and responsibilities and for boards to help plan training and development. The 'NOS' – as they are sometimes referred to – are explored in more detail in chapter 17.

**Further information:**
National Occupational Standards for Trustees and Management Committee Members is available from the UK Workforce Hub website (see resources section).

I am a new trustee.
How can I find out more about my roles and responsibilities?

The Good Trustee Guide covers all of the main areas of a trustee's responsibility. You can use the Guide as a reader to find out more about your responsibilities, as a reference guide to check individual issues as they arise or as a guide to develop your board or review its effectiveness. The Guide also provides links throughout to more detailed and comprehensive sources of guidance – for example, the Charity Commission provides more detailed advice on some of the areas covered in this chapter regarding trustee eligibility.

Remember, trustees are not expected to be experts in every topic confronting the board. But they are expected to understand their duties and responsibilities. All trustees should be provided with an introduction, or induction, into their responsibilities as a trustee, covering the essential information needed. Turn to section 20.3 to find a sample induction programme and checklist.

# 2 Legal structures and charitable status

## 2.1 Introduction

As a trustee, you take ultimate responsibility for your charity. This and the next chapter introduce what this means in practice. They cover:

- what a charity is
- the legal structure of your organisation
- the duties of trustees
- trustee liability
- the structure of the trustee board and where it fits into the organisation.

# 2.2

## Charitable status

### What is a charity?

The modern concept of charity has evolved from an Elizabethan statute of 1601, which defined as charitable *'the relief of aged, impotent and poor people, the maintenance of schools of learning, the repair of bridges, churches and highways, and the relief or redemption of prisoners or captives'* among other things. This was developed over the years by the courts. In 2006, a new Charities Act restated the charitable purposes and set out a separate public benefit requirement and a range of other changes.

### Charities have exclusively charitable purposes

Today, charities are organisations that are set up with purposes that are exclusively charitable. Charitable purposes are set out in the Charities Act 2006 (a change from the previous Good Trustee Guide). The purposes of a charity will be set out in its 'objects' clause in its governing document and must fall under one or more of the following:

a) the prevention or relief of poverty

b) the advancement of education

c) the advancement of religion

d) the advancement of health or the saving of lives

e) the advancement of citizenship or community development

f) the advancement of the arts, culture, heritage or science

g) the advancement of amateur sport

h) the advancement of human rights, conflict resolution or reconciliation or the promotion of religious or racial harmony or equality and diversity

i) the advancement of environmental protection or improvement

j) the relief of those in need, by reason of youth, age, ill-health, disability, financial hardship or other disadvantage

k) the advancement of animal welfare

l) the promotion of the efficiency of the armed forces of the Crown, or of the efficiency of the police, fire and rescue services or ambulance services

m) other purposes currently recognised as charitable and any new charitable purposes which are similar to another charitable purpose.

### Charities must benefit the public

All charities must be able to demonstrate how their purposes benefit the public. For a charity to benefit the public it must be able to demonstrate:

- that it provides a clear, identifiable benefit related to its aims, the benefit being balanced against any detriment or harm and
- that the benefits are to the public, or a section of the public, and that there not unreasonable restrictions such as high fees preventing any opportunity to benefit.
- Any private benefit must be incidental to a charity's work. This includes the restrictions over how far trustees can benefit personally from a charity (see section 3.8) and the benefits to members in a membership charity.

The Charity Commission has published guidance on the Public Benefit Requirement which is available on the Commission website[5]. Under the Charities Act 2006 trustees must have regard to this. Trustees must also now set out in the Trustees Annual Report how they have carried out their charitable purposes for the public benefit.

[5] Charity Commission *Charities and Public Benefit* statutory guidance (available on the Charity Commission website under 'About Charities' – 'Public benefit')

### When are organisations required to register with the Charity Commission?

To register as a charity, you apply to the Charity Commission. The Charity Commission exists to regulate and support charities. If your organisation's annual income is over £5,000 per year and you meet the criteria for registration then your organisation is viewed to be a charity and must register. Two categories of charities, excepted charities (including many individual churches) and exempt charities (including charitable Industrial and Provident Societies and universities and colleges) have not been required to register. Under the Charities Act some of these will now have to register with the Commission.

Remember that when an organisation registers a charity, it is gaining charitable status – not a new legal structure. Charitable status and legal structure are different. An organisation will firstly establish itself with a legal structure, such as a company or association structure (see section 2.3) and then, if eligible, register as a charity. This means that it is common for an organisation to be both a charity and, say, a company at the same time. This is sometimes a cause of confusion.

### What are the advantages of charitable status and charity registration?

All charities, whether or not they are registered, can get some relief from direct taxes such as income tax, corporation tax, stamp duty and capital gains tax. There are also some limited concessions on VAT.

Charities can claim back any income tax paid on donations made through Gift Aid and can benefit from the payroll giving scheme whereby payments can be made to charities from employees before deduction of tax They are also entitled to 80 per cent business rate relief on any premises they occupy, and this can be extended to 100 per cent at the discretion of the local authority.

Registration enables a charity to apply for grants from trusts or donors who have a policy of giving only to registered charities.

Registered charities may also benefit from an improved public image because they are regulated and have a charity number.

### What are the disadvantages of charitable status – or what should I be aware of?

Charitable status brings with it restrictions and requirements:

- Charities are only permitted to undertake charitable activities or to fund the charitable activities of another organisation, which does not have to be a charity. This places restrictions on
  - the type of work charities can carry out or fund – all activities must further or support the charity's objects
  - political activities undertaken by the charity (see over) and
  - trading activities undertaken by the charity (see over)
- Charities must comply with regulatory requirements, including those relating to the preparation of annual accounts and returns (see chapter 7).
- The governing body of the organisation take on the duties and responsibilities of charity trustees (see chapter 3). There are restrictions over how far trustees can personally financially benefit from their role (see section 3.8).

**Further information**
on charitable status is available in the Charity Commission publication *Registering as a Charity* (CC21) or from the About Charities pages of the Charity Commission website.

### The Charities Act 2006

The Charities Act 2006 followed years of extensive consultation and scrutiny and originally came out of the NCVO Charity Law Reform Advisory Group. It introduced a number of different reforms. It modernised the definition of charity, updated the structure, objectives and powers of the Charity Commission, introduced registration for some exempt and excepted charities and introduced a Charity Tribunal to hear appeals from decisions of the Commission. It also introduced a new incorporated legal structure for charities and a range of measures to provide more flexibility and less bureaucracy for trustees. Finally it introduced a new regime for the licensing of public charitable collections.

Most of the provisions are now in the force. The only outstanding ones are the registration of some excepted charities due in October 2008 and exempt charities due in 2009, the introduction of the charitable incorporated organisation due in 2009 and the new public charitable collections regime where there is, as yet no date.

### Charitable status – political activities

Whether you are trying to save a local community centre from closing or lobbying government, campaigns are created to produce change and make an impact.

Campaigns are *'organised actions around a specific issue seeking to bring about changes in the policy and behaviours of institutions and or specific public groups.'*

Campaigning is the 'mobilising of forces – such as resources or capacity – to influence others in order to effect an identified change'.

**Further information**
see NCVO's *Good Campaigns Guide: Campaigning for Impact* by Jim Coe and Tess Kingham 2005.

As a charity trustee, you are responsible for ensuring that your charity complies with the law relating to political activities by charities. Guidance has recently been clarified by the Charity Commission to enable charities to have greater confidence and clarity in campaigning to realise their charitable purpose.

Following consultation with the sector, the Charity Commission issued guidelines in 1995 to clarify that, while under English law charities cannot have political purposes – that is they cannot, as their main purpose, seek to change a law or government policy either in the UK or abroad – they can carry out political activity (seek to change a law or policy both in the UK and abroad) that supports the delivery of its charitable purposes. Charities can never engage in party political activities (i.e seeking to persuade members of the public to vote for against a candidate or political party).

To help clear up the confusion around campaigning law – and to give trustees more confidence when their charity engages in campaigning – the Charity Commission recently brought out further guidance in the form of Speaking Out – Guidance on Campaigning and Political Activity by Charities (Version March 2008). The guidance makes an important distinction between campaigning which is mainly about changing public attitudes and political campaigning which is about changing law or government policy. It also clarifies that:

- a charity can devote all of its resources to a campaign that seeks to raise awareness, education or behaviour change and can also campaign to change a law or policy provided that this activity does not become the charities' sole or continuing purpose
- a charity can campaign using emotive or controversial material where it is lawful and justifiable in the context of the campaign
- campaigning against a private company and behaviour change of corporations is not a political activity
- special rules apply in the context of an election

### Why do some charities have a separate, non-charitable arm for political activities?

Charity Commission regulation states that 'political activity can only be a means of supporting or contributing to the achievement of its charitable purposes. It cannot be a charitable purpose in its own right, or the only means by which the charity pursues its objects.'

Some charity trustees decide to set up separate non-charitable companies or associations to carry out their policy work and political activities so that they will not be subject to restraints imposed on by charity law.

### Charitable status and political activities: what role should I play as a trustee?

You should ensure that you and your fellow trustees take the major decisions about the educational, policy and campaigning work of your charity. Depending on the size and complexity of your operations, this could involve some or all of the following activities:

- Ensure that staff and volunteers understand the guidelines and restrictions on political activities, if campaigning work is delegated to them
- Put mechanisms in place to review your charity's policy statements and reports to ensure that all political activities comply with charity law (see definition above)
- Discuss the degree to which engaging with political activities would help achieve your charity's aims – it can help to set clear and measurable objectives and have in place an appropriate campaign strategy from the outset
- Decide how much of your charity's resources it is appropriate to use in this area of work – this may vary depending on internal priorities and the external environment in which your organisation is operating
- Ensure independence and transparency when working with politicians and political parties
- Ensure that you have procedures in place to monitor and evaluate political activities
- Enhance organisational learning and build confidence – campaigning is not always successful but when it is the impact on the lives of beneficiaries can be great. This means that it should be acceptable to make a mistake in your campaigning work – but not to keep making the same mistakes!
- Regularly review membership of any campaigning alliances and coalitions to ensure that your charity's involvement in such alliances is part of a coherent campaign strategy and might be reasonably be expected to further your charity's objectives.

**Further information:**
It is recommended you refer to checklist in the Charity Commission's Speaking out guidance.

Do charities have the right to trade?

According to HM Revenue and Customs, trading describes *'activities, which involve the provision of goods or services to customers on a commercial basis. When deciding whether a trade exists, it is of no relevance that you do not intend to make a profit or that you intend profits to be used only for charitable purposes.'*[6]

If your organisation is a registered charity, there is no reason why charity and tax law should stop it from engaging in all kinds of trading. But you will have to be certain that you take thorough legal advice. Don't let the law deter you. Do make sure you're clear how it works.

This is because trading implies a risk to funds that have been given for charitable purposes, not speculation. The fact that all profits may be applied to charitable purposes is irrelevant when determining 'trade'. It is the activity, not the outcome, that is under scrutiny.

A charity's trading profits are exempt from corporation or income tax if it falls under one of the following categories:

1 Carrying out the charity's primary purpose – trading that carries out a primary purpose as stated in the charity's governing rules or constitution (for example a residential care home charging its residents), where the actual work of trading is carried out by the charity's beneficiaries or where it is undertaken in the course of carrying out the primary purpose (for example a theatre charity selling food and drink to the members of the audience. This is known as ancillary trading).

2 Selling donated assets – if a charity sells donated goods, land, buildings and investments this is not regarded as trading so long as the donations have been given specifically to raise funds for the charity (significant alterations – turning donated fabric into clothing for example – would render the sale outside allowable activity).

3 Comes within the small scale exemption – charities are exempted from income or corporation tax on trading profits where the annual turnover for non primary purpose trading is below a financial threshold. At present (July 2008) this is £5,000 for charities with a total income under £20,000, 25% of total income for charities between £20,000 to £200,000 and £50,000 for all charities over £200,000.

4 Falls within the Extra statutory Concession– applies to fundraising events such as car-boot sales, dances, film showings, firework displays or fetes. There are detailed rules which must be followed.

Full details of all these exemptions can be found on the HMRC website.

If your charity intends to trade in a way that does not fit any of these four categories you will be required to hive off trading activity into an arm's-length trading subsidiary which donates all profits back to the parent charity (see chapter 2.4 for more information).

**Further information:**
Available from the Charity Commission's publication Trustees, trading and tax (CC35)

[6] HMRC Charity trading and business activities website page

## Stating charity and company status on documents

The Charities Act 1993 requires certain registered charities to state their charitable status on certain documents. Separate provisions are also in place for companies, laid down in the Companies Act 2006.

The detail of these provisions depends on the income level of your charity and include a wide range of items from fundraising appeals to letterheads, cheque books and emails. The provisions also contain restrictions on what information should be displayed.

The provisions are quite detailed and beyond the scope of this guide. NCVO has a briefing sheet on its website providing more details (see Resources section).

What happens if the charity fails to comply?
The trustees and staff of charities or companies who are involved in the issue of any document without the necessary details are committing an offence and can face criminal prosecution.

**Further information**
about charity requirements is in Charity Commission publication *Charities and Fundraising* (CC20) and company requirements in Companies House guidance booklet *Company Formation* (GBF1).

## Checklist

Have you checked the Charity Commission's guidance on public benefit to see how it may affect your charity?

If you are not a registered charity, have you checked the criteria and threshold for charity registration? Do you think you may need to register?

Does your board need to review its campaigning activities to be satisfied that it complies with charity law?

Does your board need to review the trading activity of your charity to be satisfied that it complies with charity and tax law?

Have you checked the requirements for stating charity and (if appropriate) company status on documents?

# 2.3

## Legal structures

When an organisation is formally established it will adopt a governing document or set of rules. The governing document is the legal structure for the organisation. The document usually sets out:

- the name of the organisation
- its purposes, or 'objects'. This is a statement of what the organisation is set up to do. It is usually worded in quite formal terms – for example, an organisation providing training for young people may have for its object *'the advancement of education of young people'.*
- its powers – how it carries out its purposes. As a trustee, you are responsible for the control and management of the administration of the charity and everything you do must further that. Some activities – appointing staff, managing premises and so on – are not in direct furtherance of your objects so to operate effectively powers are normally set out in your governing document allowing trustees to carry out indirect tasks and delegate work. Some powers are also set out in law.
- provisions around membership of the organisation, if relevant
- provisions around who can be a trustee and how they are elected or appointed
- procedures for calling meetings, both general meetings (of members) and trustee board meetings
- provisions for amending the governing document or closing the organisation.

If the organisation is a charity and meets the criteria to register as a charity (see section 2.2) the governing document must be in a form acceptable to the Charity Commission.

Broadly speaking, there are three common forms of legal structure for charities, each with its own type of governing document (there are also a number of other, less common legal forms):

- Trust
- Unincorporated association
- Company Limited by Guarantee

**Further information:**
about legal structures and charitable status is available in the Charity Commission's publication Choosing and Preparing a Governing Document (CC22).

## Trust

A trust is the traditional structure used for setting up a charity. It establishes a relationship between three groups of people: donors, trustees and beneficiaries.

Many older charities are established as trusts and the structure is typically used today to set up:

- grant-giving trusts
- church restoration or building repair funds
- some smaller service-providing organisations
- organisations not requiring a membership structure.

### Advantages

- relatively cheap to set up and run with no ongoing costs
- simple to administer as minimal formalities are required
- board is often self-perpetuating

### Disadvantages

- Trusts are unincorporated bodies so property cannot be held in the name of the charity; it has to be in the names of the trustees Contracts are also in the names of the trustees
- When the trustees resign or new trustees are appointed, trust assets have to be transferred into the names of the new group of trustees, which incurs legal expense (although this can be avoided by appointing a corporate body as custodian trustee, which holds the assets in its name for an indefinite period)
- Trustees of charitable trusts do not have the protection of limited liability, which trustees of charitable companies enjoy. If the trust has insufficient assets to pay its debts or incurs any other liabilities, for instance arising from negligence or libel or under contract, the trustees will personally have to pay them (see section 3.9).
- If the trust deed does not contain a power of amendment it may only be altered by an order of the court or of the Charity Commissioners
- A trust does not have a membership like an association and so may find it harder to demonstrate accountability to users
- Unless the trust deed includes a power to remove trustees, it can be difficult to remove an unsuitable trustee, or one who has behaved improperly, if they are not willing to resign.

### Governing document

A charitable trust's governing document is usually a declaration of trust or a trust deed. This sets out the:

- names of the first trustees
- initial trust fund
- name in which the trust will be administered
- charitable objects
- trustees' powers
- eligibility for trusteeship
- procedures for appointing trustees, holding meetings, voting, etc.
- amendment and dissolution procedures.

### Trustee appointment

The boards of charitable trusts are normally self-perpetuating although they can be appointed for fixed terms by outside bodies. New trustees are appointed by the existing trustees, in accordance with eligibility criteria and procedures laid down in the trust deed.

### Closing down

Some trusts, such as a church restoration fund, close down once they have reached their target and the assets have been used. Others cease to be financially viable or their purpose becomes out of date, or beneficiaries can no longer be found. Some close down because they need to change to a more appropriate legal structure, such as a charitable company limited by guarantee.

If the trust deed does not stipulate what happens to any remaining assets in the event of the charity closing down, the trustees should approach the Charity Commissioners to transfer the assets to another charity with similar objects.

## Unincorporated association

A charitable unincorporated association is a group of people who come together to pursue a shared aim.

It is a particularly suitable structure for membership organisations, where it is important for the members to have close involvement with the running of the charity. It is typically used by:

- self-help groups
- local societies
- local campaigning organisations.

### Advantages

- simple to set up and inexpensive to run
- very flexible as the constitution can be tailored to suit the needs of the organisation, so control can lie in the hands of either the membership as a whole or a smaller group of trustees (frequently called the management committee) elected by the members
- constitution can include a power to alter its terms, usually subject to the approval of a certain percentage of its membership.

### Disadvantages

- no legal personality so legal transactions cannot be carried out in the name of the charity. A small group of holding trustees or a custodian trustee (a corporate body such as the Official Custodian) who do not have any of the responsibilities of trusteeship must be appointed to hold the assets in their names
- trustees have unlimited liability so if the association has insufficient assets to pay its debts, or incurs any other liabilities (e.g. arising from negligence or libel or under breach of contract) the trustees will personally have to pay them (see chapter 3)
- in exceptional instances the personal liability can extend to the wider membership
- Relevant law is quite complicated as there is no statute applicable such as Companies Act.

### Governing document

An unincorporated association will usually have a constitution, which sets out:

- the name in which the association will be administered
- charitable objects
- trustees' powers
- criteria for membership and voting rights
- procedures for electing trustees, holding meetings, etc.
- financial matters
- amendment and dissolution procedures.

### Trustee appointment

Trustees will normally be elected from the membership following procedures set out in the constitution. They are also often appointed by outside bodies such as a local authority or may be ex officio that is they are automatically trustees because of the office they hold, e.g. Mayor or Vicar. There is often a power enabling the board to co-opt a certain number of trustees in addition to the elected and appointed trustees.

### Closing down

Some unincorporated associations close down because they have grown considerably and now employ staff and occupy premises so the limitation of trustees' liability offered by a company limited by guarantee becomes desirable. Others close as members lose interest, or when the value of their innovative services is recognised, and their provision is taken over by a statutory body such as a local authority.

If the constitution does not stipulate what happens to any remaining assets in the event of the charity closing down, the trustees should apply to the Charity Commission for guidance to transfer the assets to another charity with similar objects.

## Company Limited by Guarantee

A charitable company is a limited company set up to carry out charitable activities. The trustees of a charitable company enjoy the protection of limited liability.

### Advantages

- has legal status of being incorporated with its own legal personality
- property can be owned by the charity, so names on legal documents do not have to be changed every time there is a change of trustees
- has membership instead of shareholders, and members all guarantee to pay a nominal sum of usually £1 or £5 if the company becomes insolvent
- trustees and members of charitable companies have limited liability (see section 3.9 for more information).

### Disadvantages

- extra cost of setting up a company
- additional bureaucracy involved in meeting the requirements of company law
- names and addresses of trustees must be available for public inspection (which sometimes deters individuals from taking on trusteeship).

### Governing document

The document which sets out the purpose of a charitable company and the way in which it will run its affairs is in two parts: the memorandum of association and the articles of association.

The memorandum of association states:

- the charity's name
- the charitable objects or aims
- the powers of trustees to achieve the objects
- special powers, such as provision for worker-trustees or power to use the charity's assets to pay for trustee liability insurance
- the fact that members' liability is limited
- the amount of the members' guarantee
- details of what happens to the assets if the company is wound up.

The articles of association give the rules and regulations which govern the internal proceedings of the company. These usually include:

- membership of the company
- the number of trustees, how they are elected, for what period, and any restrictions on who can become a trustee
- procedures for holding meetings – including annual and extraordinary general meetings, and for voting
- financial and auditing procedures
- procedures for appointing auditors
- powers to delegate to staff or sub-committees
- administrative provisions, e.g. notices, indemnities, standing orders.

Under the Companies Act 2006 most of the detail now in the Memorandum of Association will be in the Articles and the Memorandum will become a short document mainly for the purpose of incorporation.

### Trustee appointment

The articles set out the procedures for the nomination and election of trustees, whether from within or outside the membership, and/or the appointment of trustees by outside bodies.

The articles also set out who can become a member of the company, the procedure for becoming a member and the procedure for expelling a member.

Confusion can arise if care is not taken when using the term 'member' to differentiate between those who are in a strict legal sense the members of the charitable company, usually entitled to elect the trustees, and when the term is used more colloqually to mean someone who pays an annual 'membership' subscription or is receiving services from the charity, who may be only 'affiliate' or 'associate' members with no legal status

### Closing down

If a charitable company goes into voluntary liquidation the surplus assets must be distributed for exclusively charitable purposes. A formal winding-up process must be carried out by a duly appointed liquidator but more usually a shorter striking off procedure will be followed.

## Charitable Incorporated Organisation

A new legal structure for charitable companies is included in the Charities Act 2006. The Charitable Incorporated Organisation (CIO) structure will, when implemented, allow charities to have the benefits of incorporation and be regulated solely by the Charity Commission and not by Companies House. The advantage of this new form of legal structure for charities is that the structure is designed specifically for charities, and charities will no longer need to be regulated by two separate bodies.

Charities wishing to take advantage of this new structure will need to convert from an existing charitable company to a CIO.

At the time of updating the Good Trustee Guide, the provisions relating to the CIO were due to be implemented in 2009. In the meantime, charities are generally advised that, if they need to incorporate, they should not wait for the new legislation but incorporate using existing legislation.

**Further information**
is available on the Charity Commission website (search for CIO).

## Industrial and Provident Society (IPS)

An IPS is another form of incorporation. Until the Charities Act 2006 it could not be a registered charity but could have charitable status as an exempt charity. Under the Charities Act 2006 some IPSs will retain their exempt status (including housing associations, but others will now be required to register with the Charity Commission). An IPS is defined as a society for the benefit of the community and should carry on a business, industry or trade. This legal framework is commonly used by housing associations. Further information is available on the Financial Services Authority website.

## Drawing up a governing document

To simplify the process of drawing up a governing document, the Charity Commission has approved:

- Model governing documents, containing many of the standard provisions suitable for charities
- Approved governing documents for the branches or affiliated organisations of certain national bodies
- Model objects clauses.

**Further information:**
is available at the Charity Commission's website under About Charities.

## Amending a governing document

There may be times when a charity finds its original purposes – perhaps agreed many decades ago – no longer fully reflect the environment in which it operates. Or, that its procedures for electing or appointing trustees have become unwieldy. Changes in legislation may also mean that an organisation's procedures for, say, holding general meetings are no longer up to date.

These are all examples of situations where a charity may look to review and, if necessary, amend provisions in its governing document. In particular, it has been quite common recently for charities to review their governing document in the light of the significant number of changes brought in by the Charities Act 2006 and Companies Act 2006.

Amending your charity's governing document is a significant piece of work, involving the approval of members (if your charity has a membership) and in some cases the prior approval of the Charity Commission.

### Where is our amendment clause in our governing document?

Companies Limited by Guarantee have a statutory power of amendment in the Companies Act. This means that there may not be an amendment clause in your governing document.

Some trust deeds contain a power to vary the deed. Similarly, the constitution of many unincorporated associations will include a power to alter its terms, usually subject to the approval of a certain percentage of the membership. If as an unincorporated charity you do not have the power to amend your governing document, you will have to apply to the Charity Commission for a scheme. This is easier for very small charities.

### Is Charity Commission approval required to amend our governing document?

Most charities will require the consent of the Charity Commission to any change to the objects and provisions conferring benefits to the trustees. In the case of charitable companies this is a statutory requirement.

### Do we need to call a general meeting to approve changes?

If your charity has a membership, then members will normally be required to approve any proposed change to the governing document at a general meeting. Usually, the procedures for calling a meeting and the percentage of members present and voting required to approve the amendment are set out in the governing document.

### Who should we notify?

The Charity Commission must be informed of the change and may need to give prior approval.

Companies Limited by Guarantee must inform Companies House of the change.

**Further information** on amending your charity's governing document is available from the Charity Commission's publication *Changing your Charity's Governing Document* (CC36).

# 2.4

## Incorporation

It is quite common for charities to move from an unincorporated association or trust structure to a company limited by guarantee structure. This is because the company structure can be more suitable as an organisation grows in size and complexity. If your organisation is unincorporated but employs staff, occupies property and / or has significant contractual arrangements, you may consider moving to a company structure. In a company, the organisation has its own legal identity, which means that contractual arrangements can be made in the name of the company, not the name of the trustees, and hence provide trustees some (although not comprehensive – see chapter 3) protection from personal financial liability.

The process of moving to a company structure is called 'incorporation', and involves setting up a new company limited by guarantee, registering it as a charity, and then transferring assets and liabilities from the unincorporated organisation to the new company organisation. Because of the complexity of the process it is recommended you seek professional advice before taking any action.

**Further information**
is available from the Charity Commission's *Setting up a company to replace an existing charity* webpage (see About Charities).

## Checklist:

Have all trustees received a copy of the governing document?

Are all trustees familiar with the objects of the organisation?

Do trustees understand the provisions of your governing document?

Have you reviewed your governing document recently to ensure the objects reflect your current and planned work, and the administrative provisions (appointment of trustees and so on) are workable and meet your needs?

Are you confident that your organisation's current legal structure best meets the organisation's needs?

Do you need to consider changing your legal structure?

## Branches and subsidiaries

Branches

Many charities have local groups or branches. These may fundraise only, provide services, carry out advice and campaigning work or operate as self-help groups. Some of these may not themselves be charitable – for example social clubs for the benefit of members but which also raise funds for the main charity. The degree of control and autonomy varies considerably from charity to charity.

Are trustees responsible for the activities of local groups?

If you are a trustee of the national or 'parent' charity, you need to know what the relationship is to any local groups.

In some instances the local group will be part of the national charity. If this is the case, then the trustees of the national charity will be responsible for all the activities and actions of the local groups or branches.

Other charities, such as Age Concern and Mencap, have a structure in which all local groups are separate, autonomous organisations, each registered as a charity. Each local group has its own trustees and the trustees of the national charity are not responsible for the activities of the local groups. Many such organisations have membership agreements between the national charity and local organisations.

If you are not sure about the relationship between the national charity and local branches, check your governing document. If you are still unsure, seek advice from the Charity Commission.

If you are a trustee of a national charity with dependent local groups you should:

- establish an adequate system for overseeing and monitoring local groups
- consider having a written code of conduct for each of the local groups
- ensure that local groups state that they are a registered charity on all their stationery, appeal documents, cheques, invoices and receipts
- provide accounting returns which have to be consolidated into the national accounts
- consider the needs of local groups when allocating reserves.

If you are a trustee of an autonomous local organisation you should:

- have your own governing body and produce your own accounts
- register with the Charity Commission if your organisation has exclusively charitable purposes and meets the minimum requirements for registration
- comply with legislation for PAYE, VAT and other fiscal or legal requirements
- consider having a written agreement between autonomous local groups and the 'parent' charity.

Trustees of autonomous local organisations should be aware that mismanagement of their affairs could result not only in their personal liability but also in adverse publicity that could be damaging for the national charity.

## Checklist:

Are you a trustee of a charity with branches?

Are the branches separate legal entities?

If your charity has dependent branches, does your board need to review how it exercises its responsibilities for the activities of the branches and how the branches ensure their accountability to the trustees?

If you charity has branches that are separate legal entities, does your board need to review the relationships between local branches and the national charity – for example membership agreements that may exist between the national charity and local branches?

Subsidiaries

Some charities have a separate, non-charitable subsidiary. This can occur if your charity wishes to benefit from continuous trading activity that is not directly related to its objects or where they want to isolate the risk. Trustees should obtain detailed legal advice before setting up a wholly owned trading company. Some charities have separate charitable subsidiaries. For example, a 'parent' charity could establish one or more charitable subsidiaries to deliver a range of specialist or complex services. The charitable subsidiaries would have their own boards of trustees to provide a focus on the subsidiary's work but would also benefit from the support of the parent charity.

**For further information**
see Charity Commission's publication Collaborative working and mergers: an introduction (CC34).

Trading

Trustees should obtain detailed legal advice before setting up a wholly owned trading company. In particular, advice should be sought on any deeds of covenant and the circumstances in which a charity can lend money to its trading arm. The charity's governing document will need to include powers for the trustees to invest in the shares of a private company. The consent of HM Revenue and Customs may be required if the charity is not to lose some tax exemptions. Expert advice will be needed on dealing with the financing of the wholly owned trading company.

As a matter of charity law and good practice you should ensure that:

- the financial structures of the charity and any trading subsidiaries are kept separate
- the interests of the charity do not become dominated by those of the trading subsidiary
- any loans made to a trading subsidiary are within the terms of the charity's governing document, are at a commercial rate of interest and are properly secured
- if the charity and the trading subsidiary share premises, equipment or staff, care is taken to apportion costs accurately between them, to avoid any hidden subsidy of the trading company by the charity.

## Checklist:

Does your charity have a non-charitable trading subsidiary?

Have you carried out a review of your subsidiaries?

Are your non-charitable trading subsidiaries or associates adequately capitalised without putting the funds of your charity at risk?

Would you be able to recover your entire investment if you now disposed of your trading company?

# 3

# Duties and responsibilities of trustees

## 3.1

### Introduction

As a trustee you must make sure that your organisation:

- pursues its objects or purposes, as set out in its governing document
- uses its assets exclusively to pursue those aims
- acts in the interests of its beneficiaries.

You should also:

- take an active part in the charity
- avoid conflict with your personal interests
- not profit from your role unless it has been authorised

More guidance on the role of the board and its relationship with staff can be found in chapter 11.

# 3.2

Where day-to-day management and operations are delegated to staff or volunteers, your board remains responsible for supervising the chief executive (and sometimes other staff) and ensuring that the organisation is being well managed and operating within agreed policies, the law and its budget.

In order to carry out its role the board must:

- meet as often as is necessary for the proper administration of the charity
- consider the need for professional and other expert advice where necessary.

**Tip:** it is a good idea to draw up a role description for a trustee, setting out their duties and responsibilities. A model role description, including role descriptions for trustees with specific roles are available in section 4.1.

## Duty to comply with the governing document

Trustees must comply with the provisions of their governing document (see section 2.3). They should be familiar with its provisions; and in particular with the stated charitable objects.

Trustees have a duty to act within the objects of the charity, and to apply the charity's assets exclusively to pursue those objects. It is a breach of trust to undertake any activities outside the objects. You could be held personally liable to repay to the charity any monies spent on activities outside the objects.

In addition to your statutory powers and limitations, you will usually have additional powers to pursue the charity's aims as set out in the governing document. For example, the governing document usually defines the powers trustees have to delegate work to sub-committees or staff, but this does not mean that they have to delegate. You should make sure that you know your powers to act and do not exceed them.

Some organisations also have written rules or standing orders for internal procedural matters such as the conduct of board meetings, the composition of the board and other committees, and the election or appointment of new trustees. You will need to be familiar with and follow these rules, which must not contradict or repeal anything contained in the governing document. The standing orders can be amended in accordance with the procedure set out in the governing document.

# 3.3

## Duty of care

The Charity Commission state that trustees must *"use reasonable care and skill in their work as trustees, using their personal skills and experience as needed to ensure that the charity is well-run and efficient; and*

*consider getting external professional advice on all matters where there may be material risk to the charity, or where the trustees may be in breach of their duties".*[7]

*"use reasonable care and skill"* means allowing for:

- any special knowledge or experience a person has or says they have; and
- any special knowledge it is reasonable to expect from a business or professional person when acting in either capacity.

The level of competence and proficiency required of a trustee will vary according to the level of expertise the person has.

If you do not seek advice on matters on which you are not an expert, be they legal, financial or managerial, you could be regarded as having acted imprudently and you may be personally liable for the consequences. The Charities Act 1993 requires you to seek professional advice in some instances, for example, in relation to certain land transactions. When you do seek advice, you should keep copies of relevant correspondence and/or notes of conversations.

The Trustee Act 2000 introduced a new statutory duty to create certainty and consistency to the standard expected from a trustee in relation to investment powers (see chapter 7 on investment for more details).

# 3.4

## Duty to comply with the law

Trustees must ensure the organisation complies with laws that may be relevant to its work. Such laws will vary from organisation to organisation depending on size and activities, but often include:

a) charity law and the requirements of the Charity Commission (see below);

b) company law and the requirements of Companies House (see below);

c) Industrial and Provident Society law, and the requirements of the Financial Services Authority;

d) employment law (see chapter 11);

e) health and safety legislation (see section 9.3);

f) data protection legislation (see section 10.2);

g) legislation against discrimination on grounds of race, disability, gender and other factors (see section 12.1); and

h) any other legislation which may apply to particular organisations, such as that relating to fundraising, the protection of children or vulnerable adults, the provision of health or care services, the provision of financial advice, housing and tenancy law and others.

[7] Charity Commission publication *The Essential Trustee: What you need to know* (CC3). Crown Copyright.

# 3.5

As a trustee you are not expected to have a detailed knowledge of this legislation. However, you should be aware that legislation exists and, where necessary, you should be satisfied that someone is responsible for making sure that effective compliance systems are in place. The Code of Governance recommends that trustees put in place *"policies, procedures and reporting mechanisms in place to ensure compliance with applicable legislation."* [8]

## Charity law

Under charity law all trustees must be eligible for trusteeship (see section 1.1). You must follow the Charity Commission's disclosure, reporting and accounting requirements, including those introduced in the Charities Act 1993. Failure to do this is a criminal offence. You must keep within the law on trading, political activities and fundraising.

## Company law

As a trustee of a charitable company, trustees are also company directors and you must comply with the legal requirements relating to company directors. You must ensure that your charity keeps up to date with its company returns and record-keeping.

You must act in the best interests of the company even where this conflicts with your private or other interests. You must not continue trading as a company if you know, or should have known, that your company is insolvent.

[8] *Good Governance: A Code for the Voluntary and Community Sector* (Governance Hub, 2005).

The Companies Act 2006 introduced a set of statutory duties of company directors. These are:

- to act within the company's powers
- to promote the success of the company for the benefit of its members as a whole. In the case of a charitable company this will mean to achieve its charitable purposes including the need to consider the company's actions on the community and environment
- to exercise independent judgment
- to exercise reasonable care, skill and diligence

  – these all came into force in October 2007
- to avoid conflicts of interest
- not to accept benefits from third parties
- to declare an interest in proposed transactions and arrangements

  – these will come into force in October 2008

## Checklist

If your charity is established a company, have you made all trustees aware of their statutory duties as company directors?

Does your board need to check that there is someone responsible for ensuring that the charity complies with the law, and in particular with the requirements of the Charities Act 2006 and Companies Act 2006?

**Further information**
Companies House Directors and Secretaries Guide (GBA1).

## Duty to protect the charity's property

Trustees have a duty to protect all the assets belonging to the charity, for instance by ensuring that there are adequate financial controls and that any land or buildings the charity owns are well maintained and insured.

Any funds, land, buildings or other assets which form part of the charity's permanent endowment (that is, property which the trustees may not spend as if it were income) cannot usually be expended without the Charity Commission's consent in accordance with new provisions of the Charities Act 2006 . If they are investment assets they should be invested to produce a good income while protecting the real value of the capital. In some cases authority can be obtained from the Charity Commission to adopt a total return approach to investment and spend part of the capital gain. This is a complex area and more detail can be found on the Commission's website.

Trustees also have a duty to protect the charity's reputation and its intellectual property such as trade-marks and databases.

**Further information:**
Charity Commission Operational Guidance *Endowed charities: a total return approach to investment* (OG83)

# 3.6

## Duty to act in the interests of beneficiaries and avoid conflicts of interest

When you sit down at the board meeting table, all of your outside interests have to be left outside or, if they can't, they need to be properly managed.

The law is quite clear – your first duty as a trustee is to the charity's beneficiaries, which means you must act in the interests of the charity as a whole. You must remain independent and not come under the influence of another organisation. Anything that might conflict – or be perceived to conflict – with your duty as a trustee should be managed using a conflicts of interest policy. A good test is to ask if the charity's reputation would be damaged if your connection with a member of staff, a firm of professional advisers, or a building company, for example, were made public.

## Situations where a conflict of interest may occur

- Where a trustee may stand to benefit personally. Trustees cannot benefit beyond what is allowed by law and permitted in the charity' governing document. This restriction also applies to persons connected with the trustee. This situation could include, for example
  - when a trustee receives payment for a particular service they provide to the charity, or
  - where a trustee also uses the charity's services and stands to benefit personally (eg receive a grant)
- Where a trustee's loyalties are divided between the charity and another organisation (or perhaps a personal situation). Inevitably, in practice, trustees have a wide range of interests in private, public and professional life, and these interests might, on occasions, conflict. For example, local councillors sometimes sit on the boards of organisations that are funded by the local authority to which they are members.

## Dealing with conflicts of interest

Any potential conflict of interest should be carefully considered and managed in the correct way. It is good practice to have an agreed policy and an agreed practice which trustees should follow when considering conflicts of interest. This can include:

- A code of conduct for trustees (see the end of this chapter)
- Register of interests disclosing potential personal interests
- A procedure for identifying conflicts and withdrawing from discussion and decision and the minuting of such a process (this should also extend to the discussion and decisions).

## An example conflicts of interest procedure

- Any trustee who has a financial interest in a matter under discussion should declare the nature of his/her interest and withdraw from the room, unless s/he has a dispensation to speak.
- If a trustee has any interest in the matter under discussion which creates a real danger of bias, that is, the interest affects him/her, or a member of his/her household, more than the generality affected by the decision: s/he should declare the nature of the interest and withdraw from the room, unless s/he has a dispensation to speak.
- If a trustee has any other interest which does not create a real danger of bias, but which might reasonably cause others to think it could influence their decision, s/he should declare the nature of the interest, but may remain in the room, participate in the discussion, and vote if s/he wishes.
- If in any doubt about the application of these rules, s/he should consult with the chair.
- It is recommended that trustees' interests are listed in a register.

If conflicts of interest are so frequent as to limit an individual's usefulness as a trustee, then s/he must stand down from one of the posts.

## Conflicts of interest: other issues to consider

The Companies Act 2006 will introduce new provisions for conflicts of interest for company directors. These will come into force in October 2008. There are duties to avoid conflicts of interest, not to accept benefits from third parties and to declare an interest in proposed transactions. There is also a requirement to disclose the nature and extent of interests in an existing transaction or arrangement. This includes transactions between the company and the directors where there are special rules for charitable companies. There are detailed rules for this and the procedures required for disclosure. It is good practice to include on every board meeting agenda an item for disclosure of any interest.

If the company's Articles (in its governing document) include provisions for dealing with conflicts of interest and the directors follow them they will be protected from breach of their statutory duties.

The Articles may also include a provision for the directors to authorise a conflict. Again , there are detailed rules for this situation which are outside the scope of this book.

It is good practice for trustees of unincorporated charities to inform the board of situations where they, or people connected with them, may have an interest in a contract or transaction.

## Checklist

Do you have a conflicts of interest policy for trustees?

If you are a charitable company are you aware of the new provisions under the Companies Act 2006 and do your articles include procedures to deal with conflicts of interest?

**Further information**
Charity Commission online guidance *A Guide To Conflicts of Interest For Charity Trustees* (linked from *The Essential Trustee* publication).

# 3.7

## Duty to act collectively

Trustees are jointly and severally responsible for the activities of the charity and must act together. No trustee acting alone can bind his or her fellow trustees, unless specifically authorised to do so.

Trustee boards operate collectively and decisions are taken as a body. The board's decisions do not have to be unanimous. Therefore the majority bind the minority, and you are bound by the decisions of your fellow trustees even if you were absent from a meeting. If you vote against a decision, make sure your vote is recorded in the minutes and if the matter is serious, for example if you think the charity is going to spend resources on something outside its objects (which would be a breach of trust), you should consider resignation (but see section 3.9 on liability).

Meetings are the formal setting for all trustee decisions. Trustees should meet often enough to carry out their business of governing the charity. Trustees act collectively and they cannot act individually in their role as trustee unless authorised. In practice trustees are often involved in aspects of a charity's work (for example, sub-committees, as advisers, or as volunteers to specific services) and this should be encouraged but it should also be made clear which role the trustee is in.

There are restrictions over the use of electronic or 'virtual' meetings (see chapter 21).

# 3.8

## Duty not to financially benefit unless authorised

The voluntary principle – that trustees serve primarily to benefit others, rather than for personal gain – is one of the defining principles that distinguish charities from other types of organisation. According to the Charity Commission, the vast majority of trustees in the country carry out this principle by serving on their boards without receiving payment of any kind – perhaps with only their basic out of pocket expenses covered.

What does the voluntary principle of trusteeship mean in practice? According to the Charity Commission, it means that "trustees must not put themselves in a position where their personal interests conflict with their duty to act in the interests of the charity unless authorised to do so".[9]

In practice, the voluntary principle means that there are restrictions over how far trustees can receive benefits from the charity. Restrictions on benefits cover the following:

1) Payment for serving as a trustee. There is no general power in law to allow this type of payment, and special authority would need to be given by the Charity Commission or the courts. Any organisation considering paying their trustees to 'be a trustee' would need to demonstrate that it is "clearly in the interests of the charity and provides a significant and clear advantage over all other options". Authority to pay a trustee in this way is only given in exceptional circumstances – an example is where a charity's work is very complex and trusteeship carries a very high burden.

2) Where an employee of the charity is also a trustee. It is rare for a trustee to also be an employee and there is no general power to allow this. Authority would need to be given by an express clause in the governing document or by the Charity Commission. There are some types of charity where this situation is more common – for example, schools often include the head teacher as a trustee and religious charities often include the spiritual leader as a trustee. There have also been recent cases where the Charity Commission has authorised a chief executive to serve as a trustee in the same organisation. It is important to note that, if a trustee resigns in order to take up a paid position in the charity, Charity Commission approval may also be needed (see Charity Commission publication CC11 – see below). Approval must also be obtained where a trustee's spouse or partner becomes a paid employee if they have shared finances.

3) Payment to a trustee for services provided for the charity (e.g. providing legal advice or electrical services). The Charities Act 2006 allows trustees to be paid for goods or a service they may provide to the charity (not as an

[9] Charity Commission publication *Trustee expenses and payments* (CC11). Crown Copyright.

employee), provided that the governing document does not expressly prohibit payment and provided that certain conditions are met. These conditions include that the payment is reasonable and in the best interests of the charity, ensuring a written agreement exists over the payment, that the trustee to be paid is not involved in the decision, and that a minority of trustees are not paid (there are other conditions and it is recommend you consult Charity Commission publication CC11).

4) Payment to 'connected persons' or businesses – most of the restrictions over payment also apply to family members or businesses connected with a trustee.

5) Payment in kind – payment does not just involve a financial transaction. For example, payment could include where a trustee is given free use of office space for their business in return for joining the board; or where a trustee is also a service user and receives free use of facilities for which users normally have to pay.

6) Payments which may sometimes be perceived as being expenses – for example payment for loss of earnings or 'honoraria' payments are considered to be payments.

Can I claim back out of pocket expenses?

Yes, provided the organisation's governing document does not expressly prohibit this (which is unusual).

Expenses which may be reimbursed are actual costs which a trustee has incurred in their role and can include such items as travel, meals, childcare whilst at trustee meetings, postage and telephone calls. Payments trustees above actual expenses incurred and which do not relate to legitimate trustee activities cannot be treated as expenses. Examples of these are travel costs for a spouse or payment of telephone bills unrelated to the charity.

Any payment which are excessive or are not genuine and reasonable out of pocket expenses will be treated as income and be subject to tax as with other forms of income. A trustee who receives an unauthorised payment may be required to pay it back to the charity. The Charity Commission provide further guidance on what are permitted expenses in *Trustee Expenses and Payments* (CC11).

Payments – issues to consider

The Charity Commission recommend that any departure from the voluntary principle of trusteeship should be given very careful consideration, and be carried out with the proper authority. This may involve seeking prior Charity Commission approval.

## Drawing up a trustee expenses policy – good practice guidelines

- Set out which items are legitimate expense claims – e.g. travel, childcare, accommodation, etc.
- Only reimburse actual costs – and pay against receipts. Extra money may be regarded as taxable income (see above).
- Include an expenses claim form with every agenda. Trustees can always donate their expenses back and if they are a taxpayer the charity can reclaim the tax under Gift Aid.

## Considering paying a trustee? Checklist (from the Charity Commission):

- Who will receive the payment – will it be a trustee, or a person or business connected with a trustee?
- What is the payment expected to cover?
- Is the payment clearly in the best interests of the charity?
- Is there a legal authority for it?
- What conditions must be met if the payment is to be made?
- How will any conflict of interest be managed?

**Further information**
It is recommended you consult the Charity Commission's publication *Trustee expenses and payments* (CC11).

## Checklist

Is payment of trustees likely to be an issue for your board?

If so, have you checked your governing document to see what it says about payment of trustees?

If so, have you familiarised yourself with the Charity Commission guidance and ensure that it is followed?

# 3.9

## Trustee liability

Trustees are often concerned about their personal liability. This section summarises the types of liability which trustees may incur.

### Remember ... keep it in perspective!

Before describing the different types of liability that trustees may incur, it is important to point out that very few trustees who have acted honestly suffer financial loss as a result of their trusteeship. There are risks, but they should be kept in proportion. When breaches of trust (see below) have been committed as the result of an honest mistake, or when trustees have been found wanting in the degree of control they exercised over staff, the Charity Commission has rarely required trustees to make good any loss. Insurance will not protect you from liability incurred as a result of a breach of trust knowingly committed.

### What are the personal liabilities of trustees?

Trustees of all types of charities can be held personally liable for:

- breach of trust under charity law (this includes spending the charity's money on an activity which is outside the charity's legal objects, carrying out unpermitted political activity, fraud, serious negligence or a trustee receiving personal benefit) (see below);
- acting as charity trustees when disqualified;
- failure to comply with relevant statutory requirements in areas such as health and safety, trade descriptions and financial services;
- failure to deduct an employee's PAYE.

The degree of risk of personal liability will vary according to the activity of your charity. In general, charities engaged in service provision will face greater risks than those involved in grant-making.

### Liability for breach of trust

Trustees may be liable for a breach of trust, for instance if they distribute assets on causes falling outside the express objects of the charity, or fail prudently to protect the trust property. If trustees are found to be in breach of trust, then they may be required by the Charity Commission or the court to make good the losses to the charity which arose as a result of breach of trust.

All trustees, regardless of the charity's legal structure, may be jointly and severally liable for a breach of trust. However, it is important not to get the risk of being found in breach of trust out of proportion; and it is unlikely that the trustees of a well-run charity will be found personally liable if they have acted honestly and reasonably. Indeed, trustees can apply to the Charity Commission for relief from personal liability if they have acted honestly and reasonably.

The Charity Commission's position is even more robust. In its booklet *The Essential Trustee* (CC3), it states that

*"If trustees act prudently, lawfully and in accordance with the governing document, then any liabilities (ie debts or financial obligations) that they incur as trustees can normally be met out of the charity's resources."* [10]

Steps you can take to minimise the risk of acting in breach of trust include:

- Ensuring the organisation acts in accordance with the requirements of its governing document
- Ensuring the organisation is well-managed and follows good practice
- Complying with all relevant legislation
- Taking appropriate legal or other professional advice when you don't have enough information to make a decision.

[10] Charity Commission publication *The Essential Trustee* (CC3). Crown Copyright.

### Liability for the debts and liabilities of the organisation

As well as for breach of trust, trustees may in some circumstances be personally liable for the debts and other liabilities of the charity. The extent to which this is the case depends on whether the charity is a trust, an unincorporated association or a company.

### Trusts and unincorporated associations

Trusts and unincorporated associations do not have their own independent legal personality. This means that the trust or unincorporated association cannot contract on its own account. If the trustees enter into any contractual or other arrangements they must do so by contracting in their capacity as trustees. As a result of this, they are personally liable to settle any debts or other liabilities which occur as a result of the arrangement entered into. Liabilities of this type might include fees for professional services, repairing covenants or rent under a lease, damages for breach of contract, etc.

Provided that the trustees have acted honestly and reasonably they will usually be entitled to be indemnified against their liability from the assets of the trust or unincorporated association. However, if the charity does not have sufficient assets to meet the liability, then the trustees will still be jointly and severally liable to make good any shortfall. If trustees are concerned about any potential liability of this type – for example, if the organisation is taking on significant responsibilities such as employee or premises – then one option is to incorporate as a company limited by guarantee (see below).

### Charitable companies

Charitable companies have their own legal personality, so that contracts and other legal relationships can be entered into by the company. Charitable companies also afford trustees limited liability. This is because the members of the company (who may or may not also be trustees/company directors) will typically guarantee that, in the event of the winding up of the company, they will contribute a nominal amount, usually £1 or £5, towards its assets.

This means that, unlike with an unincorporated association or a trust, the trustees of a charitable company cannot be personally liable for the debts of the company, or liable in contract or tort (a legal term covering civil wrongs such as negligence or liability).

However, the benefits of becoming an incorporated charity and limiting liability are not as comprehensive as is sometimes thought. Trustees of a charitable company can still be personally liable for the activities of the organisation in certain circumstances, as this section of the Good Trustee Guide illustrates, and can be held liable for certain breaches relating to their duties as company directors, including:

- breach of their fiduciary and statutory duties as company directors (examples are using the charitable company's assets to procure an unauthorised benefit for the trustees);
- wrongful trading under the Insolvency Act 1986 (that is, continuing to trade when you know, or ought to have known, that there was no reasonable prospect of avoiding going into insolvent liquidation (this has never yet happened to trustees of a charitable company);
- fraudulent trading – where a trustee deliberately seeks to defraud a creditor when the company is insolvent or about to become insolvent;
- acting as a company director when disqualified;
- other breaches listed in 'what are the personal liabilities of trustees?' above

### How does liability relate to trustees' terms of office?

Normally the Charity Commission expects new trustees to assume responsibility for decisions made by the board of trustees in the past. However, new trustees do not have to assume responsibility for past breaches of the charity's trusts. If new trustees discover, on assuming office, that the charity is currently acting in breach of trust, they must take steps to remedy the situation or else they too will become liable for the breach.

Trustees do not cease to be liable for their actions in breach of trust upon retirement or resignation. You will remain liable for any breaches of trust committed during your term of office. This means that if the Charity Commission instigates an enquiry into the activities of a charity during 2003 and judge that, for example, the trustees had spent some of the charity's assets on activities outside their charitable objects, then they could require the people who were trustees in 2003 to repay to the charity the sum judged to have been misspent.

### What should trustees do if a bank asks for a personal guarantee?

If your charity approaches a bank or other lender for a loan the trustees may be asked for personal guarantees in addition to any agreement with the charity. If the charity subsequently gets into financial difficulty, you can be left with a personal liability. You should always take legal advice before agreeing to provide a personal guarantee.

### What steps can trustees take to protect themselves?

There are a number of ways in which trustees can limit the risk of personal liability:

- Good management practice – particularly financial management and clear procedures – is the starting point for risk limitation.
- Clear roles and responsibilities – job descriptions and induction procedures for trustees are important, as are clear lines of responsibility, budgetary guidelines and good communication.
- Records of decisions taken – you should make your own notes of the board's decisions and check them against the minutes before agreeing them. The minutes are the legal record of the board's decisions.
- Provisions in your governing document – you can have express provisions inserted in the governing documents that exempt trustees from personal liability to the charity if they have acted reasonably and made an honest mistake that results in loss to the charity.
- Insurance – trustees may take out trustee liability insurance. They may pay the premiums themselves or now under the charities Act 2006 in most circumstances (unless prohibited by the governing document) the costs can be met by the charity (For more information, see section 9.2).
- Incorporation – becoming a company limited by guarantee can offer protection to trustees against liability for debts incurred by the charity.
- Contingency funds – these can be built up so that sufficient reserves exist to meet potential liabilities such as premature termination of leases or staff redundancy costs.
- Professional advice – this should be obtained by the board if there is any doubt about the correct course of action to be taken.
- Board development – your board should consider implementing a continuous programme of board development – trustee training and governance reviews – to keep abreast of changes in law and practice.

### Can trustees limit their liability by distancing themselves from decisions?

If you are in disagreement with your board over an issue and are concerned about your liability, you should withdraw from the decision and ensure that your disagreement is minuted. However, trustees are judged to act jointly so it could be argued that your continued membership of the board will not remove your liability.

**Further information**
The Governance Hub publication *Reducing the Risks: A Guide to trustee liabilities* (available from NCVO) provides further information on this topic. The Charity Commission's *The Essential Trustee* (CC3) is also a useful source of information.

## Checklist

Are all trustees aware of their roles and responsibilities?

Do you have trustee role descriptions?

Do you have an induction process for new trustees?

Have you conducted a risk assessment of the personal liability of your board of trustees?

Are you confident that your management practices and board practices limit this risk as far as is reasonably possible?

Does your board seek expert advice when faced with a complicated legal or technical issue which it is not confident to deal with?

Do trustees understand their personal liabilities?

Have you considered taking out trustee liability insurance?

Does your trustee board have a development programme which includes a regular review of its role and effectiveness?

Does your board need to consider incorporation (unincorporated charities only)?

## A Code of Conduct for trustees

A trustee code of conduct is an agreement between the charity and individual trustees that spells out the standards of behaviour expected from trustees. Trustees sign up to the code when they join the board. When they do so, they are pledging to uphold its standards.

The governing board, using input from other parts of the charity, writes the code to establish a set of organisational values – for example integrity, honesty, transparency. It also asks for specific behaviours from trustees designed to put these principles into practice.

NCVO recommends that every charity institute a trustee code of conduct. In brief, a trustee code of conduct, well formulated and properly implemented, can be a powerful tool for improving quality of trustee board governance:

- The very act of writing a code can have a good effect on the board by bringing concerns into the open and inspiring debate.
- Codes of conduct provide basic protection for the organisation by defining inappropriate behaviour on the part of its trustees.
- Codes can be used to improve trustee recruitment, induction, assessment, training and development.

NCVO's model codes are intended to offer a place for boards to begin the vital process of policymaking. They are not intended as templates for policy for all organisations. A policy authored by anyone other than the board (even by NCVO) and adopted without discussion won't necessarily suit the organisation. It's the board's responsibility to know the special needs of its organisation and tailor policy to fit.

### Fostering trustee ownership

For implementation to be effective, the board must feel that the code of conduct comes from them, reflecting their concerns and expressing their wishes. This sense of ownership is born during the writing process when the board formulates the code. Once a code has been created, this feeling of ownership has to be kept alive. New trustees have to buy into existing codes of conduct and serving ones need to keep them in mind.

## A Model Trustee Code of Conduct

### Organisational values

As a trustee of [organisation] I promise to abide by the fundamental values that underpin all the activity of this organisation. These are:

### Accountability

Everything [organisation] does will be able to stand the test of scrutiny by the public, the media, charity regulators, members, stakeholders, funders, Parliament and the courts.

### Integrity and honesty

These will be the hallmarks of all conduct when dealing with colleagues within [organisation] and equally when dealing with individuals and institutions outside it.

### Transparency

[Organisation] strives to maintain an atmosphere of openness throughout the organisation to promote confidence of the public, stakeholders, staff, charity regulators and Parliament.

Additionally, I agree to the following points:

### Law, mission, policies

I will not break the law or go against charity regulations in any aspect of my role of trustee.

I will support the mission and consider myself its guardian.

I will abide by organisational policies.

### Conflicts of interest

I will always strive to act in the best interests of the organisation.

I will declare any conflict of interest, or any circumstance that might be viewed by others as a conflict of interest, as soon as it arises.

I will submit to the judgment of the board and do as it requires regarding potential conflicts of interest.

### Person to person

I will not break the law, go against charity regulations or act in disregard of organisational policies in my relationships with fellow trustees, staff, volunteers, members, service recipients, contractors or anyone I come into contact with in my role as trustee.

I will strive to establish respectful, collegial and courteous relationships with all I come into contact with in my role as trustee.

### Protecting the organisation's reputation

I will not speak as a trustee of this organisation to the media or in a public forum without the prior knowledge and approval of the chief executive or Chair.

When prior consent has not been obtained, I will inform the Chair or chief executive at once when I have spoken as a trustee of this organisation to the media or in a public forum.

When I am speaking as a trustee of this organisation, my comments will reflect current organisational policy even when these do not agree with my personal views.

When speaking as a private citizen I will strive to uphold the reputation of the organisation and those who work in it.

I will respect organisational, board and individual confidentiality.

I will take an active interest in the organisation's public image, noting news articles, books, television programmes and the like about the organisation, about similar organisations or about important issues for the organisation.

### Personal gain

I will not personally gain materially or financially from my role as trustee, nor will I permit others to do so as a result of my actions or negligence.

I will document expenses and seek reimbursement according to procedure.

I will not accept substantial gifts or hospitality without prior consent of the Chair.

I will use organisational resources responsibly, when authorised, in accordance with procedure.

### In the boardroom

I will strive to embody the principles of leadership in all my actions and live up to the trust placed in me by [organisation].

I will abide by board governance procedures and practices.

I will strive to attend all board meetings, giving apologies ahead of time to the Chair if unable to attend.

I will study the agenda and other information sent me in good time prior to the meeting and be prepared to debate and vote on agenda items during the meeting.

I will honour the authority of the Chair and respect his or her role as meeting leader.

I will engage in debate and voting in meetings according to procedure, maintaining a respectful attitude toward the opinions of others while making my voice heard.

I will accept a majority board vote on an issue as decisive and final.

I will maintain confidentiality about what goes on in the boardroom unless authorised by the Chair or board to speak of it.

### Enhancing governance

I will participate in induction, training and development activities for trustees.

I will continually seek ways to improve board governance practice.

I will strive to identify good candidates for trusteeship and appoint new trustees on the basis of merit.

I will support the Chair in his/her efforts to improve his/her leadership skills.

I will support the chief executive in his/her executive role and, with my fellow board members, seek development opportunities for him/her.

### Leaving the board

I understand that substantial breach of any part of this code may result in my removal from the trustee board.

Should I resign from the board I will inform the Chair in advance in writing, stating my reasons for resigning. Additionally, I will participate in an exit interview.

This Code of Conduct is taken from the NCVO publication *Best Behaviour: Using trustee codes of conduct to improve governance practice* (Tesse Akpeki, edited by Marta Maretich, 2004).

# 4

# Board and committee structures

## Introduction

This chapter looks at the make-up of the board, where the trustees fit in and where sub-committees fit in. As for the rest of Part One, this section concentrates on defining the role. After reading this section you can visit Part Three to look at practical ways of enhancing the effectiveness of meetings and sub-committees.

# 4.1

## Who's who in the boardroom

| Who they are | What they do | Special features |
|---|---|---|
| Board Members (may be called the trustee board, committee, the board of directors, the executive committee, the board of governors etc) | Work as a team to make most important decisions for their charity<br>Take overall responsibility | Don't get paid<br>Team of equals<br>Unique kind of group leadership |
| The Chair (also called the chairman, chairwoman or chairperson of the board) | Board member chosen to run meetings; may also work closely with the chief executive and be in charge of providing information to board members | Important job<br>Runs meetings<br>Helps all board members' opinions be heard<br>Acts as facilitator to the board |
| The chief executive or head of staff (if one is appointed – may be called chief executive officer , CEO, director, co-ordinator, manager, director-general, executive etc) | Responsible for the day-to-day running of the charity; puts the board's decisions into practice | Gets paid<br>Rarely a board member<br>Hired (and may be fired) by the board<br>Supported and evaluated by the board<br>Reports to the board |
| Board Sub-committee | Small group assigned by the board to focus on a particular task or area (such as finance, internal audits and so on) and advise the board | Can contain non-board members<br>Can't make decisions unless authorised<br>Reports to the board<br>Can add value to governance |
| Advisory Group | Group of non-board members which advises the board | No official role<br>No voting power<br>Can provide valuable information and expertise |

## Board meetings

Meetings are the formal setting for all trustee decisions. The quality of your decisions will depend on planning, preparation, efficient running and chairing of board meetings and the time you devote to team building. Trustees should of course make an effort to attend all board meetings. If you are unable to attend you should send your views and comments to the chair prior to the meeting.

Many charities will have a quorum (the minimum number of people who must be present for the meeting to take place) laid down in their governing document. Some governing documents contain clauses requiring trustees to resign if they have been absent without sufficient reason from a specified number of meetings.

Procedures in your governing document regarding the calling of meetings must be followed. You may also have procedures governing the conduct of meetings (see chapter 21 for more on effective meetings).

## On the board

### Honorary officers

Many boards find it useful to have a number of trustees who take on specific roles. Trustees with specific roles may:

- deal with matters needing attention between meetings of the full board
- take a lead in preparing issues in readiness for board meetings

In charities that employ staff they sometimes

- act as an effective link between the staff and the board of trustees
- share with the chief executive the task of representing the charity
- sit on recruitment panels for senior staff appointments
- sit on disciplinary panels
- act as a final court of appeal for serious disciplinary matters.

Trustees with specific roles are often called 'honorary officers'. Honorary officers can only carry out aspects of the charity's business if they are authorised to do so. Honorary Officers commonly comprise a chair, vice-chair, secretary and treasurer. The roles of chair and treasurer are particularly common.

The honorary officers are sometimes elected by the members of the board of trustees or by the charity's membership. Unless the board has explicitly delegated decision-making powers to honorary officers, they should act in an advisory capacity and must take care to report their activities fully to the board to prevent the other trustees feeling excluded by an inner group. This is particularly important if honorary officers meet as a group in between board meetings. The governing document may give honorary officers specific roles, functions and responsibilities.

### The chair

The role of the chair is to chair the meetings of the board of trustees. The chair sometimes also take a number of other, wider roles (although not exclusively so: in some charities these roles are undertaken by other trustees). When staff are employed, the chair may work closely with the head of staff – chief executive or manager – to support him or her in achieving the aims of the charity and acting as the channel of communication between the trustees and staff. The chair may act as a figurehead of the charity and represent it at functions, meetings and in the press and broadcasting media. Other tasks may include authorising action to be taken between meetings of the full board, signing cheques for amounts above those for which authority has been delegated to staff and signing legal documents.

### The vice-chair

The vice-chair may either be a chair designate (i.e. a person in waiting to be chair) or somebody who will deputise for the chair.

### Vice-chair as deputy chair

The vice-chair acts for the chair when the chair is not available and undertakes assignments at the request of the chair. To ensure continuity, every charity should ensure that key people have a deputy who can assume their responsibility and is familiar with their work should a sudden absence occur. The vice-chair fulfils this role for the chair. The charity should also consider other key roles that require deputies, for example the chief executive.

### The secretary

In charities with staff, most of the secretarial duties involved in running the board – sending out agendas and board papers, taking minutes, checking that a quorum is present, booking the meeting room and so on – are commonly undertaken by staff. The role of the secretary is confined to taking minutes of meetings from which all staff are excluded, being consulted by the chair in between meetings and undertaking other duties delegated to the honorary officers or at the request of the chair.

Where there are no paid staff, the honorary secretary has to undertake all the secretarial duties to support the board. Taking accurate minutes of meetings is a particularly important task as these form the legal record of the board's decisions (see chapter 21 for further guidance).

Under the provisions of the Companies Act 2006 Charitable Companies are no longer required to have a company secretary unless their Articles specifically provide for one. If they do have a company secretary their duties are to ensure that the charity complies with the requirements of company law, including keeping the Register of Members, Register of Directors and Register of Charges up to date and notifying Companies House of any changes in trustees, preparing and filing the annual return and making sure that the company documents are kept safely. In charities with staff, the role of company secretary is not normally assigned to the honorary secretary but delegated to a member of staff.

### The treasurer

The treasurer takes the lead in overseeing the financial affairs of the charity. The treasurer will assist other trustees to perform their financial duties, by interpreting and explaining accounting requirements, ensuring that the board receives reports containing the information trustees need in an 'easy to understand' format, and helping trustees guide any other professional advisers they have appointed.

The precise tasks of a treasurer will depend on the size of the charity, the governing document and/or the remit given to the treasurer by the trustee board. In most charities the treasurer's duties are likely to include:

- presenting financial reports to the board in an understandable form
- keeping the board aware of its financial responsibilities
- ensuring that the charity's accounts are prepared in a suitable format
- ensuring that the accounts and financial systems are independently examined or audited if required
- liaising with the auditors/ independent examiners.

In smaller charities the treasurer may personally maintain the financial records and prepare budgets and financial reports. The treasurer should have sufficient technical expertise to guide the financial affairs of the charity. For example, if the charity has large investments the treasurer should have sufficient knowledge to ensure that they are earning the best possible return. The treasurer should also be willing and able to give authoritative advice that protects a charity's financial position but may conflict with the aspirations of the board to expand the charity's work.

**Tip:** it is a good idea to draw up a role description for each honorary officer, setting out their duties and responsibilities. Model role descriptions are available overleaf.

Patrons (these are not trustees)
Patrons are people who lend credibility or support to the cause of a charity or voluntary organisation. They are not involved in any way in its management, nor do they have any legal responsibilities. Patrons can thus be helpful in fundraising and public relations; for instance, they may be prepared to be named on letterheads or in annual reports, and can help to gain media coverage if they are willing to attend events.

Presidents (they are not usually trustees)
The role of president or vice-president is usually a figurehead role distinct from that of a trustee. A president or vice-president may be formally elected or appointed or may be informally chosen as a figurehead in a similar way to a patron. Presidents sometimes have specific duties such as the chairing of the annual general meeting.

Presidents or vice presidents are not usually trustees and have a quite separate role to the trustees' role – unless the governing document states otherwise (for example, the term president is used in some countries to refer to the chair of the board).

## Checklist

Does your charity have written role descriptions for its honorary officers?

Does your board need to review the honorary officers' role descriptions in the light of the needs and legal duties of your charity?

## Model role descriptions

Model job description for a trustee
The following specimen trustee role descriptions and person specifications can be adapted to meet your charity's particular needs.

Role description – the roles, responsibilities and tasks which trustees are expected to carry out.

Person specification – the skills, experience and qualities which are expected from trustees. Again these will vary depending on what specifically you are looking for – they could include technical skills, experience of the community you work with or of a particular culture. These may have come from a board review or skills audit. Again, however, all trustees should be able to demonstrate basic qualities of commitment and integrity which are needed to be a trustee.

## Trustee role description

Title: Trustee of ______________________________________________

The duties of a trustee are:

- To ensure that the organisation complies with its governing document (i.e. its trust deed, constitution or memorandum and articles of association), charity law, company law and any other relevant legislation or regulations.
- To ensure that the organisation pursues its objects as defined in its governing document.
- To ensure that the organisation applies its resources exclusively in pursuance of its objects (ie the charity must not spend money on activities which are not included in its own objects, no matter how worthwhile or charitable those activities are).
- To contribute actively to the board of trustees' role in giving firm strategic direction to the organisation, setting overall policy, defining goals and setting targets and evaluating performance against agreed targets.
- To safeguard the good name and values of the organisation.
- To ensure the effective and efficient administration of the organisation.
- To ensure the financial stability of the organisation.
- To protect and manage the property of the charity and to ensure the proper investment of the charity's funds.
- If the charity employs staff, to appoint the chief executive officer and monitor his/her performance.

- In addition to the above statutory duties, each trustee should use any specific skills, knowledge or experience they have to help the board of trustees reach sound decisions. This may involve scrutinising board papers, leading discussions, focusing on key issues, providing advice and guidance on new initiatives, or other issues in which the trustee has special expertise.

Trustee person specification

- a commitment to the organisation
- a willingness to devote the necessary time and effort
- strategic vision
- good, independent judgement
- an ability to think creatively
- a willingness to speak their mind
- an understanding and acceptance of the legal duties, responsibilities and liabilities of trusteeship
- an ability to work effectively as a member of a team
- Nolan's seven principles of public life: selflessness, integrity, objectivity, accountability, openness, honesty and leadership.

## Role description for a chair

Title: Chair of ____________________________________________

Role description

In addition to the general responsibilities of a trustee:

Additional duties of the chair
(the list below are examples – see section 4.1)

- Planning the annual cycle of board meetings
- Setting agendas for board meetings
- Chairing and facilitating board meetings

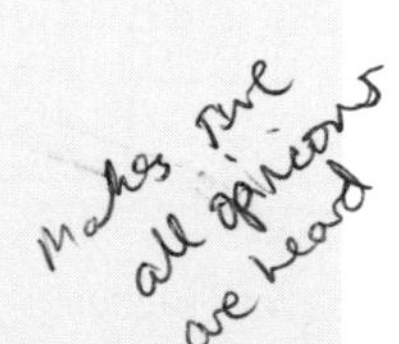
Makes sure
all opinions
are heard

- Giving direction to board policy-making
- Monitoring that decisions taken at meetings are implemented
- Representing the organisation at functions and meetings, and acting as a spokesperson as appropriate
- The vice-chair acts for the chair when the chair is not available and undertakes assignments at the request of the chair

- Where staff are employed
  - Liaising with the chief executive to keep an overview of the organisation's affairs and to provide support as appropriate
  - Leading the process of appraising the performance of the chief executive
  - Sitting on appointment and disciplinary panels
- Liaising with the chief executive officer to develop the board of trustees
- Bringing impartiality and objectivity to decision-making
- Facilitating change and addressing conflict within the board and within the organisation, liaising with the chief executive (if staff are employed) to achieve this.

Person specification
In addition to the person specification for a trustee:

**Role of chair**

- leadership skills
- experience of committee work
- tact and diplomacy
- good communication and interpersonal skills
- impartiality, fairness and the ability to respect confidences.

In most circumstances it would also be desirable for the chair/vice-chair to have knowledge of the type of work undertaken by the organisation and a wider involvement with the voluntary sector and other networks.

## Role description for a secretary

Title: Secretary of ________________________________________

Role description
In addition to the general responsibilities of a trustee:

Additional duties of the secretary

The role of the secretary is to support the chair by ensuring the smooth functioning of the board. Tasks will include the following (either by carrying them out directly or delegating to a member of staff and ensuring that they have been carried out):

- preparing agendas in consultation with the chair and chief executive
- making all the arrangements for meetings (booking the room, arranging for equipment and refreshments, organising facilities for those with special needs, etc.)

- preparing agendas in consultation with the chair and chief executive officer and circulating them and any supporting papers in good time.
- receiving agenda items from other trustees/staff
- checking that a quorum is present
- minuting the meetings and circulating the draft minutes to all trustees
- ensuring that the minutes are signed by the chair once they have been approved
- checking that trustees and staff have carried out action agreed at a previous meeting
- circulating agendas and minutes of the Annual General Meeting and any special or extraordinary general meetings
- in organisations which are companies, acting as company secretary where this role is not delegated to a member of staff
- sitting on appraisal, recruitment and disciplinary panels as required.

Person specification
In addition to the person specification for a trustee:

**Role of secretary**
- organisational ability
- knowledge or experience of business and committee procedures
- minute-taking experience, if this is not being delegated to staff.

## Role description for a treasurer

Title: Treasurer of ______________________________________

Role description
In addition to the general responsibilities of a trustee:

**Additional duties of the treasurer**
The overall role of a treasurer is to maintain an overview of the organisation's affairs, ensuring its financial viability and ensuring that proper financial records and procedures are maintained. In small charities without paid staff the treasurer may take a greater role in the day-to-day finances of the organisation.

- overseeing, approving and presenting budgets, accounts and financial statements
- being assured that the financial resources of the organisation meet its present and future needs
- ensuring that the charity has an appropriate reserves policy

- the preparation and presentation of financial reports to the board
- ensuring that appropriate accounting procedures and controls are in place
- liaising with any paid staff and volunteers about financial matters
- advising on the financial implications of the organisation's strategic plans
- ensuring that the charity has an appropriate investment policy
- ensuring that there is no conflict between any investment held and the aims and objects of the charity
- monitoring the organisation's investment activity and ensuring its consistency with the organisation's policies and legal responsibilities
- ensuring the organisation's compliance with legislation
- ensuring that equipment and assets are adequately maintained and insured
- ensuring that the accounts are prepared and disclosed in the form required by funders and the relevant statutory bodies, e.g. the Charity Commission and/or the Registrar of Companies
- if external scrutiny of accounts is required, ensuring that the accounts are scrutinised in the manner required (independent examination or audit) and any recommendations are implemented
- keeping the board informed about its financial duties and responsibilities
- contributing to the fundraising strategy of the organisation
- making a formal presentation of the accounts at the Annual General Meeting and drawing attention to important points in a coherent and easily understandable way
- sitting on appraisal, recruitment and disciplinary panels as required.

Person specification

In addition to the person specification for a trustee:

**Role of treasurer**

- financial qualifications and experience
- some experience of charity finance, fundraising and pension schemes
- the skills to analyse proposals and examine their financial consequences
- a preparedness to make unpopular recommendations to the board
- a willingness to be available to staff for advice and enquiries on an ad hoc basis.

## Checklist

Do all trustees have a copy of their role description and person specification?

Are all prospective trustees sent copies of a trustee role description?

# 4.2

## Delegation

Trustees are required to act in person and any decisions affecting the charity must be made by the trustees acting together. However, in practice, most but the very smallest charities will delegate day to day matters to

- individual trustees – for example delegating the role of financial oversight to the treasurer
- sub-committees – for example to investigate a particular issue in more detail
- staff or volunteers – the day to day running of the charity

### What matters should be reserved for the trustee board?

It is recommended that some tasks should not delegated from the trustee board but instead be the subject of a board decision.

ICSA (the Institute of Chartered Secretaries and Administrators) has produced a specimen list of such items, Matters Reserved for the Board of Trustees, aimed at charities with a senior management team.

## Sub-committees

### Can trustees delegate to committees?

Trustees are required to act in person and any decisions affecting the charity must be made by the trustees acting together. If your governing document gives you the power to do so, you may delegate authority to a sub-committee of your board for a particular aspect of the charity's work, or delegate authority to a task group or committee whose members need not necessarily all be trustees.

However, any decisions made by such groups remain the responsibility of the whole board of trustees. The terms of reference and reporting-back procedures of any committees, sub-committees or task groups should be laid down in writing and agreed by the board of trustees.

For many charities monthly, bimonthly or quarterly meetings of the board of trustees are sufficient to carry out its work. But as organisations become larger, take on more staff and expand into new areas or activities, boards sometimes establish sub-committees or working groups which can allow more time to be spent on certain issues and involve people from outside the trustee board.

### Sub-committees – good practice

- Boards must have a power in their governing document to delegate decisions
- Boards can delegate decisions to sub-committees but the board is ultimately accountable for decisions taken
- The role and accountability of the sub-committee should be clear to all members of the sub-committee and the board
- Sub-committees should be reviewed to ensure they are effective.

### Do you have the power to set up sub-committees?

Check your governing document to see what it says about board and committee structure. Is there a clause giving the board of trustees power to establish sub-committees? Does the power allow the delegation of decision-making? Are there rules governing the membership of sub-committees? (For example, sub-committees with decision-making power may require a majority of trustees as members.)

Trustees who serve on a sub-committee should be able to distinguish between their role as board member and their role as sub-committee member. For more guidance on good practice in the use of sub-committees see chapter 21.

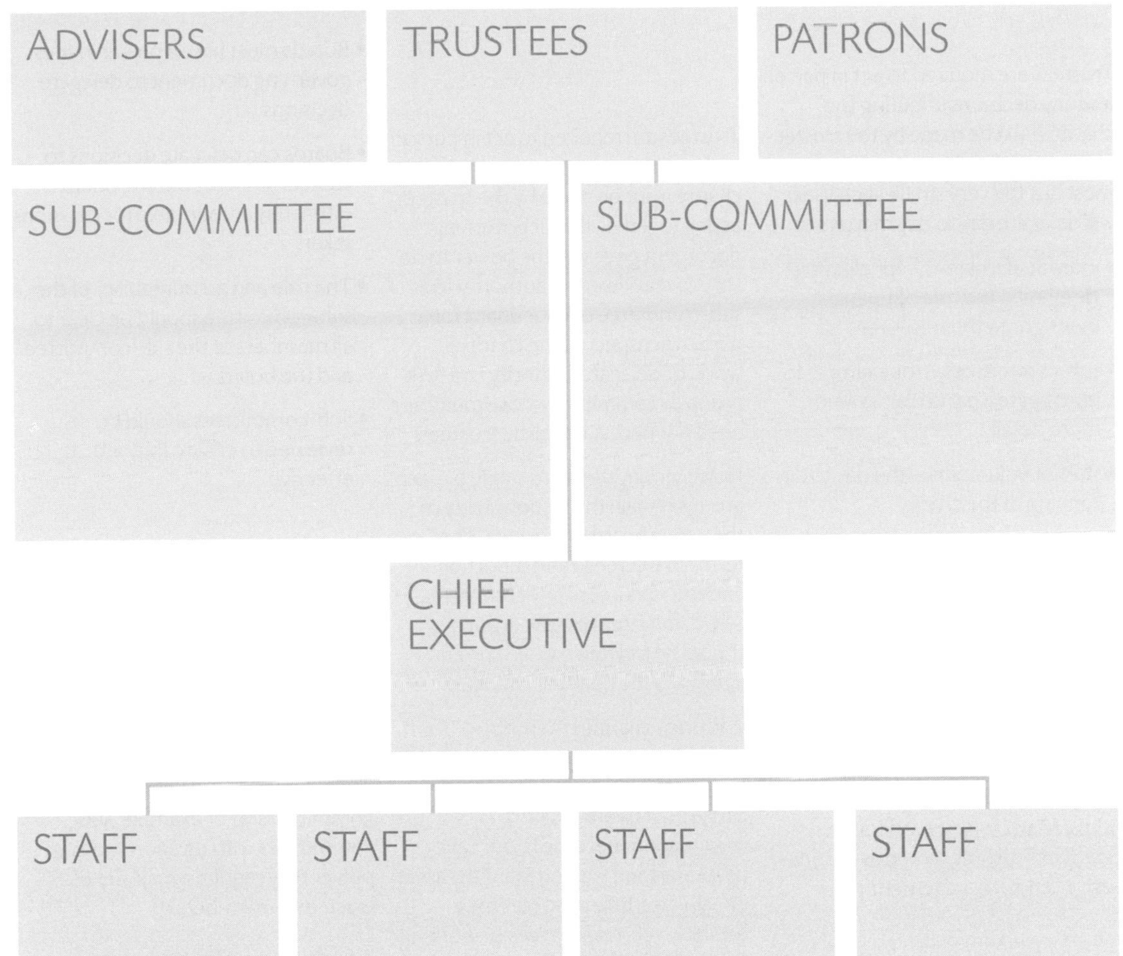
ADVISERS
TRUSTEES
PATRONS
SUB-COMMITTEE
SUB-COMMITTEE
CHIEF EXECUTIVE
STAFF
STAFF
STAFF
STAFF

## Boards of trustees and sub-committees compared

| Board of trustees | Sub-committee |
| --- | --- |
| Ultimate responsibility for the charity. | May specialise in certain areas of the board's work – for example, finance, fundraising, staff pay or board recruitment. |
| Can delegate decision-making and ratify recommendations of sub-committees if it has the power to do so. | The remit and any decision-making power is set by the board of trustees and the governing document. |
| May invite non-voting observer members to meetings who are not trustees. | Can have a mix of trustees, staff, volunteers and external advisers. |

## Checklist

Does your governing document include a power to establish sub-committees?

Do all your committees and working parties have written terms of reference?

When trustees join sub-committees are they briefed about their role on the sub-committee?

## Staff and volunteers

### What can trustees delegate to staff and volunteers?

Charities have a power to employ agents. All trustees can delegate implementation of their decisions, but a power is required to delegate executive (decision-making) powers.

If your charity is of a sufficient size, and your governing document gives you the power to do so, you may delegate the day-to-day management of the charity and all its operations to employed staff and/or volunteers. The scope of delegated authority should be set down in writing, and decisions made by staff and/or volunteers on important matters must be reported to the board of trustees as quickly as possible. The board remains legally responsible for all activities of the charity, including matters delegated to staff and/or volunteers – and it is recommended that some duties are never delegated to others.

What is appropriate to delegate to staff and/or volunteers will vary with the size of the charity. For example, the trustees of a small grant-giving trust would be expected personally to examine all grant applications, but this would be impractical for the trustees of a charity whose grants run to many millions of pounds.

The trustees of such charities should produce written guidelines setting out their grant-giving policy, and then delegate to staff and/or volunteers the authority to make grants within those policy guidelines up to a specified amount. The trustees should be given a report of any grants made. Similarly, the boards of trustees should make major policy decisions.

The trustees of a national network of self-help groups may decide that all helpline volunteers must be trained, but could delegate to local groups decisions about the hours each helpline should be staffed. Trustees of a charitable company running charity shops may decide whether properties should be purchased or rented but will delegate decisions about shop location and layout to local staff and/or volunteers.

### Can trustees take on other roles?

Trustees can, and sometimes do, play several roles in their charity. In addition to their volunteer role as a member of the governing body, they act as volunteers in other ways, for example, running fundraising events, doing the accounts, or delivering the service provided by the charity.

If you have a number of different roles, it is important to be aware of when you are acting in a particular role. In your role as a trustee, you are responsible for setting objectives for the chief executive officer's work plan, but if you are in another volunteer role, you must be prepared to take direction from the person with responsibility for supervising that area of the charity's work. For example, if your charity runs a community centre that has a paid manager, when you are in your role as a trustee the manager will be accountable to you, but when you work as a volunteer helping to run the community centre's crèche, you will be accountable to the centre's manager.

**Tip:** if you are a trustee and take on other roles in the charity – for example volunteering in the office or organising events, think of yourself as having different "hats" – in this case a trustee hat and a volunteer hat.

## Checklist:

Do trustees delegate day to day running to others?

Have you agreed the scope of delegated authority in writing (for example in job descriptions or policies)?

When were these last reviewed?

# Part Two:

# Good Governance

# 5

# What is governance?

Your charity's success depends on how it meets the needs of its beneficiaries, its vitality, its standing in the voluntary sector and its ability to manage change. Achieving this success depends to a large extent on the way you and your fellow trustees govern effectively.

It is essential for your board to be able to stand back and take the wider view of your charity. Are you clear about why your charity should exist? Do you know where the organisation is going in the future? And is the charity meeting its objects in the most effective way?

Perspective and leadership are vital whatever the management structure of your organisation. If your organisation does not employ staff, you will be involved in the day-to-day management of its work, so stepping back helps give trustees the 'big picture'. Where staff are employed, your responsibility will be to ensure that the charity is well managed – rather than being actively involved in running it – and well monitored.

## What is governance?

Trustees take overall responsibility for everything the charity does and they act collectively to govern the organisation. The term often used to describe this role is "governance". What is governance?

Chris Cornforth describes governance as

*"the systems and processes concerned with ensuring the overall direction, effectiveness, supervision and accountability of an organisation"*[1].

Sandy Adirondack defines governance as

*"the process by which a governing body ensures that an organisation is effectively and properly run... Governance is not necessarily about doing; it is about ensuring things are done"*[2].

### Principles of good governance

The twelve essential responsibilities of trustees, set out in chapter 1, are underpinned by seven principles of good governance, as set out in the Code of Governance. Drawn up in 2005 by a number of different support and membership bodies in the voluntary and community sector, the Code sets out a statement of best practice in governance. The seven principles are:

### 1. Board leadership

**The key principle:**
Every organisation should be led and controlled by an effective Board of trustees which collectively ensures delivery of its objects, sets its strategic direction and upholds its values.

**Supporting principles:**
The role of the Board: Trustees have and must accept ultimate responsibility for directing the affairs of their organisation, ensuring it is solvent, well-run, and delivering the outcomes for which it has been set up.

Strategic direction: Trustees should focus on the strategic direction of their organisation, and avoid becoming involved in day to day operational decisions and matters (except in the case of small organisations with few or no staff). Where trustees do need to become involved in operational matters, they should separate their strategic and operational roles.

### 2. The Board in control

**The key principle:**
The trustees as a Board should collectively be responsible and accountable for ensuring and monitoring that the organisation is performing well, is solvent, and complies with all its obligations.

**Supporting principles:**
Compliance – The Board must ensure that the organisation complies with its own governing document, relevant laws, and the requirements of any regulatory bodies.

Internal controls – The Board should maintain and regularly review the organisation's system of internal controls, performance reporting, policies and procedures.

Prudence – The Board must act prudently to protect the assets and property of the organisation, and ensure that they are used to deliver the organisation's objectives.

Managing Risk – The Board must regularly review the risks to which the organisation is subject, and take action to mitigate risks identified.

Equality and diversity – the Board should ensure that it upholds and applies the principles of equality and diversity, and that the organisation is fair and open to all sections of the community in all of its activities.

[1] *The Governance of Public and Non-profit Organizations: what do boards do?* (Cornforth, CJ (ed.) – Routledge, 2003).

[2] *The Good Governance Action Plan for Voluntary Organisations* (Adirondack, Sandy – NCVO, 2002).

## 3. The high performance Board

**The key principle:**
The Board should have clear responsibilities and functions, and should compose and organise itself to discharge them effectively.

**Supporting principles:**
Trustee duties and responsibilities – Trustees should understand their duties and responsibilities and should have a statement defining them.

The effective Board – The Board should organise its work to ensure that it makes the most effective use of the time, skills and knowledge of trustees.

Information and advice – Trustees should ensure that they receive the advice and information they need in order to make good decisions.

Skills and experience – The trustees should have the diverse range of skills, experience and knowledge needed to run the organisation effectively.

Development and support – Trustees should ensure that they receive the necessary induction, training and ongoing support needed to discharge their duties.

The Chief Executive – The Board should make proper arrangements for the supervision, support, appraisal and remuneration of its Chief Executive.

## 4. Board review and renewal

**The key principle:**
The Board should periodically review its own and the organisation's effectiveness, and take any necessary steps to ensure that both continue to work well.

**Supporting principles:**
Performance appraisal – The Board should regularly review and assess its own performance, that of individual trustees, and of sub-committees, standing groups and other bodies.

Renewal and Recruitment – The Board should have a strategy for its own renewal. Recruitment of new trustees should be open, and focused on creating a diverse and effective Board.

Review – The Board should periodically carry out strategic reviews of all aspects of the organisation's work, and use the results to inform positive change and innovation.

## 5. Board delegation

**The key principle:**
The Board should set out the functions of sub-committees, officers, the Chief Executive, other staff and agents in clear delegated authorities, and should monitor their performance.

**Supporting principles:**
Clarity of roles – The Board should define the roles and responsibilities of the Chair and other honorary officers, in writing.

Effective delegation – The Board should ensure that staff, volunteers and agents have sufficient delegated authority to discharge their duties. All delegated authorities must have clear limits relating to budgetary and other matters.

Terms of reference – The Board should set clear terms of reference for sub-committee, standing groups, advisory panels, etc.

Monitoring – All delegated authorities must be subject to regular monitoring by the Board.

## 6. Board and trustee integrity

**The key principle:**
The Board and individual trustees should act according to high ethical standards, and ensure that conflicts of interest are properly dealt with.

**Supporting principles:**
No personal benefit: Trustees must not benefit from their position beyond what is allowed by the law and is in the interests of the organisation.

Dealing with conflicts of interest: Trustees should identify and promptly declare any actual or potential conflicts of interest affecting them.

Probity: There should be clear guidelines for receipt of gifts or hospitality by trustees.

Trustees who are directors must also comply with the rules of conflict of interest imposed by the Companies Act.

## 7. Board openness

**The key principle:**
The Board should be open, responsive and accountable to its users, beneficiaries, members, partners and others with an interest in its work.

**Supporting principles:**
Communication and consultation: Each organisation should identify those with a legitimate interest in its work ('stakeholders'), and ensure that there is a strategy for regular and effective communication with them about the organisation's achievements and work.

Openness and accountability: The Board should be open and accountable to stakeholders about its own work, and the governance of the organisation.

Stakeholder involvement: The Board should encourage and enable the engagement of key stakeholders, such as users and beneficiaries, in the organisation's planning and decision-making.

**Further information:**
*Good Governance: A Code for the Voluntary and Community Sector* is available from the NCVO website (see resources section).

## Hallmarks of an Effective Charity

The Charity Commission's Hallmarks of an Effective Charity set out "the standards that will help trustees to improve the effectiveness of their charity, and the principles that our regulatory framework exists to support."[3]

Further information can be found in the Charity Commission's publication *Hallmarks of an Effective Charity* (CC10).

[3] Charity Commission publication *The Hallmarks of an Effective Charity* (CC10). Crown Copyright.

Governance is concerned with leadership and direction. It is about ensuring your charity has a clear, shared vision of its purpose, what it is aiming to achieve and how in broad terms it will go about doing it, and that it maintains a sense of urgency about its work.

As trustees, you must set clear aims and objectives, establish priorities, safeguard the charity's assets (money, property – including intellectual property – equipment and human resources) and use them effectively and exclusively for the benefit of those the charity exists to help.

Trustees take ultimate responsibility for the governance of their organisation. However, governance is not a role for trustees alone. More, it is the way trustees work with chief executives and staff (where appointed), volunteers, service users, members and other stakeholders to ensure their organisation is effectively and properly run and meets the needs for which the organisation was set up.

The Good Trustee Guide aims to show you how you can use various approaches; clarifying board/staff relations, planning trustee recruitment and induction, organising board development and conducting board reviews – to energise and enhance the effectiveness of the way your board works. Many of these draw on the Code of Governance as a set of principles.

# 6

# Strategic planning

A key responsibility of your board is to ensure that your charity makes a difference while working within the objects in its governing document. What does this mean in practice?

It means agreeing, usually every three to five years:

- the ideal state your charity wants to see (the vision)
- the role it will play to work towards the vision (the mission)
- the changes it hopes to bring about (the outcomes)
- how it will act (the values), and
- what it actually plans to do (the activities and outputs).

# 6.1

## Objects and mission

What is your mission?

Your mission should sum up in clear, non-legal language the medium-term goals of your charity. It should be consistent with your objects as defined in your charity's governing document (see section 2.3), but may refine them and outline how they will be met in the coming years.

It should be short, just one or two sentences, and set out:

- the purpose of the charity – what changes do we want to bring about?
- the beneficiaries or cause – who or what are we here for?
- how and where the charity will work – how do we do it?

Example:

The Worcestershire Association of Carers exists to relieve the stresses experienced by carers and people with physical, mental or sensory impairment within the family or home in the county of Worcestershire, through the provision of information services, support centres and the promotion of needs of carers.

# 6.2

## What is strategic planning?

Strategic planning involves:

- clarifying your charity's purpose
- reviewing your charity's situation
- opening up options and choices
- making decisions
- making sure the right people know what has been decided, and what it means for them.

Strategic planning may not always seem relevant to a small association or grant-giving trust. However, the trustees of even the smallest groups will benefit from standing back and questioning whether their charity should carry on doing what it has always done or if it should be making changes. In fact, the smallest charities may have the most to gain: strategic planning can help them to keep nimble and make the most of new opportunities.

This five-step process is taken from NCVO's *Thinking Ahead: An introduction to strategic planning*:

| | | |
|---|---|---|
| 1 | Get ready | Prepare: decide on the process and timescale you want your strategic planning to follow and form a group to take the lead and to share tasks |
| 2 | Clarify your organisation's purpose | Consider your vision, mission and values: what your organisation is going to be like and how it's going to act<br>Consider the outcomes and changes your organisation exists to make<br>Analyse and build your knowledge of your user group |
| 3 | Open up options and choices | Look internally: consider the organisation's strengths, weaknesses, competencies and capacity<br>Look out: consider how external trends and issues will influence how and to what extent the organisation can deliver its mission in the future |
| 4 | Make decisions | Refine options for the future and discuss them with stakeholders<br>Develop detailed priorities |
| 5 | Communicate, implement and review | Communicate your strategy internally and externally<br>Weave strategy into team and individual work plans<br>Track the progress of the strategy and judge its success in strengthening your organisation |

# 6.3

## Case study

Dorset Agenda 21 (DA21), a community-based forum on sustainability issues, wanted a new strategy. It was keen to take advantage of the emergence of environmental issues on the mainstream political agenda, but it had very limited resources. The charity's trustees led the strategic planning process and began with a special informal meeting to explore the charity's mission, vision and values, as well as members' needs. After this review, the trustees planned to propose amendments to their vision and mission at the next annual general meeting. They also organised a stakeholder consultation meeting to generate ideas for new projects, which they later explored and refined. DA21 has now become more focused on its identity as a delivery agent rather than an advocacy body, and collaborative working is a priority to enable it to punch above its weight. DA21 has been particularly effective in communicating its strategy to stakeholders, who are now much more aware of its role and its openness to partnership working.

## The strategic plan

A strategic plan sets out how your charity will move from the present position to the one it aspires to reach by the end of the identified period. The format of your plan will depend on your charity's needs and who you are communicating the plan to. There is no hard and fast rule about what a strategic plan should look like or what it should contain. It should be as long or as short, as detailed or as light-touch, as it needs to be.

### Types of plan

Here are five different suggestions of what a strategic plan could look like:

**Story:** A plan that tells a powerful and convincing narrative about where your charity has come from and provides an exciting vision for the future.

**Roadmap:** A technical plan that gives your charity a route to a destination, highlighting landmarks you will pass, potential hazards you may encounter on the way and resources you'll need.

**Logbook:** A framework that sets out what your charity wants to be and how it will act, but gives the space for the charity to record and capture the pattern of strategic choices it makes in the coming years.

**Flyer:** A short snappy plan that is designed to promote your charity's successes and future intent to an external audience.

**Library:** Not so much a single plan in itself as a store that pulls together plans, budgets and information about the charity's environment for staff to draw on.

You might also want to consider creative ways of communicating your plan. For instance, some charities have found events, posters, visual diagrams and even 3D models of their strategy effective.

If you find it helpful to have a written plan in a single document, consider including the following elements:

- A clear statement of the charity's vision and mission and the specific changes it wants to deliver
- A summary of its performance so far and reasons for this
- An analysis of potential opportunities and challenges in the future
- Priorities and aims for the coming years
- Plans for how the whole organisation will change to deliver these priorities
- An outline of how the organisation will track the progress of this strategy, including milestones and indicators of success.

### Keeping the strategy alive

Strategic planning is an ongoing process. Even once a plan has been agreed, you and your fellow trustees should review it at regular intervals:

- to monitor progress against targets
- to check that any assumptions made are still valid
- to see if the plan should be modified.

You will also need to communicate the plan in different ways to reinforce the ideas behind it and to ensure that all your stakeholders not only understand your direction, but support your goals and help you to achieve them. Updates on progress are equally important.

Your strategic plan should form the basis of all your charity's operational planning. Operational planning translates your high level strategic plan into a more detailed description of who will do what and when. Operational plans usually relate to the short to medium term, maybe one to three years, and may apply to your whole charity, or a particular project or area of work. Business plans, annual plans, project plans, action plans and individual work plans are all different types of operational plan. Don't worry too much about these terms; the important thing is to develop plans which will help you to deliver your work and keep on track.

# 6.4

## The board's role in strategic planning

- The board should lead the strategic planning process with the chief executive (if you employ one). This is a crucial part of your remit: making sure the charity is achieving the most for its beneficiaries or cause.
- You are removed from the day-to-day 'firefighting' and can take a holistic approach to your organisation and offer perspective
- It is the trustees' role to regularly assess how the charity meets its purposes – including a review of how far its purposes reflect the current operating environment and whether they need to change (see also section 2.3)
- You can help to draw together the views of different stakeholders
- In particular, the board should ensure that stakeholders such as staff, volunteers and users have the opportunity to feed into the strategic planning process. If you do, your ideas are likely to be richer and the links between your board's strategic level work and day-to-day operations can be improved, making a plan really robust.

How strategic planning can help the board improve its own work

- It provides the overall framework for the board to assess the charity's progress
- It provides an opportunity for your board to review its own role and performance
- It can help to identify board priorities
- It can provide opportunities for board meetings, sub-committees and working parties to be remodelled around strategic priorities
- The experience can help identify board member interests and expertise and form the basis of board recruitment (around particular skills, experience, etc needed to fulfill the plan)
- The process can help to strengthen the relationship between your board and chief executive.

**Further information**
*Thinking Ahead: An introduction to strategic planning* (Eliot, Jake – NCVO, 2008)

## Checklist

Does your charity have an up-to-date vision and mission?

Does your charity have a strategic plan?

Is the strategic plan reviewed at regular intervals?

Has the strategic plan been communicated to the right stakeholders in the right way?

Does your board need to review its strategic planning process?

If you employ staff and a chief executive, does your board and the chief executive have a clear understanding of the level of leadership expected from the chief executive?

# 7

# Resources

# 7.1

## Financial responsibilities

### Introduction

What financial responsibilities do trustees have?

Trustees are legally responsible for the financial resources entrusted to the charity.

Charity accounting changed in the 1990s with the official recognition that charity operations were very different from commercial companies. Since the 1990s, the Charities Acts of 1993 and 2006, along with a framework for charity accounting – the Statement of Recommended Practice or SORP – have brought in clearer guidance and requirements to ensure trustees are able to discharge their responsibilities effectively.

Charitable companies are also subject to company law and trustees must ensure that the accounting procedures set out in the Companies Acts are followed.

Key financial responsibilities of trustees include:

- ensuring proper accounting records are kept
- ensuring annual reports and accounts are produced in a form that satisfies the requirements of regulators and the charity's governing document, and are filed with regulators as required.
- approving and monitoring budgets
- ensuring that proper control is exercised over both income and expenditure in particular monitoring continued solvency
- monitoring fundraising policy and activities
- overseeing any trading activities
- ensuring that the tax affairs of the charity are managed effectively
- ensuring that any investments earn the best possible return without putting the capital at risk
- ensuring investments are invested:
  - in accordance with the charity's powers of investment as set out in its governing document
  - in accordance with any agreed socially responsible policy
- ensuring that the charity's assets and income are used exclusively to pursue its objects
- ensuring that reasonable steps are taken to prevent and detect fraud and other irregularities. If your charity is large enough to warrant having internal audit staff, these staff should report directly to your board.

### I am new to finance. What role should I play as a trustee?

Financial information can seem daunting to the inexperienced or the non-financial expert: don't let it. As a trustee you have a duty to ask questions and take advice when you need to.

All trustees should either have, or be prepared to develop, basic skills in financial management. In particular, trustees should know how to:

- read budgets and accounts so they know if the annual accounts properly summarise their charity's activities and state of affairs
- interpret financial reports and advise on appropriate action in response
- guide professional advisers entrusted with property and financial reserves
- assist and monitor fundraising activities
- recognise actual or threatened insolvency.

Some trustees will not have previous experience of dealing with a charity's finances. They should be given support by the Honorary Treasurer or the charity's finance officer or in some other way. This chapter of the Good Trustee Guide also aims to give trustees basic information about their financial responsibilities.

Trustees can be personally liable for the misuse of charity funds or the liabilities of an insolvent charity so you should make sure you and your board members understand their wide-ranging financial responsibilities.

### Getting meaningful information

Trustees should ask for financial information to be presented in a form which they can understand (e.g. tables, charts, graphs) and the information should be accompanied by a written commentary. Some charities give new trustees a glossary of the terms used in their accounts (see part five).

### Key questions to ask

Are we running a gain or a loss?

Are key expenses under control?

Do we have sufficient reserves?

Is cash flow adequate?

Where are we compared to budget?

Is our financial plan consistent with our strategic plan?

Are the staff satisfied and productive?

Are we filing reports on a timely basis?

Are we fulfilling our legal obligations?

Can financial responsibilities be delegated to an honorary treasurer, financial advisers, staff or volunteers?
Your charity may well have an honorary treasurer, financial advisers or a sub-committee that co-ordinate financial management, and you may appoint staff, volunteers or an outside agency to undertake day to day financial duties (such as book-keeping or payroll). All trustees, however, should take an active interest in the financial affairs of the charity and exercise care when appointing or supervising anyone to manage its finances. You cannot escape your financial responsibilities by delegating control and supervision of the finances to someone else. You remain responsible for the financial affairs of the charity and would share liability for any financial wrongdoing.

How will the financial management exercised by trustees be judged?
Two related sets of criteria may be used to judge your performance in fulfilling your financial responsibilities.

**'Proper care and diligence'**
A trustee will not, for example, be held personally liable for wrongdoing by any financial agents if the board of trustees has given proper attention to the appointment, duties and supervision of the agents.

**'Prudence of ordinary men and women of business in the management of their own affairs'**
This requires trustees to satisfy themselves that the financial affairs of the charity are being properly handled in the same way that they would manage their own finances or those of someone else for whom they were morally responsible. Ignorance of what is happening, or the absence of dishonesty on the part of a trustee, is not accepted as prudent behaviour. As a trustee it is your responsibility to find out all relevant information. Charities which are companies have detailed general duties which must also be observed (Chapter 2 Companies Act 2006).

The requirements of charity accounting are detailed and well beyond the scope of this book. This chapter can only very briefly outline these requirements – for more detailed guidance you can consult the Charity Commission's resources on their website or via their helpline or consult NCVO's *Good Financial Management Guide* (see Resources section).

## Checklist

Do any members of your board need support in understanding the charity's financial affairs?

Examine your governing document. Does it give you powers to delegate financial matters?

Do you know the terms on which individuals or sub-committees have been delegated financial responsibility by the board of trustees?

Are you satisfied that the charity's financial agents are properly supervised and accountable to the board?

Have you made sure that you know who is responsible for each aspect of your charity's financial management?

Have you made sure that reporting requirements have been agreed and maintained?

Does your board need to organise any training to strengthen the financial skills of the trustees?

Does your charity give all trustees a guide to its accounts, covering such items as any designated or restricted funds, and giving any necessary explanations, for example clarifying if amounts raised at fundraising events are shown at gross or net value?

Does your charity give all trustees a list of any significant assets, and any obligations attached to them?

## Accounting records

Charity trustees must ensure proper accounting records are kept of all the charity's transactions (including, in particular, all monies received and paid and all assets and liabilities).

The accounting records should disclose with reasonable accuracy at any time the financial position of the charity.

Trustees are not required to keep the records personally, but can delegate this task to staff, volunteers or, for example, an agency.

Accounting records must be kept for at least six years.

In addition, Gift Aid records must be kept for six years in line with guidance from HM Revenue and Customs.

Your charity's choice of accounting system and should be proportionate to the needs of your charity. For example, a very simple book-keeping system, perhaps operated by the treasurer or volunteer book-keeper, should suffice for a small community group with a few thousand pounds of income each year.

On the other hand, a large charity with significant income and expenditure, several projects or services and large numbers of monthly transactions is likely to require a complex system which could include online billing and invoicing systems, with day to day financial management delegated to staff.

In both examples, however, the treasurer has an important role in presenting financial information to trustees, ensuring trustees understand the financial picture of the charity and can make informed decisions.

## Budgeting

The board of trustees is responsible for ensuring that the income and expenditure, and assets and liabilities, of the charity are managed in an efficient and effective manner. As a trustee, therefore, you are responsible for taking financial decisions and exercising financial controls. You will need to ensure that the financial management information you work with is accurate, up to date and sufficiently detailed.

### Introduction to budgeting

Trustees are responsible for scrutinising and approving a charity's budget. Budgets are simply estimates of future income and expenditure. They perform three central roles:

- controlling activities involving income and expenditure relating to both capital and revenue items
- monitoring financial performance
- planning future operations.

Budgets must be more than guesswork. They should be based on the agreed operational plan for the year and be realistic about expected income. You and your fellow trustees should be given details of any assumptions made, such as the rate of inflation, and details of any underlying calculations should be available if you want to investigate any particular item.

The budget should build on the accounts for the previous year and include estimates for all significant items of income and expenditure, and an estimate of the surplus or deficit that is expected at the end of the budget period. If the expected income is very uncertain, for example if it depends on the success of several fundraising events, two or three budgets may have to be drawn up prioritising the work your charity will be able to do at different levels of income.

### Budget monitoring and reporting

Totals for income and expenditure in the budget should be monitored on a regular basis. A comparison should be made between budgeted income and expenditure and actual income and expenditure.

Trustees should receive reports showing this comparison and explaining the reasons for any material difference between actual and budget figures and giving up-to-date forecasts of income and expenditure for the rest of the financial year. The reports, which should be made at least every three months, should also advise trustees of any action that may be required to bring income or expenditure into line with the budget or forecast. These reports are sometimes called management accounts.

Although management accounts will vary in complexity depending on the size of a charity, all trustees should expect to be able to quickly identify key financial issues from a board financial report – you shouldn't have to wade through pages of figures. You may find that a summary narrative report drawing out key points can help interpret the figures. The treasurer has an important role here to help the board interpret reports and focus the board on the bigger picture.

On the basis of these reports you should authorise appropriate management action and, if necessary, agree changes to the main budget itself. Exception reporting, that is reports which highlight the items on which there has been a significant over- or under-spend or a significant excess or deficit in income, can help trustees concentrate their attention on areas where action may be needed.

### Should individual activity budgets be monitored?

If your charity has several different activities then you should consider having separate income and expenditure budgets for each activity. Reports should also be prepared for each budget on the same basis as that described for a single budget. Trustees will then be able to compare the financial performance of different activities and will be alerted to any financial problems resulting from a particular activity. Individual activity monitoring can help trustees to make informed decisions and can also help identify where the costs of activities are not being fully covered. Charities are encouraged to adopt a 'full cost recovery' method for budgeting individual activities wherever possible (see box).

## Full cost recovery

'Full cost recovery' is a method of understanding the full costs of a particular project, activity or service (the word project is used in this box for clarity), including the proportion of overheads used by that project.

Why use a full cost recovery approach? Such a method can help charities to be more sustainable by ensuring project budgets cover both direct costs along with a fair overhead contribution.

Full cost recovery can also help monitor overhead costs and ensure the best use of a charity's resources – for example by identifying disproportionately high overhead costs.

Finally, full cost recovery also makes common sense. How can you make rational decisions and future plans without knowing the true cost of a project or service and how it impacts on overhead costs or reserves? For example, understanding the full costs of an activity can help trustees identify where a particular activity is not fully funded. If trustees are to decide to run a project or activity at less than full cost – for example as a pilot, loss leader or for raising profile – they need to do so knowingly.

The full cost recovery method involves:

- identifying the overhead costs of the charity – sometimes called 'core costs', they are the costs which cannot be directly attributable to a service or activity. An example might be the costs of a finance officer or the rent of a general office.
- identifying the direct costs associated with a particular activity or service – for example the salary costs of a project worker.
- allocating overhead costs to specific projects. Rather than, say, allocating a percentage of all overheads to each project, a 'full cost recovery' method can enable you to apportion costs in a sophisticated way that can help better reflect the true cost of a service.

A straightforward example of apportioning overhead costs is to divide the rental costs of a general office between projects based on the floorspace used by each project.

A more complex example is the apportioning of governance and strategic costs between projects in a large organisation. The first step involves identifying the governance and strategic costs themselves, including the proportion of the chief executive's time (and hence salary and proportion of their own overhead costs) spent on this activity along with activities like the cost of organising trustee board meetings. The second step is to allocate the governance and strategic costs between projects, for example by the relative size of each project.

Useful tools exist to help charities adopt full cost recovery. A detailed analysis of the approach is outside the scope of this book and further information is listed in the resources section.

## Cashflow

What are cashflow forecasts?
A cashflow forecast indicates – usually on a monthly basis – when in the year payments are made or received by the charity. It may be, for example, that expenditure will be higher than income in the first half of the year, but in the second half, income will exceed expenditure. A cashflow forecast will warn the board of trustees of any cash shortage that might occur as a result of the timing of payments and enable you to plan accordingly, e.g. by negotiating a temporary overdraft with your charity's bankers.

## Financial controls

What are internal financial regulations?
In order to provide a point of reference for staff and financial agents, and to ensure continuity of good financial practice, trustees should draw up regulations for the conduct of the charity's financial affairs.

It is important that the regulations are appropriate to the size of your charity and should not be unduly bureaucratic. If you have engaged an independent examiner or auditor, they may be able to help you decide what measures are suitable for your charity. In general, however, trustees should ensure that internal financial regulations include:

- details of responsibility for maintaining financial records and preparing reports
- the basis on which trustees delegate responsibilities for financial matters to paid staff, volunteers, subcommittees or financial agents
- procedures for preparing and approving financial plans and budgets
- the charity's banking arrangements
- the payment of staff and other agents of the charity
- policies and procedures for purchasing goods and services
- procedures for authorising expenditure on behalf of the charity
- a detailed description of the duties and responsibilities of the honorary treasurer
- procedures for controlling, opening, listing and distributing incoming post, including monies received
- procedures for authorising and controlling activities concerned with raising or generating funds by or on behalf of the charity. The board should review these regulations from time to time to ensure that they are in keeping with the changing needs of the charity.

## Checklist

Do you have a copy of your charity's budget for the current financial year?

As a trustee do you know how well the charity is performing against its budget?

How regularly do you receive financial monitoring reports and how old are the reports when you get them? (Every month/every three months/less frequently than every three months?)

Have you taken appropriate action to deal with any budget deficiencies?

Does your board need to review the financial reports you receive to ensure that they provide sufficient details of the financial performance of individual activities undertaken by your charity?

Do the budget monitoring reports you receive include:

- a comparison of actual and budgeted income and expenditure?
- an explanation of any differences between the actual and budget figures?
- revised forecasts of income and expenditure?
- recommended action (including revisions to the budget) to address any divergence from the budget?

Do you adopt a full cost recovery approach to project budgeting?

Does your board need to check that your charity's financial regulations are comprehensive and relevant to the needs of the charity?

If required, do you ask your independent examiner or auditor to comment on the charity's financial controls?

# Annual reporting and accounting

### Introduction

The preparation of a trustees' annual report and accounts is:

- a crucial document for public accountability (see chapter 14)
- a good opportunity to review your charity's purposes and progress (or lack of progress) towards them.

### What are the minimum regulatory requirements?

All charities must prepare accounts covering each financial year. All charities, except exempt and excepted charities (see page 81) must prepare an annual report.

### Who should receive copies of the trustees' annual report and accounts?

All charities must make the accounts and annual report (where required to prepare one) available to the public on request. A reasonable charge may be made. Registered charities with an income or expenditure over £10,000 per year must file the report and accounts with the Charity Commission within ten months of the financial year end (although early filing is encouraged). Please see page 82 for details of changes expected to this threshold.

Charities with a formal membership are likely to have requirements in their governing document regarding the circulation of annual reports and accounts to members.

A funder may require a copy of the annual report and accounts.

Charitable companies are subject to company law and must submit a directors' report, including the charity's annual accounts, to Companies House, within ten months (within nine months for financial years beginning on or after 6th April 2008) of the end of the charity's financial year. Company law also requires that the annual reports and accounts are circulated to members. For financial years beginning before 6th April 2008, these must be circulated 21 days before the Annual General Meeting; after this date, the documents must be circulated before the charitable companies files its accounts and reports at Companies House (although the governing document may have a stricter requirement which must be followed or amended).

It should be noted that the information in this section principally covers the minimum regulatory requirements placed upon charities with regard to the production of annual reports and accounts. In practice, trustees may wish to go beyond these requirements. For example, trustees often want to ensure that their annual report and accounts are circulated as widely as possible to all those with an interest in the charity, not just to those required by the law and governing document. Trustees also often produce a shorter and more accessible 'annual review' to help with this process (see page 81).

### What information should be contained in the annual report and accounts?

The annual report and accounts consist of two sections: the annual report, summarising the charity's achievements over the financial year; and the annual accounts, summarising the charity's financial position over the financial year.

### The SORP

The requirements for the preparation of annual reports and accounts are contained in The Charities (Accounts and Reports) Regulations. These regulations are interpreted for charities in the form of the Statement of Recommended Practice (SORP) on Accounting by Charities.

Published by the Charity Commission and most recently revised in June 2008, the SORP provides recommended guidance on charity accounting and is a mechanism to help charities comply with the charity accounting regulations.

Although the SORP is described as 'recommended', it is based on the charity accounting and reporting regulations and, therefore, charities are expected to follow the guidance in the SORP. However, the extent to which an individual charity is expected to follow the SORP depends on the charity's size, legal structure and status (some charities such as universities or registered social landlords have a specialist SORP which must instead be followed).

For example, a charity with an annual income over £100,000 is expected to prepare accounts in accordance with the SORP, whereas a small unincorporated charity with an annual income under £10,000 is only expected to follow the SORP in so far as the simplified requirements around the content of the annual report – and may instead prepare accounts on a receipts and payments basis (see below).

All charitable companies are expected to prepare accounts and an annual report in accordance with the SORP and also, in accordance with the requirements of company law to prepare a directors' annual report and accounts. In practice, charitable companies often prepare a modified directors annual report and accounts that is in accordance with the SORP.

## Excepted, exempt and voluntarily registered charities

The accounting and reporting requirements for except and exempt charities are slightly different and trustees of these charities should consult the Charity Commission's CC16 guidance.

Charities registered voluntarily must meet the same requirements as those of registered charities.

### The annual report

The annual report is an opportunity to reflect on the charity's progress over the year, celebrate achievements and explore challenges.

Some of the content of the trustees' annual report is mandatory. The specific requirements for charity annual reports are contained in the Statement of Recommended Practice (SORP) on Accounting by Charities – the SORP now places emphasis on the narrative section of the annual report and accounts as well as on the format of financial information.

The Charity Commission's CC15 guidance includes a helpful section H summarising the SORP requirements by way of a list of information that must be included in a trustees' annual report. The requirements vary depending on the size of a charity.

Charitable companies must comply both with the regulations for charity annual reporting and with the regulations under the Companies Acts to produce a directors' report. However, rather than produce two annual reports, many charitable companies in practice produce a directors' report that is suitably modified to contain information that complies with the requirements of charity law.

However, the Commission encourage organisations to go beyond the mandatory list and look to ensure that the report accurately reflects the charity's achievements during the year.

The Annual Report need not be lengthy – it should set out the purposes of the charity and how it has gone about achieving those purposes over the year. A good annual report, in the words of the Charity Commission, should "bring the charity to life"[4]. It is a good opportunity to reflect on the progress, achievements and challenges over the year and to highlight the public benefit of the charity's activities.

### Our charity publishes an annual review. Is this the trustees' annual report?

Not necessarily. Some organisations produce a trustees' annual report and accounts that satisfy regulatory requirements, and a separate 'annual review'. Such a review may be in a 'glossy' format that provides information about a charity's work for supporters, donors, potential funders and beneficiaries. The SORP includes guidance on the production of summary financial statements or information in such a review.

[4] Charity Commission publication *Charity Reporting and Accounting; The Essentials* (CC15). Crown Copyright.

## The annual accounts

Introduction

The required format of a charity's accounts varies depending on the charity's annual income, level of assets, legal structure, status (ie registered, excepted or exempt) and provisions in its governing document. The circumstances of each charity will determine

- the type of accounting method which must be used in the preparation of the annual accounts
- how far the charity should prepare accounts in accordance with the SORP
- the level of external scrutiny required of the annual accounts
- what needs to be sent to the Charity Commission and Companies House

A summary of the requirements for registered charities is set out below. However, it is strongly recommended that trustees check the Charity Commission's clear and helpful guidance CC15 Charity Accounting and Reporting: The Essentials to pinpoint their charity's exact requirements.

## Accounting thresholds

Changes to accounting thresholds

The guidance below is relevant for financial years beginning on or after 1st April 2008. For guidance on financial years beginning before 1st April 2008, please refer to the Charity Commission's CC15 guidance on their website (see resources section).

In August 2008 the government announced further changes to charity accounting and reporting thresholds. These changes are expected to take effect in time for the 2009/10 financial year:

- Preparation of accruals accounts for unincorporated charities – rise in threshold from £100,000 to £250,000
- External scrutiny of accounts – rise in threshold from £10,000 to £25,000
- Submission of annual accounts and trustees' annual report to the Charity Commission – rise in threshold from £10,000 to £25,000

Unincorporated charities

| Income per annum | Type of accounting method | Minimum statutory requirements for external scrutiny of accounts | Accounts prepared in accordance with SORP ? | What to send annually to the Charity Commission |
|---|---|---|---|---|
| £0– £10,000 | Can be receipts and payments method | None | Not if receipts and payments method used | Annual Update form * |
| £10,001–£100,000 | Can be receipts and payments method | Independent examination | Not if receipts and payments method used | Annual return, report and accounts |
| £100,001–£500,000 and total assets up to £2.8m | Accruals method | Independent examination | Yes | Annual return, report and accounts |
| Over £500,000 (or total assets over £2.8m and income over £100,000) | Accruals method | Audit | Yes | Annual return (plus Summary Information return if income over £1m), report and accounts |

* Although very small charities are not obliged to submit an annual information update, by doing so the trustees will meet their charity's legal obligation to keep the Charity Commission informed of changes to the charity.

Charitable companies

| Income per annum | Type of accounting method | Minimum statutory requirements for external scrutiny of accounts | Accounts prepared in accordance with SORP ? | What to send annually to the Charity Commission | What to send to Companies House ** |
|---|---|---|---|---|---|
| £0–£10,000 | Accruals method | None | Yes | Annual Update form | Annual return, report and accounts |
| £10,001–£100,000 | Accruals method | Independent examination | Yes | Annual return, report and accounts | Annual return, report and accounts |
| £100,001–£500,000 and total assets up to £2.8m | Accruals method | Independent examination | Yes | Annual return, report and accounts | Annual return, report and accounts |
| Over £500,000 (or total assets over £2.8m and income over £100,000) | Accruals method | Audit | Yes | Annual return (plus Summary Information return if income over £1m), report and accounts | Annual return, report and accounts |

** Note: Charitable companies are required to comply with a number of company law reporting requirements, including the filing of an Annual Return (this is separate from the Charity Commission's annual return), report and accounts and registering changes to the directors, company secretary and the company's registered office as they occur. Please refer to Companies House guidance for further information (the Directors and Secretaries guide is a useful introduction – see resources section).

### Format of accounts

Accounts must be prepared either on a receipts and payments, or accruals, basis:

**Receipts and payments** accounts are a simpler form of accounts, summarising income and expenditure during the year along with a statement of assets and liabilities.

**Accruals accounts** must be prepared in accordance with the SORP and the 2008 regulations and are designed to show a 'true and fair view' of the accounts. They consist of a balance sheet (see page 87), a statement of financial activities (see page 86) and explanatory notes.

Charitable companies must prepare accruals accounts in accordance with company law and the SORP. In practice charitable companies often produce a modified set of company accounts that is in accordance with the SORP.

The Charity Commission produce template accounting packs to help non-company charities follow the receipts and payments or accruals methods. Because of the extra requirements placed on charitable companies, the accounting packs are only suitable for non-company charities.

### Scrutiny of accounts

**Independent examination**

The 'independent examination' is designed to give small- to medium-sized charities a way of scrutinising their accounts, but without the formality of having a professional audit. The regulations have specific requirements over who can carry out an independent examination, and the type of report. If a charity's income exceeds £250,000 the independent examiner must be a member of a body specified under the Charities Act 2006.

**Professional audit**

A professional audit (rather than an 'informal' audit) as required by the Charities Act 1993.

**Your charity's own requirements**

Your charity's own rules may differ from statutory requirements and may set a higher standard than either legislation or the SORP. As trustees, you must comply with your governing document (although you may want to consider amending the governing document to bring your charity into line with the above requirements). You may also want to consider amending your governing document if your document just refers to an 'audit' because this may not make it clear what type of audit is required. If the wording is unclear, trustees can consult with the Charity Commission for guidance.

A full professional audit may also be a requirement of a funding agreement you have. If this is the case, it must be followed regardless of the legislative requirements above.

Finally, the Charity Commission may require an audit in exceptional circumstances even where one is not a statutory requirement.

## Group accounts

Charities with subsidiaries (either charitable or non-charitable) must prepare group accounts where the group's annual income – after eliminating intra group transactions and consolidation adjustments – is over £500,000. See the Charity Commission's CC15 guidance.

### Statement of Financial Activities (SOFA)

The SOFA is an annual statement of financial activities and is prepared in accordance with the SORP for organisations preparing accruals accounts. The SOFA is a development from the traditional income and expenditure account and recognises the distinct reporting needs and requirements of charities. It recognises that charities do not usually have one indicator of performance comparable to the bottom line for commercial businesses. The SOFA shows, in summary form, the charity's funds and how they have been used:

- all the charity's funds
- all its incoming resources
- all its revenue expenditure
- all transfers between funds
- all recognised and unrecognised gains and losses on investments
- how the fund balances have changed since the last balance sheet date

Income and expenditure in the SOFA is in a columnar format, separating unrestricted funds, restricted funds, permanent endowments and total funds. Income and expenditure is classified under standard SORP headings (although smaller charities are not required to use these headings) including, for incoming resources:

- voluntary income
- activities for generating funds
- investment income
- incoming resources from charitable activities
- other incoming resources

and for outgoing resources (resources expended):

- cost of generating funds (broken down between generating voluntary income, cost of goods sold, investment management costs etc.)
- charitable activities
- governance costs

## The balance sheet

The balance sheet is a 'snapshot' of assets (what the charity owns), creditors (what the charity owes) and funds (what resources the charity has available to use to meet its charitable objects) at a particular date. A specimen balance sheet is shown on page 88. See the glossary below or in part five for an explanation of terms.

Charities that are required to prepare their accounts in accordance with the SORP must prepare their balance sheet according to SORP guidelines.

Charities preparing accounts on a receipts and payments basis may prepare a statement of assets and liabilities. This is not the same as a balance sheet, since there is no requirement to balance.

## What do trustees need to look out for in a balance sheet?

If you think your charity may be in financial difficulty you should apply the simple balance sheet test for insolvency:

*Are your assets less than your total liabilities?*

Bear in mind that the fixed assets are not generally available to provide short-term funds and balance sheet figures are not an indication of what might be obtained for the assets in a forced sale.

If 'provisions' are included in your accounts, it is important that you determine whether or not these provisions are realistic and relevant to the accounts in which they are made. For example, if there is a legal case pending against the charity, your lawyers may estimate that the costs and penalties will add up to £1,000.

Trustees should look at the net current asset position, because it gives some indication of the charity's ability to meet its short-term financing needs. But remember that a balance sheet shows the charity's position at one point in time. It should not be relied upon in isolation to assess a charity's ability to fund its current and future activities. This must be done by proper cashflow forecasting and budgeting which should use the balance sheet as its starting point.

The distinction between restricted and unrestricted funds is crucial. Misapplying restricted funds amounts to a breach of trust and could result in the trustees having personally to make good the misspent funds. It is recommended that assets and liabilities representing the funds are analysed between restricted and general funds to ensure that each fund is separately represented by adequate and appropriate assets. Such an analysis would normally be disclosed in the Notes to the Accounts. Because of the vital importance of solvency, advice should be taken if doubts linger.

Specimen balance sheet

Key to terms used

**Accruals** – expenses listed in a report that have been incurred but which remain unpaid at the date of the report

**Debtors** – money owed to the charity.

**Deferred income** – income listed in a report which has been received but relate to a period following the date of the report

**Liabilities or creditors** – money owed by the charity, either short term – expected to be paid within a year (eg debts to pay) – or long term (eg loans).

**Provisions** – charges listed in a balance sheet for costs or expenditure which cannot be precisely calculated.

## Statement of financial activities – example

**Care Home Trust Limited**

Consolidated statement of financial activities (including an income and expenditure account) for the year ended March 2006

| **Consolidated balance sheets as at 31 March 2006** | **Notes** | **Group 2006 £'000** | **Group 2005 £'000** |
|---|---|---|---|
| Fixed assets | | | |
| Tangible assets | 10 | 830 | 850 |
| Investments | 4 | 137 | 129 |
| | | 967 | 979 |
| Current assets | | | |
| Stocks | 11 | 217 | 213 |
| Debtors | 12 | 290 | 287 |
| Cash at bank and in hand | | 423 | 319 |
| | | 930 | 819 |
| Creditors: amounts falling due within one year | 13 | 242 | 195 |
| Net current assets | | 688 | 624 |
| Total assets less current liabilities | | 1,655 | 1,603 |
| Creditors: amounts falling due after more than one year | 15 | 46 | 56 |
| | | 1,609 | 1,547 |
| Funds | | | |
| Unrestricted funds | | | |
| General | 16 | 1,430 | 1,363 |
| Designated | 16 | 167 | 167 |
| Restricted funds | 17 | 12 | 17 |
| | | 1,609 | 1,547 |

Approved by the board on 13 June 2006 and signed on its behalf by:

S.A. Bloggs, Chairman

## Checklist

Does your board need to review if your charity is keeping records of accounts in a form that will satisfy your legal obligations?

Are you sure that the most recent accounts and trustees' report were properly authorised by the whole board and that your charity has a procedure for authorising future reports and accounts?

Does your board need to review its procedures for ensuring that an annual return and trustees' report and accounts (if required) are submitted to the Charity Commission?

Does your board need to review its procedures for ensuring that an annual return and trustees' report and accounts are sent to the Charity Commission and Companies House?

Does your charity need to have its accounts scrutinised? If so, has your charity appointed an independent examiner or auditor to audit its current year's accounts?

If you already have an independent examiner or auditor are you sure you have taken due care in their selection?

If you appoint an auditor, has your board agreed proper terms of engagement with the current auditor?

Does your board regularly review the guidance in the SORP?

## Investments

What is an investment?
in this section, 'investments' include shares, rental or lease of land, loans and units in collective investment schemes. Investments do not include the process of purchasing items such as land for future sale which are more accurately described as trading.

What are trustees' main responsibilities with regard to investment?
Trustees have a responsibility to maximise the financial return on a charity's investments while minimising the charity's exposure to risk. They should also bear in mind the long term future of the charity by protecting its capital from the effects of inflation. You should, therefore, avoid investments that are speculative, that is, those which carry a high risk of loss, and ensure that your charity's funds are diversified. A diversified portfolio of investments is one in which investment funds are spread across a number of different investments thereby reducing the risk attached to any single investment.

Trustees are also under a duty to obtain impartial, written advice when investing funds. The advice must come from someone whom the trustees are satisfied has adequate experience of investment matters. This could be an accountant, bank manager, stockbroker, a member of the charity's staff or one of the trustees. However, trustees who give investment advice should consider the extent of any professional negligence liability which they may incur by doing so.

What are the investment powers of trustees?
The governing document of your charity should define the powers you have to invest.

### Unincorporated charities

If the trust deed or constitution of your unincorporated charity does not specifically restrict your power of investment or where a trust deed or constitution refers to the Trustee Investments Act 1961, the Trustee Act 2000 (the "TA 2000") will apply. The TA 2000 was introduced to replace the limited powers granted in the Trustee Investments Act 1961 (the "TIA 1961") giving trustees wider powers of investment.

Trustees are now able to make the kind of investments, which an absolute owner would have the power to do. A range of new powers to appoint agents, nominees and custodians, to insure trust property and to pay professional trustees supports the wider powers of investment.

The powers provided by the TA 2000 are default powers, designed to facilitate trustees governed by old or poorly drafted trust instruments. Some trust instruments may contain wider powers of investment than those conferred by the TA 2000, in which case, these powers would apply.

## Charitable companies

The TA 2000 does not apply to charitable companies in respect of the company's property. A company's charitable powers are derived from and governed by the provisions of the company's governing documents.

Trustees of charitable companies have similar obligations to those listed in the Trustee Act 2000, even though the Act does not apply to them expressly. They must act to promote the purpose of the company and not in their own interest. As a result, when making investments in respect of a charitable company, subject to any specific requirements about investments in the company's governing documents, trustees must act prudently within their power to maximise the return on the invested assets and in the best interest of the company.

The TA 2000 may apply to other funds held on charitable trust for which the company acts as trustee. For example, a charitable company could administer trusts set up by donors for charitable purposes and the Act would apply to these if the trust deed did not either specify specific restrictions or give a wide power of investment.

## Unincorporated charities

### Common law and statutory duty of care

The Trustee Act 2000 introduced a new statutory duty to create certainty and consistency to the standard expected from a trustee in relation to investment powers. The statutory duty applies to trustees of both existing and new trusts. However the duty can be excluded or amended by the trust instrument (see section 3.3 for more information on the general duty of care for trustees).

The Trustee Act 2000 provides that a trustee "must exercise such care and skill as is reasonable in the circumstances, having regard in particular:

1) to any special knowledge or experience that s/he has or holds herself/himself out as having, and
2) if s/he acts as trustee in the course of business or profession, to any special knowledge or experience that it is reasonable to expect of a person acting in the course of that kind of business or profession."

There are two parts to this test. Firstly, what is reasonable in the circumstances given the knowledge and experience the trustee has or hold themselves out as having. The greater your experience and knowledge, the higher the standard of conduct expected. Secondly, if you are acting in the course of business, i.e. as a professional trustee, your conduct would be assessed with the skills normally possessed by such a person.

### Exercising your investment powers

Trustees of unincorporated trusts exercising their power of investment, whether under the TA 2000 or the trust's constitution, have a duty to consider the "standard investment criteria" and a duty to take advice. The standard investment criteria require trustees to consider:

- the suitability of the general investments of the trust and of particular investments
- the need for diversification, both in terms of risk and to balance income and capital growth.

These duties cannot be excluded or limited by the trust instrument. It is necessary for you to demonstrate that you have considered these criteria and there is also a duty to review the investments held by the trust from time to time.

Before exercising any power of investment or making a review of investments held by a trust, you must obtain "proper advice", unless you reasonably conclude that, in all the circumstances, it is unnecessary or inappropriate to do so. The person who gives this advice must be, in the reasonable opinion of the trustees, someone qualified to give it by his or her ability and practical experience of financial and other matters relating to the proposed investment.

### Delegation of investment powers

Under the TA 2000, an agent can be appointed by the trustees to exercise their investment powers. Such an agent would be subject to the duty to consider the standard investment criteria.

If the agent is someone who would be a person to give proper advice, s/he would not be under an obligation to obtain and consider proper advice.

Where trustees delegate asset management powers, the agency contract must be in writing and must require the agent to comply with a policy statement. The policy statement sets out the objective of the trust to guide the agent and must ensure that the investment function will be exercised in the best interest of the trust.

There is a duty to review the arrangement of the delegation, and as a matter of good practice this should take place every twelve months and in some cases a more frequent review may be necessary.

### Socially responsible investment

A socially responsible approach can help ensure that a charity's investment policy is consistent with its charitable objects.

Socially responsible investment is wider than ethical investment. Whilst ethical investment usually involves selecting negative criteria to avoid certain forms of investment, socially responsible investment can be both positive and negative and also includes selecting investments that further the charity's objects and values as well as providing a financial return.

There is growing pressure for trustees to adopt a socially responsible investment policy for their charities. For example a 2001 NOP survey for the Charities Aid Foundation found that over 40% of respondents would prefer to support a charity that invested ethically[5].

### Are responsible or ethical investment policies permitted?

Yes, provided that guidelines are followed. Normally, trustees should exercise investment powers to prudently provide the greatest financial benefit for the charity. A socially responsible or ethical investment approach can be entirely consistent with this duty.

The Charity Commission's CC14 Investment of Charitable Funds guidance sets out three situations where it may be possible for trustees to avoid certain investments:

- avoiding investing in companies which are directly contrary to the purpose of the charity. For example, it would be correct for the trustees of a charity whose objects include health promotion to decline to invest in tobacco companies. It will usually be possible to identify alternative investments with a similar potential return.
- avoiding investing in companies that could alienate beneficiaries or supporters

where the two circumstances above do not apply, but where trustees still wish to invest ethically on moral grounds, trustees should be satisfied that a moral approach to investment does not put the charity at risk of significant financial detriment as a result of investment choices.

[5] Quoted in *The Good Investment Guide for the Voluntary Sector* (Catherine Wood – NCVO, 2007).

### What is involved in socially responsible investment?

There are three common strategies for socially responsible investment:

1) Screening – drawing up criteria (both positive and negative) governing the selection of investments – for example, companies with good environmental policies (positive) or companies involved in tobacco (negative)

2) Preference – identifying environmental, ethical or social guidelines that trustees would like companies to follow

3) Engagement – encouraging companies to make improvements in their environmental, ethical or social performance.

In developing a socially responsible investment policy, trustees should make decisions in the interests of the charity and not based on their own personal ethical concerns. However, given that a socially responsible investment policy should satisfy the charity's stakeholders, it is important to debate the ethical views of trustees and stakeholders as part of the development of a policy.

Socially responsible investment is a complex topic and may be a new issue for trustees. Further information can be found in NCVO's *Good Investment Guide for the Voluntary Sector*, the Charity Commission publication *Investment of Charitable Funds: Basic Principles* (CC14) or *Investing Responsibly – a guide for Charity Trustees* (EIRIS Foundation, 2005) (the latter available from the NCVO website).

## Other investment issues

### How should assets be treated?

Trustees have a general duty to ensure that the assets of a charity (for example, property owned by the charity) are managed efficiently, securely held and that income is used in pursuit of the charity's objects. You should be provided with details of the assets owned by the charity and given information on any special, restricted categories of funds, such as permanent endowments or appeal funds, that may not be used for the general purposes of the charity and details of the safeguards in place to protect them.

See section 3.5 for guidance on investment of assets which form part of the charity's permanent endowment.

### Are there any investment funds designed specifically for charities?

Common investment funds for charities have been established with the approval of the Charity Commission. They are similar to unit trusts but take advantage of charities' tax position. They allow charities to pool their funds so that they can be invested in a wide spread of investments by specialist investment managers, thus spreading the management costs and risks.

### Tax issues

While most forms of investment income of charities is exempt from tax, not all is. For example, loans to or investments in a private company such as a trading subsidiary are not exempt. Advice should be sought.

### Can trustees be held personally liable for investment decisions?

The Charity Commission's guidance states: "Trustees are not liable to make good the charity's loss simply because an investment made by them is unsuccessful. However, trustees may be liable if, in making or retaining the unsuccessful investment, they have acted outside the scope of their powers, or have failed to discharge the[ir] duties"[6].

### Should trustees agree an investment policy?

Yes. It is strongly recommended by the Charity Commission that trustees agree an investment policy in writing and keep it under regular review. Such a policy is a legal requirement if investment is delegated to an investment manager. An investment policy can help trustees ensure they are fulfilling their duty to make good use of a charity's funds. See chapter 8 for guidance on the policy-making role of trustees.

[6] Charity Commission publication *Investment of Charitable Funds: Basic Principles* (CC15). Crown Copyright.

## Checklist

Does your board need to satisfy itself that the charity's investments are sanctioned by the terms of your governing document?

Do trustees understand their duties and responsibilities as regards investment? Does your charity have a written investment policy?

Does your policy make reference to ethical or responsible considerations?

Have you got a copy?

Is it updated on a regular basis?

Does your board need to check the terms on which advisers or investment managers have been consulted about your charity's investments?

Are you satisfied that any investment managers employed by your charity are properly supervised and holdings appropriately safeguarded?

Do you have up-to-date records of your charity's assets and restricted funds?

## Reserves

### What are reserves?

Reserves are defined by the Charity Commission as funds that are freely available. This definition excludes funds where use is restricted or funds that have been designated for a particular purpose.

### What are trustees' responsibilities with regard to reserves?

Trustees have a duty to spend the income of the charity within a reasonable time unless they have a power to do otherwise. This power may be explicit in the governing document or implicit.

Trustees should explain and justify the level of reserves their charity holds and, to fulfil this duty, should agree a reserves policy (see below).

### Why have reserves?

Any charity requires a minimum level of reserves to cover contingencies and to provide a level of working capital. Reserves can ensure the charity has, for example sufficient funds to provide its service, pay its staff and creditors, allow for possible maternity, sickness or redundancy payments, keep its property in good repair, pay for insurance and replace equipment and, if necessary, to close down in a controlled way.

Indeed, the existence of reserves is a sign of good financial management. You could be judged to be acting negligently if you do not ensure that your charity has adequate reserves.

However, allowing reserves to build up without good reason could lead to bad publicity and funders being unwilling to grant further funding, and ultimately could amount to a breach of trust or trigger tax liabilities.

### What should a reserves policy cover?

A reserves policy should cover:

- why the charity needs reserves
- the level of reserves believed to be required
- how the reserves will be maintained at the agreed level
- arrangements for monitoring and reviewing the reserves policy

Drawing up a reserves policy involves:

- conducting an analysis of existing funds, income streams, expenditure and cashflow
- analysing the need for reserves
- calculating the reserves level
- drawing up and formally agreeing the reserves policy.

The reserves policy should be based on the assessment of the following four areas:

- the level, reliability and source of future income streams
- a forecast of future, planned expenditure
- an identification of future circumstances – needs, opportunities, contingencies and risks – which are unlikely to be met out of income
- identifying the likelihood of each future circumstance and the consequences of the charity in not being able to meet them.

### What must trustees do?

All charities that are required to produce a trustees annual report must include a paragraph about the level of reserves held and the reasons for holding reserves. This requirement is listed in the Statement of Recommended Practice (see page 80) and is included in the list of items all charities must include in their annual report[7].

For more information see the Charity Commission's CC19 – *Charities' Reserves.*

## Checklist

Does your charity have a policy on the level of reserves?

Is the policy reviewed each year?

Are new trustees given a copy of the policy? Does it meet regulatory requirements?

[7] Charity Commission publication *Charity Reporting and Accounting: The Essentials* (CC15). Crown Copyright.

## Insolvency and wrongful trading

If your charity is unincorporated the rules explained below will not apply. But the trustees and members of such charities will face unlimited personal liability for the debts and obligations of the charity if it can not meet those debts. Trustees of unincorporated charities, where there is a risk of insolvency, should consider incorporation.

### What is the law concerning insolvency and wrongful trading?

Wrongful trading is defined in the Insolvency Act 1986. It takes place if a company continues to operate when the company directors knew, or ought to have known, that there was no reasonable prospect of the company avoiding going into insolvent liquidation – which is the equivalent for a company of becoming bankrupt. The only defence to the claim is that the company directors took every reasonable step to minimise potential losses to the charity's creditors.

The directors of a charitable company are the charity trustees and, when wrongful trading occurs, the term director can be extended to include shadow directors, i.e. the people 'in accordance with whose directions or instructions the directors of the charitable company are accustomed to act'. The intention is to cover those who 'pull the strings' of a company but who are not formally on the board. Therefore, in some instances, staff, such as the chief executive or finance director, could also share responsibility.

Charitable companies do sometimes get into financial difficulties. It can be tempting to continue the charity's activities in the hope that the financial situation will improve. However, the trustees of charitable companies must put the needs of the company's creditors first and always take positive steps to minimise their potential loss, especially if the charity is in danger of going into insolvent liquidation.

If your charitable company becomes insolvent you could be disqualified (for two to fifteen years) from being a company director. You and your fellow trustees can also be held personally liable by the court to repay money to creditors where you have been wrongfully trading.

### What is the law concerning fraudulent trading?

Fraudulent trading is judged to have taken place if in the course of winding up a charitable company it appears that any business of the charity has been carried on with the intent to defraud the charity's creditors or for any fraudulent purpose. An example is where trustees incur a debt knowing there is little prospect of it ever being repaid.

Fraudulent trading is both a criminal and civil offence and applies where there has been actual dishonesty in the running of the charity. Apart from any penalties a court may impose, trustees may be required to make good the creditors' losses.

Insolvency is a complex legal area, a full consideration of which is outside the scope of this guide. If your charity finds itself in any financial doubt or difficulty, then the best advice is to take advice.

If your charity is in financial difficulties you need to take advice such as from your solicitor or from an insolvency practitioner about your ability (or otherwise) to trade through the difficulties or on alternative insolvency procedures which might be pursued by or against you.

## Checklist

Are trustees aware of their responsibilities as regards insolvency and wrongful trading?

Are trustees aware of the importance of taking advice when necessary?

Are trustees clear about whether they need the protection of incorporation as a company?

## Taxation and rating

Trustees need to understand how taxation may affect their charity for two main reasons:

- an unexpected tax bill or unclaimed tax relief could have a significant effect on the organisation's financial position
- failure to manage the organisation's tax affairs properly may expose trustees to personal financial liability for its tax bills.

### Who is responsible for paying the charity's tax?

An unincorporated charity has no separate legal identity from its trustees and members. This means that you can be held personally liable for taxes arising from your charity's activities. In practice this is not a problem when the organisation has the necessary funds to pay, but personal liabilities can arise if it becomes insolvent.

Trustees of a charitable company are not liable for the charity's taxes except where personal liability arises as a result of poor administration.

### What are trustees' responsibilities with regard to tax and rates?

Trustees are responsible for ensuring that the tax affairs of their charity are properly handled in a way which gives rise to the minimum tax. This involves payment of any tax liabilities, including PAYE, capital gains, VAT and corporation tax, structuring the charity to minimise those same liabilities, and claiming all the tax reliefs available to the charity promptly. Trustees should ensure that the charity reclaims income tax paid on donations made under Gift Aid, payroll giving or other tax effective giving schemes (see page 103). You should also ensure that the charity has obtained the 80 per cent mandatory business rate relief on any premises occupied by the charity, although this does not apply to the premises of wholly owned trading companies. Some local authorities allow charities up to 100 per cent business rate relief, so trustees should ensure that applications for additional relief have been made.

### Obtaining advice

The taxation of charities can be a complex matter and professional advice may be necessary. If you fail to organise your charity's affairs in a way that minimises the tax liability you could be judged to be acting imprudently and so be personally liable to make good any resulting loss. Keep notes of any professional advice you receive. You will remain responsible for any decisions you make regarding your charity's tax and rating provision, but having sought professional advice will be a protection should problems arise.

## Checklist

Are you confident that your organisation complies with its tax obligations?

Have you kept copies of any professional advice you may have received on this subject?

## Internal audit

Internal audit is a practice that has spread across government and business, depending for its value on attributes of independence and objectivity. Although mainly identified with finance it can serve broader requirements, to give assurance of compliance and performance, of proper recording and honesty. Internal audit may be the responsibility of an audit committee or staff advisors, or a separate group who report direct to the board.

### Should charities have an audit committee?

The Code of Governance recommends that "larger and more complex organisations should set up an audit committee, and should also consider the use of an internal audit service"[8].

The need for such a committee will depend on the size of your charity and the complexity of its administration. The job of internal audit is: to review, to monitor and assure adherence to the law, to standards, to policy, etc., and to make known its findings.

Some larger charities have done this by setting up a small internal audit committee, appointed at the highest level, to fulfil that role. Those involved in internal audit are committed to act as 'protectors of the conscience' of the charity, to be guarantors of the proper stewardship of resources and the charity's integrity. The board lays down its remit and it reports directly to the board.

[8] *Good Governance: A Code for the Voluntary and Community Sector* (paragraph C15)

A small charity is unlikely to need a separate internal audit committee, as the scale of the charity's operations will be such that it will not be difficult for the whole board to keep sufficiently closely in touch with all the organisation's activities.

An audit committee is likely to work best through a small group of high-calibre members, chosen for their experience, maturity and independence of mind, drawn from varied backgrounds. A typical audit committee will have about four members and will meet perhaps four times a year.

### What are the terms of reference of an audit committee?

Audit committees assist the board by ensuring that appropriate accounting and financial policies and controls are in place. Internal audit is the process of checking that such policies are actually followed.

The audit committee will consider the reports of external auditors and the responses of staff to them, ensuring that external and internal control processes are properly co-ordinated and working effectively. In particular circumstances, the committee should be prepared to oversee the carrying out of special one-off inquiries.

# 7.2

### Should the work of the audit committee be reviewed?

The work of an audit committee can be very worthwhile providing it concentrates on essentials, avoids being a rubber stamp, and earns respect within and outside the charity. It is appropriate for the committee itself, from time to time, to be reviewed and assessed for effectiveness.

### A developing role for audit committees

Audit committees are coming to be seen as a hallmark of a healthy and responsible organisation. However, even at their best, there is a limit to the protection they can offer against serious misjudgements or the ill-advised use of resources.

Public pressures are in the direction of greater accountability and trustees need to take account of these. Some reflections of this are the development of social audits, environmental audits, and pioneer work on the concept of democratic audits.

These ideas have been brought together in the concept of the triple bottom line, adding a social and environmental bottom line to the traditional financial bottom line.

## Checklist

Have trustees reviewed the need for an audit committee?

If an audit committee is in place, is there a clear terms of reference?

Is the role of the audit committee periodically reviewed?

Is an internal audit process appropriate as a separate function and if so to whom should it report?

## Property and intellectual property

## Responsibilities for property

### Does the charity, or do the trustees, own the property or land?

Charitable companies, as incorporated organisations, have a legal personality. It is therefore possible for charitable companies to own property legally as well as beneficially.

Unincorporated charities (i.e. trusts and associations) have no independent legal existence, so they cannot legally own property. Property must be held on behalf of the charity by named individuals. As trustees change, a formal deed transferring trust property to the new trustees or the remaining trustees is essential. The details registered at HM Land Registry will also need to be amended. These procedures can be time-consuming and costly, particularly if there is a large number of trustees or the turnover is high. Many trusts and associations therefore appoint holding trustees or a custodian trustee. However, as a trustee you could still be personally liable, for example, if fundraising fails and there is not enough money to pay the rent. If you have behaved reasonably and honestly you may be entitled to an indemnity from the charity's assets, but you would remain personally liable if the assets were insufficient to meet the debts.

### What are holding trustees?

## Unincorporated charities

Holding trustees, or custodian trustees, are individuals appointed by an unincorporated charity to hold property on that charity's behalf. The holding or custodian trustees take no active part in the management of the charity, they merely carry out the instructions of the trustees. Sometimes it is difficult to find people willing to act as holding trustees and it may be preferable to appoint a corporate body to be a custodian trustee, such as a Parish Council or the Official Custodian, an official of the Charity Commission whose function is to hold land on behalf of charity trustees. The Official Custodian does not get involved in administering the property or in the management of the charity, but acts on the instructions of the trustees, for example selling or letting land. However, before carrying out the trustees' instructions, the Official Custodian will check that these are in accordance with the terms of the trust and any necessary consents have been obtained.

**Further information**
Charity Commission publication The Official Custodian for Charities' Land Holding Service (CC13).

### What are trustees' responsibilities for managing property and land?

Trustees have a duty to protect the charity's property and should make sure that any property owned by the charity, or held on the charity's behalf, is kept in a good state of repair and is adequately insured. Sufficient funds should be set aside for routine maintenance, interior and exterior redecorating and longer-term repairs, such as re-roofing.

If any property is a permanent endowment (given in perpetuity) you must make sure that it is used by the charity or earns a good income for the charity (more on permanent endowment in section 3.5). Similarly, you must regularly monitor the condition of any land owned by or held on behalf of your charity. You must make sure the boundaries are not encroached upon, provide adequate insurance and maximise the income you can earn from it without reducing its capital value.

If you want to sell or lease, even for a short period on an informal tenancy, any of your charity's land or buildings, the Charities Act 1993 requires you in most instances to obtain and consider a report from a qualified surveyor, who must act exclusively for the charity (i.e. the surveyor must not act for any other party involved in this transaction). The sale must be advertised, as advised by the surveyor, and any agreement concluded on terms which are the best that you could reasonably obtain. The surveyor's report must be in writing if the disposal is a sale or a lease for more than seven years.

If the property or land being sold or leased is subject to trusts requiring it to be used for a specific purpose of the charity (for example, an orphanage or museum), you must check if you have the power to sell the property before you put it on the market. You must then advertise what you are planning to do, to give the public the opportunity to raise any objections.

If you are unable to follow this procedure, or if you wish to sell the land to a person connected with the charity or its trustees (and you should note that the definition of a connected person for the purpose of disposing of charity land was extended by the Charities Act 2006), you must seek the consent of the Charity Commission. You are allowed to accept less than the full market price if you are disposing of land or property to another charity whose charitable objects come within the objects of your charity.

**Further information**
Charity Commission publication *Disposing of Charity Land* (CC28).

You may raise a mortgage on the charity's property provided you obtain written advice from someone experienced in financial matters who has no personal interest in the proposed loan. The person giving advice can be a trustee or an employee of the charity. The advice must include whether the loan is necessary, whether the terms are reasonable, and whether the charity can repay the loan.

## Checklist

Do you need to appoint holding or custodian trustees?

If your board is selling or leasing land or property, are you following the correct procedure?

Are you responsible for the maintenance of your property? If so, are you confident that you have set aside funds to meet the cost of repairs and maintenance?

If your responsibilities towards a property are significant, have you considered incorporating as a company limited by guarantee?

# 7.3

## Intellectual property and brands

Charities are often unaware of the value of the rights they have in so-called 'intellectual property'. This can include a wide range of things which are produced by a charity, including:

- trademarks, for example to protect the charity's name and logo
- copyright, such as copyrights in marketing and promotional materials and in computer software specially commissioned for the charity (for instance a specially written database application)
- database rights, for instance in donor and fundraising data bases
- design rights, in artistic and other designs
- patents, for instance in pharmaceutical products or a piece of equipment which might help a charity fulfil its objectives, such as a water pump.

These rights can be a valuable asset to a charity, and as a result the trustees have a duty to preserve their value and prevent them being wrongfully used or damaged by third parties.

Your charity should take steps to ensure that it properly identifies intellectual property when it is created, and then secures and preserves it. It should ensure that, if it commissions any intellectual property, it owns the intellectual property and has free access to all other materials necessary to enable the charity properly to use it. One thing to bear in mind particularly is that if anyone other than an employee creates intellectual property (for instance, a consultant), the intellectual property will generally belong to the person creating it rather than to the charity in the absence of agreement to the contrary.

If third parties are using intellectual property without authorisation then trustees should consider taking steps to stop that use, since if they do not do so it is possible that the charity may lose any rights it has over that intellectual property.

If a charity has a valuable piece of intellectual property which it wishes to preserve and protect it is often worthwhile to get appropriate legal advice about the best way to do so. It is usually easier to achieve the charity's objectives if this advice is sought before the relevant piece of intellectual property is acquired or created.

### Checklist

Does your organisation hold intellectual property?

If so, have you taken adequate steps to protect intellectual property?

## Fundraising

### Introduction

Trustees should seek to ensure that the charity has sufficient resources to pursue its aims and objectives – a duty that will require you to take an active interest in the funding base of the organisation.

We purposely use the term 'funding base' as opposed to 'fundraising' because, increasingly, charities are working beyond traditional 'fundraising' for ensuring their ongoing financial sustainability – diversifying their income streams and developing 'a mixed economy of funding' that incorporates grants and donations but also unrestricted income from trading, services and other contracts.

Sustainable organisations will spread their income base as widely as possible across the spectrum. NCVO hosts the Sustainable Funding Project dedicated to helping organisations explore how they can move away from a reliance on grants and donations and generate income from trading goods and services (see Resources section).

The trustees must ensure that the charity:

- is and will remain solvent
- uses charitable funds and assets reasonably, and only in furtherance of the charity's objects
- avoids undertaking activities that might place the charity's endowment, funds, assets or reputation at undue risk
- takes special care when investing the charity's funds or borrowing funds for it to use

These requirements have implications for fundraising as this income is part of the business model of the charity – and the trustees must be assured that the risk of unsuccessful fundraising efforts is acceptable. Trustees may be in breach of their duties if a charity invests excessively in fundraising which produces limited returns that cause the charity to become insolvent.

Trustees must also ensure that if funds are raised for a specific, defined purpose as understood by the funder/donor, the funds are treated as restricted funds as required by the charity accounting and reporting regulations (set out in the Statement of Recommended Practice – see page 80).

## Trustees' responsibilities for fundraising

Trustees are responsible for ensuring that the fundraising activity of their charity is properly controlled and accounts are kept. This involves proper budgeting, the control of professional fundraisers, and the observance of relevant legislation.

You may delegate some of the tasks to a fundraising sub-committee if your governing document gives you power to do so. However, it must be emphasised that you do not absolve yourself of your legal responsibilities. Trustees must continue to exercise control over the sub-committee and it is good practice to draw up terms of reference that define the sub-committee's objectives, and detail the reports that will be required by the board.

Trustees must ensure that fundraising activity is in accordance with the purposes and objectives of the charity and does not offend members of the public. Trustees should ensure that fundraising methods do not exploit individuals who are the designated beneficiaries of its activities

### Trustee Indemnity Insurance

The Charities Act 2006 (the Act) grants the Charity Commission the power to take away personal liability of an individual trustee for breach of duty or trust, only if the individual has acted honestly and fairly. The Act also makes it easier for charities to purchase trustee indemnity insurance (see section 9.2).

## Fundraising budgets

Fundraising budgets will help you ensure that fundraising activity is organised in an efficient and effective manner. Many charities also make a policy decision on the target ratio of fundraising expenditure to income as an additional control. Trustees should take into account the relative cost-to-income ratios of alternative methods of fundraising. As with other budgets, a fundraising budget should include targets for income and expenditure. Regular reports should be made that compare actual figures with budget figures and identify any appropriate action that needs to be taken to bring the funds raised back on target.

## Fundraising from members of the public

Much fundraising activity is governed by legislation in some form and trustees should ensure that their activities do not breach these laws or standards laid down by bodies such as the Advertising Standards Authority and the Fundraising Standards Board. Trustees should, in particular, be aware of legal requirements in respect of:

- Street and house-to-house collections (House-to-House Collections Act 1939 and the Police, Factories, Miscellaneous Provision Act 1916, which will be replaced by the relevant provisions of the Charities Act 2006 when it comes into operation – see below)
- Lotteries (Gambling Act, 2005)
- The Distance Selling Regulations and Telecommunication Regulations

## Employing professional fundraisers

Professional fundraisers are defined in Part II of the Charities Act 1992 as people carrying on a fund-raising business or someone who, for reward, solicits funds for charities. There are a number of exceptions to this definition, including the charity itself, its staff and trustees and, for most purposes, its associated companies. Charities may employ professional fundraisers and many charities that do are satisfied with their work.

When considering whether or not to employ a professional fundraiser, trustees need to balance the advantage of using someone with a good track record in successful fundraising against the disadvantage of donors possibly being less willing to give if they know that a sizeable proportion of their donation will go to paying the fundraiser. Part II of the Charities Act 1992, which includes provisions relating to the use of professional fundraisers, and the Charitable Institutions (Fundraising) Regulations 1994, stipulate that charities must:

- draw up a written agreement, in a prescribed form, between the charity and the professional fundraiser
- make a statement indicating, in general terms, the proportion of donations that will pay the fund-raiser's costs
- provide information to trustees on how the involvement of a professional fundraiser will benefit the charity
- make provision for the transfer of funds from the fundraiser to the charity.

Relationships with fundraisers can go wrong and the current rules give trustees certain powers. Charities can seek injunctions to prevent unauthorised fundraising on their behalf. This power can be used, for instance, if the fundraiser is using methods to which the charity objects. You can also seek an injunction if you do not want the charity associated with a particular venture. Lack of an agreement in the prescribed form is also grounds for an injunction. In addition, trustees must ensure that the final submission of application for funds is made by the charity and not the professional fundraiser.

## Fundraising from private businesses

Care should be taken when entering into joint promotions with commercial companies. For example, a charity supporting alcoholics should not engage in joint promotions with breweries.

Cause Related Marketing (CRM) is the most common form of charitable-corporate partnership. The charity effectively endorses a product or company by allowing a business to use their name, logo and brand credibility in promotional materials and advertising campaigns.

Examples of joint promotions are:

- charity affinity cards (credit cards )
- product promotions (e.g. where charity X receives a donation for every pack of Brand Y soap powder sold)
- 'relationship' marketing (e.g. a service partnership between a charity and a company).

Part II of the Charities Act 1992 requires that there must be a written agreement between the charity and the commercial company, who are known as commercial participators, and trustees should take particular care when entering into a joint promotion with such a company. Any arrangement must be in the best interests of the charity and on terms advantageous to it. The terms of the arrangement must be precisely defined by the trustees and their implementation kept under review.

Cause related marketing agreements are becoming increasingly sophisticated, and ideally there should be more provisions in any CRM agreement than the bare minimum required by the Charities Act 1993 and by the Charitable Institutions (Control of Fundraising) Regulations. There may also be significant VAT and tax implications, so it is always best to ensure that any material contract with a corporate partner is reviewed by an appropriately qualified lawyer.

Under the Charities Act it is likely that any corporate partner will be a "commercial participator" and obliged to comply with certain minimum requirements set out in the 1993 Act and in the Charitable Institutions (Control of Fundraising) Regulations. You should note that, even though under the legislation it is strictly the corporate partner's obligation to ensure compliance, the Charity Commission takes the view that the charity has a moral obligation to brief its corporate partners fully about the legal requirements. The Charity Commission published a report Charities and Commercial Partners in 2002, which is available from its website (see resources section).

One of the major changes set out in the Charities Act 2006 is that a "solicitation statement" must be produced by professional fundraisers or commercial participators that includes more detail available to the public. For a professional fundraiser this means that when soliciting for money or goods the following must be documented:

- the 'notifiable amount' of their remuneration; and
- the method by which their remuneration is to be calculated.

These requirements do not apply to individuals who are paid less than £5 a day or less than £500 per annum. These requirements do not apply to unpaid trustees or volunteers.

This means that where there is a fixed fee and this is known at the time the statement is made, the professional fund-raiser has to state this as well as stating the method by which his/her remuneration has been calculated. The statutory requirements will not be met if the fund-raiser makes a statement simply to provide his/her hourly or daily rate.

However, if the fund-raiser is being paid on daily or hourly rate and the time the person is likely to work on this campaign is variable depending on the requirement of the campaign (i.e. it is not known at the outset exactly how many days or hours the fund-raiser will be required to work) then the fund-raiser must state his daily or hourly rate as well as provide an estimate of the amount of time he/she is likely to remunerated in total. This estimate should be as accurate as possible.

## Tax-effective giving

Should trustees promote tax effective giving?
Yes. This is a key responsibility.

Since 2000, the government has introduced a number of schemes which allow charities to reclaim the tax already paid, by UK taxpayers, on money which is donated to charity. These include Gift Aid, share giving, payroll giving and others.

Over £2bn of income is generated for charities in the UK each year as a result of Gift Aid, but it is estimated that charities miss out on a further £600m by not taking advantage of the schemes[9].

More information is available from the Institute of Fundraising (see resources section).

Trustees of charities with one or more trading subsidiaries must be aware of the advantages of tax-effective giving in order to make the most of fundraising. In particular they need to remember, in all decisions made in regard to a trading subsidiary, that the interests of the charity are paramount. The interests of a trading subsidiary, its directors, creditors or employees, must all be secondary to those of the charity.

[9] *Trustees Guide to Fundraising* (Institute of Fundraising, 2007); *Introductory Pack on Funding and Finance – 3 – Fundraising* (Institute of Fundraising – Finance Hub, 2006)

## Loan finance

Loan finance is playing an increasingly important part of the 'mix' of funding and financing sources available for charities.

Loan finance is different from an income source and should be seen as a financial tool or enabler. Loans require repayment and interest will be charged in most circumstances. Arrangement fees may apply.

Loans may not be suitable for all organisations, or for all projects, but trustees should be aware of what loan finance can offer and be able to weigh up the alternatives before deciding either way.

What are the advantages of taking a loan over applying for a grant?
Loans can be faster to arrange than grants. Applying for a loan is not competitive, unlike increasingly over-subscribed grant programmes. Furthermore, loans are often more flexible, not being restricted to particular funder interests, often involve less reporting and monitoring and, finally, are paid in advance.

What should trustees consider when determining whether to apply for a loan?
The three considerations below are a good stating point to determine whether a loan may be suitable: for a particular project, within a particular organisation and at a particular point of its lifecycle:

1) what will the money be used for? For example, bridging grant and fundraising income cycles or investing in organisational growth.
2) how will the loan benefit the organisation? Trustees should prepare a business plan, considering how the loan will meet the organisation's mission and future sustainability and how the organisation will meet loan repayments.
3) Do you have correct organisation structures and systems in place? Does the governing document give the power to take out a loan and, potentially, to pledge assets as security? Are you confident the organisation's financial systems are sufficiently robust to manage a loan? Does your organisation include strong planning, financial and cash management skills? Do staff support the idea of a loan and understand why it is being used? Will the loan create a risk of personal liability for trustees or guarantors?

What risks are involved in taking out a loan?
In taking out a loan, trustees are legally binding the organisation to an agreed repayment schedule, terms and conditions and, possibly, security in the form of a charge on the organisation's assets. Trustees should understand the terms and conditions of the loan and the implications for the charity.

When trustees act prudently, they are not likely to be held personally liable for the loan if the organisation has limited liability or the loan terms specifically exclude such liability and personal guarantees are not given. However, they should be aware that ultimately the lender may have a charge on the organisation's assets and require them to be disposed of to make repayments due.

Your organisation can minimise the risks involved in taking out a loan by providing good project management, understanding and following the terms and conditions of the loan and always communicating clearly with the lender.

Remember – if a provider is willing to finance an organisation's project, they believe it will work. Providers work to understand an organisation's needs and undertake due diligence before taking out a loan.

### Where can our organisation take out a loan?

There are specialist loan providers willing to offer finance to voluntary and community organisations. Such providers look for both financial and social returns. Different providers take on different levels of risk, focus on different areas and have varying levels of engagement with the voluntary and community sector.

Further information on loan finance, including a selection of providers, can be found in NCVO's guide *Brief Guide to Loan Finance for Trustees*.

## Trading

Trading is one way of raising funds and earning income. The earlier section on charity law identified the restrictions on charity trading (see section 2.2).

Social enterprise is a term used to describe various types of organisation, primarily differentiated by the aim of creating a benefit for the community through running a self-sustaining trade or service. They can take on various forms of management and legal structures, depending on the organisation's purpose.

Similarly to traditional charities, they are organisations that have been created for the sole purpose of tackling social or environmental needs. Any surpluses the organisations acquire are generally reinvested back into business or community. Any profit-making for shareholders and owners is generally limited.

The different organisational structures that make up the term "social enterprise" are detailed below:

- unincorporated associations
- trusts
- limited liability companies
- some industrial and provident societies such as community benefit societies
- Community Interest Companies
- charitable incorporated organisations (when implemented – see page 25)

Most social enterprises have some form of restriction on the distribution of profit to shareholders, board members or staff. Sometimes it is a voluntary "not for profit" clause, for others a regulated obligation such as those for community interest companies or charities. Only social enterprises with charitable status are subject to the fundraising stipulations of the Charities Act 2006. Although the legislation may appear onerous, charities are able to access a far wider range of fundraising opportunities than non-charitable not-for-profit organisations. For instance, many trusts and foundations will only fund registered charities. Furthermore, charities can benefit from tax relief on profits and income from reserves, rate relief, some VAT benefits and tax-effective giving schemes.

## Fundraising and the SORP

The Statement of Recommended Practice (SORP) on Accounting by Charities (see page 80), most recently updated in 2008, makes recommendations on the treatment in accounts of fund-raising proceeds and costs. In general, voluntary income and capital funds raised by the charity or its agents should be reported in the accounts as a gross figure, and the costs of raising it, including the agents' costs, accounted for as fundraising expenditure, which could be deducted from the relevant fund to show the net amount raised.

The Statement of Recommended Practice (SORP) on Accounting by Charities requires charities to make a complete declaration of income and profits from trading activity. For example, where the primary purpose of a charity is wholly or mainly carried out by a trading activity, such as charging fees for the provision of services, the gross income from such activity and the gross expenditure should be disclosed in the Statement of Financial Activities (SOFA) (see page 86).

Where the charity does carry out permitted trading activities that are ancillary to the charity's objects, the proposals would require the charity to publish the net income from such activities and, by way of Notes to the Accounts, the full trading results. Examples of these types of trading activities include jumble sales and lotteries. Trustees need to ensure that their trading accounts are prepared in accordance with the SORP.

## Fundraising standards, codes and self-regulation

The FundRaising Standards Board (FRSB) was established in 2006 and runs a self-regulatory scheme for fundraising in the UK. Membership is voluntary and charities that join are asked to adhere to the Codes of Fundraising Practice and the FRSB's Fundraising Promise. The FRSB aims to be a mark of reassurance for the public as regards fundraising. The FRSB handles complaints from donors about fundraising issues. Contact details for the Fundraising Standards Board are listed in part 5.

By signing up to the Codes, trustees can help ensure the charity meets legal requirements and best practices in fundraising. Codes cover a range of areas including event fundraising, raffles and lotteries and fundraising from grant making trusts. Further information is available from the Institute of Fundraising (see part 5).

# 7.4

## Checklist

Have you explored the possibility of income generation in your organisation?

Does your board take proactive steps to identify emerging grant funding opportunities across all potential income sources?

Does your board need to review the fundraising activity of your charity to ensure that it complies with legal requirements?

Does your charity have a budget for fundraising?

Does your board receive regular monitoring reports?

If your charity has a fundraising sub-committee, does it have clear terms of reference for its activities?

Has your board considered whether trustees require training in the role and techniques of fundraising?

Is there more your charity could do to ensure the tax-effectiveness of its fundraising?

Is your legal structure suitable for the type of fundraising and income generation you need to carry out?

Has your board reviewed the role that loan finance could play in your organisation's funding mix?

Has your board considered signing up to the fundraising Codes of Practice and the FundRaising Standards Board?

## Public service delivery and contracting

## Public service delivery

### Why is there a focus on charities and public service delivery?

Charities have delivered public services for many years, particularly in the health and social care field. In recent years, however, the government has talked about its commitment to transforming public services – and one of the ways the government believes this transformation can be achieved is through increasing the involvement of charities and, more widely, the 'third sector' in the design and delivery of services.

In 2004/5, public service delivery accounted for almost a quarter of income received by charities[10].

It is felt that charities bring an important perspective to public services – for example, many charities have close links with their community or client groups, involving users of services in their governance arrangements and engaging with hard to reach groups.

[10] *Public service delivery: in context* (NCVO Sustainable Funding Project webpage)

### What do we mean when we talk about public services?

**Public services** are services that are funded with public money and are delivered by the state or on behalf of the state – for example by a charity.

**The public sector** consists of a number of national and local statutory bodies, including local authorities, central government and the health service.

### How can charities be involved in public services?

The design and delivery of public services can broadly involve two processes:

- commissioning – where a public sector organisation plans the provision of services based on an assessment of need
- procurement – the purchase of goods and services from an external agency.

Charities have an opportunity to be involved in both processes – in the delivery of public services and also in helping to identify needs and designing services.

Some public services are delivered under contract; some public service funding arrangements are 'greyer' consisting of service level agreements or grants. It is very important that trustees clarify the status of any funding arrangement because of the legal, financial or tax implications that may arise (see below for guidance on contracting).

### What should trustees consider in relation to public service delivery?

The choice of engaging in public service delivery is up to each charity to decide for itself, based on how trustees feel the charity can best meet its purposes via the services and activities it provides. In its publication Charities and Public Service Delivery, The Charity Commission suggest three guiding principles for trustees in deciding whether or not to deliver public services:

- stick to your mission – ensure that any decision to deliver public services furthers the charity's objects and meets the needs of beneficiaries
- guard your independence – trustees must, as at all other times, act solely in the interests of the charity
- know your worth – in setting a price or budgeting for a public service activity, trustees should understand the full cost of the service and the charity's scope to deliver the service

Trustees should consider the risks involved – to the charity's financial position, to its governance arrangements (such as conflicts of interest), to its service delivery (such as contractual issues and quality) and to its reputation.

The Charity Commission also provides a reminder of the general legal responsibilities of trustees that are relevant in relation to public service delivery:

- Charities must only undertake activities that are within their objects and powers
- Charities must be independent of government and other funders
- Trustees must act only in the interests of the charity and its beneficiaries
- Trustees must make decisions in line with their duty of care and duty to act prudently.

## The Compact

An important duty of a trustee is to safeguard the position of their charity in any public service funding agreement or contract position. One of the tools which charities and the wider voluntary and community sector can use in negotiation is The Compact. The Compact is an agreement between Government and the voluntary and community sector in England. Established in 1998, it recognises shared values, principles and commitments and sets out guidelines for how both parties should work together.

Five Codes of Practice – on topics ranging from funding and procurement to volunteering underpin The Compact and Local Compacts exist in most local authority areas. Although the Compact is not legally binding and is built on trust and mutual goodwill, its authority is derived from its endorsement by government and by the voluntary and community sector itself through its consultation process. For more information please see part 5.

## Checklist

Do trustees have an understanding of the public service delivery agenda and how it might affect the charity?

If trustees are considering delivering public services, have they ensured that:

- they are following their legal duties and responsibilities to act in the interests of the charity?
- all current and planned services are within the charity's objects and powers?
- the cost of the service is fully understood?
- risks have been assessed?

## Contracting

Traditionally local authorities, health authorities and other agencies gave grants to voluntary organisations to undertake a wide range of activities. Many of these grants have been replaced by contracts. Changing government policy has also led to voluntary and private sector organisations being invited to tender for contracts to provide many of the services formerly provided by the statutory sector (see above). Contractual agreements allow local authorities to exercise greater control over how their money is spent, and to set out and monitor quality standards in service provision.

If your charity has signed or is considering signing contracts to deliver services, it is important that trustees understand the responsibilities involved and – particularly if your charity has traditionally received grants – the differences between contracts and grants.

### What is a contract?

A contract is a legally enforceable agreement between two or more parties. For a contract to exist:

- the parties to the contract have to offer something, and accept what the other, or others, offer
- there has to be an exchange of consideration. Consideration means anything of material value, such as goods, services or money, e.g. a funder may provide money to an organisation in exchange for the organisation providing a service
- there must be an intention to create a legally binding relationship.

If these three factors exist, then the agreement is a legally binding agreement. It does not have to be called a contract. Contracts between funders and charities are sometimes referred to as service agreements, although not all service agreements are legally binding contracts. Seek clarity at the start of any discussion about an agreement as to whether it is intended to legally bind the parties.

### Do charities need a power to contract?

In order to enter into a contract your governing document must give you the power to do what is necessary to carry out the work, such as the power to employ staff. These powers could be contained in your governing document in the form of a general power to undertake activities in furtherance of the charity's mission.

### What issues need to be considered before entering into a contract?

Trustees should consider how the work proposed under the contract fits in with the charity's legal objects and its present and future plans and priorities. In order to survive in a difficult funding environment it can be tempting to offer to provide a new service for which funding is available. However, the service must fall within the charity's objects or else the trustees will be acting in breach of trust. It may be possible to modify the objects to allow the work to be undertaken or to run the contract through a separate trading subsidiary.

Trustees should consider the wider impact of providing the service on the rest of the charity's work, questioning the degree to which undertaking particular activities will contribute towards the achievement of the charity's mission. You also need to consider if the charity has the skills and resources, such as equipment and staffing, to fulfill the contract.

If volunteers are to be used, you should be clear what their role is and make sure their expenses, recruitment and training are funded. You may wish to consider inserting a clause in the contract stating that if volunteers are not forthcoming the level of service may need to be reduced. Cost estimates should include administration, start-up or closure costs, and training.

### What legal liabilities should be considered?

Before entering into a contract you should give serious consideration to all the terms and conditions and proceed only if you are certain that your charity can fulfil them.

Unincorporated charities (i.e. trusts and associations) have no distinct legal identity and therefore cannot enter into contracts in their own name. The contract will be a legal agreement between the trustees and the other contracting party or parties. Where individuals sign contracts they should state that they are doing so on behalf of the charity, or else they alone could be liable (see section 3.9 for guidance on personal liability). The trustees can be personally sued if the terms of the contract are not complied with. To protect yourself, you should include a clause in the contract that limits your financial liability to the assets of the charity. You may also wish to consider changing the charity's legal structure to become a charitable company in order to limit your potential financial liability (see section 2.3).

Charitable companies do have legal status and it is the company which is party to the contract, not the trustees.

### Will a separate trading company be necessary?

There are restrictions on the trading activities that charities are permitted to carry out (see section 2.2). However, if the service being provided under the contract is fulfilling the main objects of the charity (i.e. primary purpose trading), or arrives from work carried out by beneficiaries, this can be done by the charity and it will not be necessary to set up a separate trading company. In cases of doubt, trustees should always seek advice.

An example of primary purpose trading might be an art gallery charity selling limited edition prints, whereas an example of non-primary purpose trading might be the same charity hiring rooms for functions. It is important for each charity that has trading activities to seek legal advice or agree with HM Revenue and Customs (HMRC) what is primary and non-primary purpose before considering setting up a trading company.

The HMRC threshold for the annual turnover from non-primary purpose trading is a maximum of £50,000 or 25% of the charity's annual income, so a charity generating more non-primary purpose trading net income that this will have to pay corporation tax on net income over this amount unless a trading company is set up. Other exemptions and extra statutory concessions cover a range of fundraising and ancillary trading activities. There may also be VAT advantages in having a trading company but this depends on the specific circumstances of each charity and trustees should take professional advice.

### What is the liability for VAT?

Services provided under contract will usually be liable for VAT if your turnover is sufficiently high. You may therefore need to be registered for VAT. Prices included in any tenders or contracts should clearly state whether they are inclusive or exclusive of VAT. If the purchaser is a local authority, it will be able to reclaim in full the VAT charged on the provision of the service. The issues surrounding VAT are often complicated and detailed advice should be obtained from your local HM Revenue and Customs Office or your professional advisers.

### What is the situation when a trustee of the providing charity is an employee of the purchaser?

Local authorities and other purchasers sometimes have the right to nominate members of their staff as trustees of charities they fund. If a trustee of the charity providing or considering providing a service under contract is an employee of the purchasing organisation, a conflict of interest arises; appropriate procedures to manage this conflict of interest must be followed. When purchasers are entering into contracts with charities it may be more appropriate for a representative of the purchaser to attend the charity's board meetings in an advisory capacity than to act as a trustee. See section 21.8 for more guidance on the appointment of trustees by external organisations.

### What should a contract include?

If possible, contracts need to be negotiated. If you are asked to tender this may be difficult. You should keep control over how the work is managed to ensure that your charity's own policies, ways of working, priorities and standards are safeguarded. Contracts should include:

- names of the parties to the contract
- whether it is intended that third parties such as users can enforce the contract
- starting date and duration of the contract
- how risk will be allocated under indemnity and other provisions
- who will insure
- equal opportunities policies of the contracting parties
- service specification, i.e. what service will be provided, to whom, where and when
- quality, i.e. what standards must be achieved, how they will be measured and by whom
- monitoring, i.e. how the work will be monitored by the funder
- finance, i.e. the amount to be paid, and the method and timing of payment
- costs, indicating whether inclusive or exclusive of VAT
- staffing arrangements and rights to subcontract
- arrangements for reviewing, renewing, varying and terminating the contract
- arrangements for liaison between the funder and the providing charity
- arrangements for settling disputes, with provision for an independent, mutually acceptable mediator to be brought in if necessary
- provisions regarding intellectual property rights, data protection and confidentiality.

### Accounting treatment for contracts

Section 150 of the SORP requires that when a charity enters into a contract, it recognises any expenditure defrayed under that contract in the Statement of Financial Activities (SOFA) when the supplier has performed their obligations under the contract. The signing of the contract itself is not therefore, the point at which a liability is recognised.

## Checklist

Have you reviewed the role of your charity in relation to public service delivery and considered how public service delivery meets your organisation's charitable purposes?

Are you clear about the ways contractual funding differs from other forms of funding such as grants?

Does your governing document give you powers to enter into contracts?

Have you ensured that any contracts you have entered into fall within your charitable objects and within your powers?

How do any contracts you are considering entering into fit with your charity's plans and priorities?

Do you have the skills and resources to carry out any work to be done under contract?

Do your cost estimates include the full cost, such as recruitment, training and governance?

Do you need to be registered for VAT?

Do you need to review the role on your board of any representatives of organisations with whom you have contractual agreements?

Do you need to consider incorporation and additional insurance?

Do you need to insert clauses into any contracts limiting your liability to the assets of the charity?

# 8

# Policy

## 8.1

### Introduction

Regardless of the size of a charity, trustee boards will nearly always delegate some activities to others – to individual trustees, to staff, volunteers or advisors. One of the most important means by which a trustee board can manage its delegation is through the use of written policies and procedures setting out how the charity should be run.

What policies should there be?

Policies will inevitably vary depending on the size and type of a charity. However, all charities will have a need for policies in some areas, and the 'policy hierarachy' (see overleaf) illustrates how policies fit in to the organisation's structure, governance and operations.

## Policy hierarchy

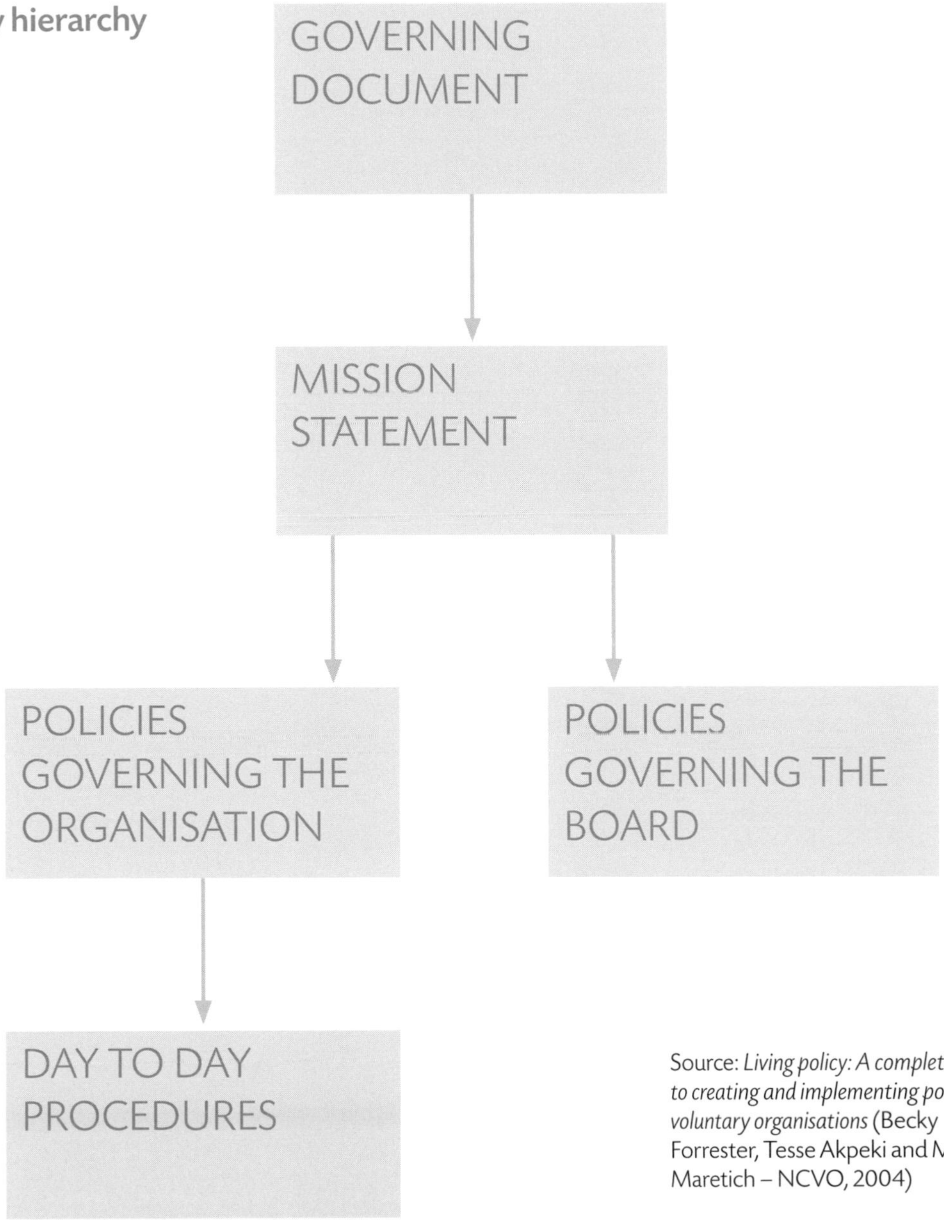

GOVERNING DOCUMENT

↓

MISSION STATEMENT

↓ ↓

POLICIES GOVERNING THE ORGANISATION | POLICIES GOVERNING THE BOARD

↓

DAY TO DAY PROCEDURES

Source: *Living policy: A complete guide to creating and implementing policy in voluntary organisations* (Becky Forrester, Tesse Akpeki and Marta Maretich – NCVO, 2004)

# 8.2

## Policies governing the organisation

Essential or 'do or die' policies. These policies cover the essentials required for a charity to operate effectively:

- **human resources policies,** if staff are employed. Human resources policies can cover a wide range of areas from working hours to discipline and grievance. They should include procedures relating to supervision and support those members of staff who may report directly to the board – commonly the chief executive (see section 11.1)
- **Volunteer management**, if volunteers are involved in your charity's work. Volunteer management policies can cover a range of areas, from role descriptions to expenses (see section 11.2).
- **financial management**. Financial policies should include internal financial controls, authorisation of contracts, procedures for the board's role in monitoring finance and policies around reserves and (if applicable) investments.
- **risk management**. A risk management policy should set out the board's overall intention to manage risk and the procedure involved (see chapter 9).

Other key policies:

- equal opportunities and diversity
- bullying and harassment
- whistleblowing[11]
- health and safety (see section 9.3)
- protection of children and vulnerable adults
- complaints procedures
- codes of conduct for staff, volunteers and service users

Operational policies, including:

- data retention and protection (see section 10.2)
- information and communications technology (see section 10.1)
- complaints (see section 14.2)
- other specialist operational policies, e.g. for charities whose work places them at some legal risk or those operating abroad
- fundraising, including working with corporates, if applicable
- campaigning and political activities (see section 2.2)

A legal audit may be useful in identifying risks and gaps in policy.

[11] The Code of Governance recommends that the board have a whistleblowing policy and procedures to allow confidential reporting of matters of concern, such as misconduct, misuse of funds, mismanagement, and risks to the organisation or to people connected with it.

# 8.3

## Policies governing the board

The trustee board should also agree policies that set out how it will operate. These policies can be useful in

- ensuring trustees understand their duties and can carry them out effectively
- clarifying 'grey' areas of board responsibility
- helping new board members get up to speed with basic procedures and working practices
- helping identify during a review whether the board is meeting its responsibilities

Essential board policies:

- Role descriptions for trustees. All trustees should have a written statement of their responsibilities (see page 51 for examples).
- Role descriptions for honorary officers (see page 52-5)
- A conflicts of interest policy and register of interests (see section 3.6)
- terms of reference for sub-committees (see section 21.9).

# 8.4

Other key board policies:

- a code of conduct for trustees, setting out the conduct and behaviour expected of trustees. You may find NCVO's model code of conduct, Best Behaviour (see page 44), a useful template. A code of conduct can be developed further by way of agreeing policies governing specific areas of trustee responsibility:
- trustee expenses policy (see page 38)
- Delineating board/staff responsibility (see section 11.3). This lies at the heart of effective governance. An agreement in this area can set out which issues should be dealt with at board level and which at staff level, and where boundaries overlap.
- Design of the board (see part 3). It may be helpful to agree a policy covering the size of the board, membership, recruitment and selection/ election procedures and terms of office (note that some of this may already be covered in your governing document so you should ensure your policy is consistent).
- Training and development (see chapter 18). A code setting out the skill audit, induction training and development of board members can help bring new trustees up to speed with what support they can receive.
- Board review or 'appraisal' (see chapter 22). The board may wish to agree a procedure governing how it is going to review its own effectiveness
- Finally, you may decide to agree other specific board policies. One example is a media policy, clarifying the role of individual trustees in acting as a spokesperson for the charity (see chapter 14).
- Board cycle or annual calendar of key activities

## Creating policy

Use the policy-making flowchart overleaf to help identify how the issue should be addressed. Many support organisations produce example, template or 'model' policies. These can be useful in giving you a starting point for a new policy, or comparing the practices of your organisation with another.

Be careful not to take wholesale another organisation's policy – their size and circumstances may not fit yours, and you may find the policy does not work for your organisation in practice.

**Further information:**
*Living policy: A complete guide to creating and implementing policy in voluntary organisations* (Becky Forrester, Tesse Akpeki and Marta Maretich – NCVO, 2004)

## Checklist

Has your board reviewed its lists of policies?

Are policies up to date?

Are new policies required?

## Policy-making flowchart

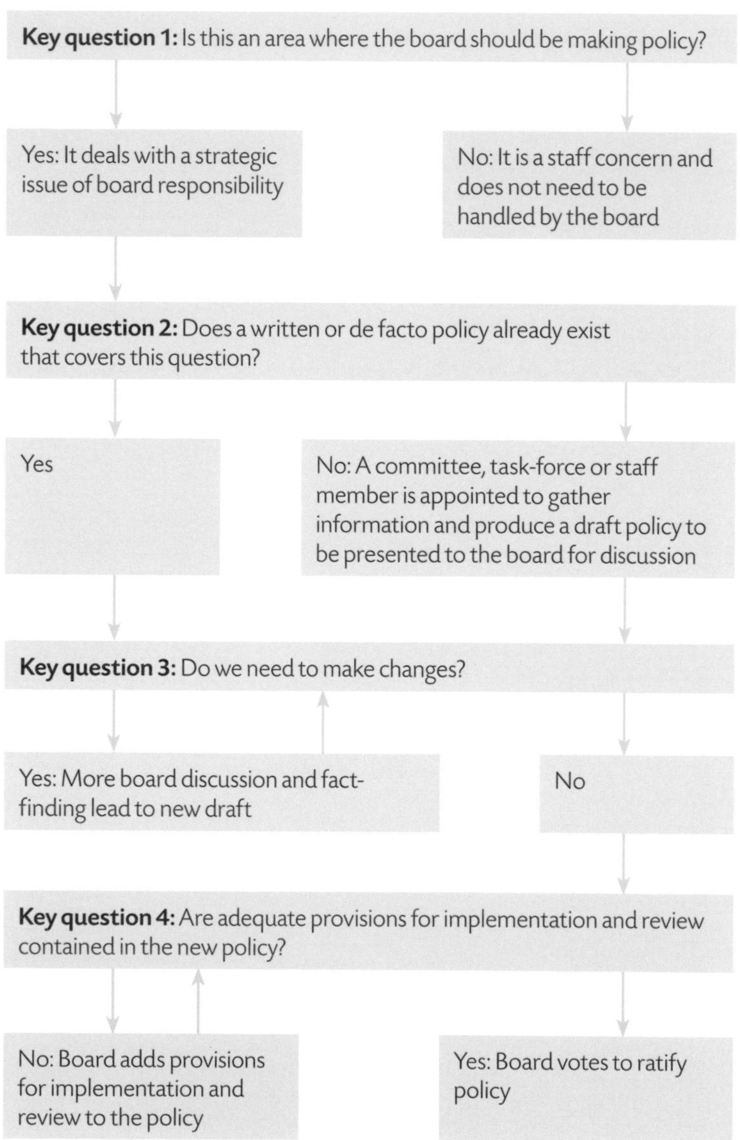
**Key question 1:** Is this an area where the board should be making policy?
Yes: It deals with a strategic issue of board responsibility
No: It is a staff concern and does not need to be handled by the board
**Key question 2:** Does a written or de facto policy already exist that covers this question?
Yes
No: A committee, task-force or staff member is appointed to gather information and produce a draft policy to be presented to the board for discussion
**Key question 3:** Do we need to make changes?
Yes: More board discussion and fact-finding lead to new draft
No
**Key question 4:** Are adequate provisions for implementation and review contained in the new policy?
No: Board adds provisions for implementation and review to the policy
Yes: Board votes to ratify policy

# 9

# Risk and safety

## 9.1

### Risk management

All charity trustees should review and put in place measures to manage the risks facing their charity. Risk management is one of the most important responsibilities of a trustee.

A risk management programme is important in meeting the mission of your charity, enabling you to seize opportunities as well as prevent disasters. The Charity Commission recommends that it is good practice for all charities to carry out a proportionate annual risk assessment and to commit to reporting on the findings.

Indeed for some charities, risk management is a requirement. For charities subject to statutory audit, the trustees' annual report is required to contain:

*"A statement confirming that the major risks to which the charity is exposed, as identified by the trustees, have been reviewed and systems or procedures have been established to manage those risks."*[12]

[12] Charity Commission publication *Charity reporting and accounting: the essentials* (CC15). Crown Copyright.

In practice this means identifying risks and describing the procedures or plans you have put in place to safe-guard against or reduce likely problems, as well as indicating how you monitor the risks and contingencies you have in place. The complexity and extent of your risk review will very much depend on the size and nature of your charity's operations.

## What is risk?

Risk is often described as the danger of something going wrong, but this is only half the story. Most risk management experts now consider risks to be potentially good as well as potentially bad. All organisations face uncertainty on a daily basis: the outcomes of events can be either positive or negative, and are usually a mix of both, to varying degrees. There will be a range of implications for your charity, whatever the outcome. You need to plan for the risks of success as well as for possible problems.

For example, in setting up a new helpline, there will be uncertainty about the take up of the service. It might receive more calls than expected but as a result, user satisfaction may be poor, as callers face a long wait for an operative. Or perhaps the service has low take up, but this could provide capacity to improve helpline procedures and invest time in promotional work.

Managing all unknowns with one approach can enable charities to be better prepared for what might happen, and is likely to be more effective than focusing only on the negative.

Risk is usually described as the danger of something going wrong. It is not only about an event however, but also about a lost opportunity. For example, if a charity's governing document is out of date and overly administratively burdensome there is a 'risk' that it may not be able to react quickly to events in order to maximise opportunities.

## Step-by-step guide to managing risk

- From key areas of uncertainty, identify the type of risks and their likely outcomes, both negative or positive, to which the organisation might be subjected
- Assess how likely or serious the risks are
- Prioritise your risks
- Agree appropriate measures to head off or manage the risks and record your plans
- Design a process for monitoring and reviewing your key risks and associated plans
- Communicate your risk management plan to highlight shared responsibility.

Below we explain a little more about each step.

### Identifying risks

A useful first stage in risk management is to explore in a systematic way key areas of uncertainty, looking at different elements of your charity's work in turn to identify possible risks. The following classification of risks is taken from the Charity Commission's Charities and Risk Management online guidance, with examples under each heading :

**Governance risks – for example**

- trustee board lacks relevant skills
- trustee board dominated by one or two individuals
- out of date governing document

**Operational risks – for example**

- ICT systems failure
- high staff turnover
- key member of staff leaving
- lack of a business continuity plan

External risks – for example

- change in government policy
- negative publicity

**Regulatory risks – for example**

- failure to comply with reporting requirements
- compliance risks
- Breach of data protection

**Financial risks – for example**

- Low level of reserves
- dependency on single source of funding

Remember to consider a range of possibilities in each area ("things that might happen") and explore the potential positive outcomes as well as the negatives. For example, the change in government policy mentioned in the list above may offer opportunities for your organisation to work in a new way.

### Analysing risks

Once a risk has been identified, you can assess:

- the likelihood of the risk happening
- the impact of the risk on the organisation if it is in fact realised.

To identify the impact of a risk, try to consider all the possible implications, some of which might not always be obvious. For example, retaining a senior manager for a long period offers stability but could lead to a lack of creative thinking in the organisation. Brainstorming together as a board could be a valuable exercise.

It can be useful to give each risk a score for likelihood – out of three perhaps, for low, medium and high – and a score for impact, and then to multiply these two scores together to give each risk a total score. You could then plot your risks on a graph like the one below.

Risk map for The Fictitious Health Care Agency

| | High Impact (3) | Medium Impact (2) | Low Impact (1) |
|---|---|---|---|
| **High Likelihood (3)** | New local authority contract<br>Requirement for same gender care<br>Senior staff member leaves<br>Difficulty recruiting support staff<br>Major health and safety breaches | Breach in appropriate user representation on board | Minor health and safety breaches |
| **Medium Likelihood (2)** | Failure to raise £100,000<br>Shift in ethnic/gender balance of users<br>Board unaware of funder priorities | Changes to record keeping on users required by funder<br>Younger clients dissatisfied with service | Changes in IT/security equipment is problematic |
| **Low Likelihood (1)** | Inadequacy of insurance<br>Destruction of office<br>Employment Tribunal claim by member of staff | Gaps in financial controls | Data protection breach |

### Prioritising risks

You can't manage every risk your charity will face, so use the analysis of likelihood and impact above to prioritise which risks you should focus on.

It's useful to determine a cut-off point, above which you will manage the risk, and below which you won't. The cut-off point could be, for example, the top five or ten risks or risks scoring six points or more. The cut-off will partly depend on how much time you will have to manage these risks. It's better to manage properly the most serious risks than to manage a full list weakly.

### Managing risks

Managing risks involves devising ways to either prevent the risk, minimise its impact, transfer the risk to a third party (for example through an insurance policy or a penalty clause), plan contingencies to come into force should the risk actually occur or accept the possible outcome. In the above example, you might

- decide that the local authority contract is too risky and choose not to take it on in the first place (prevention)
- attempt to negotiate less risky terms in the contract (minimising)
- take out extra insurance cover (transfer)
- plan a range of contingencies eg identifying agencies to provide extra cover if you are short-staffed (contingency)
- continue, aware of the risks, and see how things develop (accept the outcome).

Whichever decision you come to, make sure you have the resources to implement your approach, including those required for any contingency plans.

### Monitoring and reviewing risks

Once you have identified your key risks and decided how to deal with them, record your plans in a risk register, along with your risk map, so that you can come back to it later. You also need to decide how you will monitor and review your risks and plans, to take account of changing circumstances. Risks may come and go, or their likelihood or potential impact could change, requiring you to change the way you deal with them. It's a good idea to tie this monitoring and review process into your strategic and operational planning (see chapter 6). At the very least, review your risk register once a year and perhaps more often for large or complex projects.

### Communicating your risk management plan

Make sure everyone is aware of their responsibilities and is supported in implementing them. Consider others who could benefit from knowing how you deal with risks. For example, users may have more faith in your services if they are aware of your risk management policies and potential funders will also be looking for reassurance that their money is in good hands.

# 9.2

## The board's role

Trustees are ultimately responsible for the charity and should take the lead in ensuring that risk management is approached comprehensively and that it permeates all aspects of the charity's operations.

Risk management can be done in participation with staff, volunteers and users – this is likely to create a better analysis and stronger ownership than a 'top-down' approach.

### What can help the board?

A board which is aware of its responsibilities and works on being effective is more likely to look strategically at the risks facing the charity. A board which reviews its responsibilities regularly is more likely to be aware of the risks facing the board and the effective governance of the charity.

The good practice in Parts two and three of The Good Trustee Guide can help, particularly:

- Understanding the respective roles of board and staff
- Following good practice in recruitment and induction of board members, using a systematic approach to identifying new board members based on the organisation's needs
- Regular reviews of board and organisational performance
- Reviewing compliance with relevant laws affecting the charity
- Good management procedures and practices to develop a sense of teamwork.

## Checklist

When did you last carry out a risk management exercise?

Does your board regularly carry out a risk management exercise?

Do you report on risk in accordance with the SORP (if appropriate)?

Do you act on the findings of the exercise?

## Insurance

Trustees have a responsibility to safeguard the charity's property from loss or damage and to safeguard property from third party liabilities that might affect the charity's property. One of the means by which trustees can fulfil this duty, as a part of their overall approach to risk management, is by maintaining adequate insurance cover.

## Insurance – trustee responsibilities

### Are trustees required to take out insurance?

Some types of insurance are compulsory by law. There may also be a duty in the charity's governing document to purchase insurance.

There has been concern in recent years about the high cost of taking out insurance and has led to some trustees to question the need for certain types of insurance.

Where a form of insurance is not compulsory, trustees should form their decision to take out insurance as part their risk management exercise. The Charity Commission have produced guidance as part of their Charities and Insurance publication (CC49) to help trustees consider the circumstances where they should pass the risk onto an insurer and/or find other ways of minimising the risk.

### Can trustees be held personally liable for failing to take out insurance?

If trustees fail to take out insurance where they have a duty to do so, or unreasonably fail to take out insurance for which they have the power to do so they may be personally liable for any loss arising. Personal liability may also arise for trustees of unincorporated organisations if the organisation can not pay an uninsured claim.

Taking out insurance is one of a number ways that trustees can manage any risks facing the charity and themselves personally. Understanding duties and responsibilities as trustees, following good governance practice and putting in place sound risk management practices are also key to managing risks along with taking out insurance cover.

## Types of insurance

Cover is required or recommended for a wide range of items, including the property of the charity (such as land, buildings, furniture and computers); cash on the premises or in transit; its liabilities to employees, volunteers and the public; motor insurance; and insurance for fundraising or special events. You should regularly review the policies to ensure that the cover is still adequate and the premiums competitive. An up-to-date inventory of all property, furniture and equipment must be kept.

### Insuring property

You are responsible for ensuring that there is adequate insurance cover for the following:

- Buildings: It is advisable to choose a policy which covers what is known as 'all risks' to the building. Trustees should take professional advice on the sum for which the building is insured.
- the contents of premises. An 'all risks' policy will generally cover damage to contents from most events. If the policy is not 'all risks', additional cover against damage to contents from specified events or accidents should be taken out.
- consequential loss. This covers any costs resulting from disruption to the activities of the charity, for example as the result of a fire. The costs of renting alternative premises would be one such loss.

If a charitable company owns its premises, responsibility for insuring the property rests with the charity.

If, as a trustee, you hold property on behalf of an unincorporated charity, you are solely responsible for insurance on that property.

If your charity's premises are leased, then responsibility for insurance will generally be specified in the lease.

### Insuring for liability as employers

Trustees are required by law to insure against any liability for personal injury or illness sustained by their employees as a result of their employment. As a trustee you must ensure that employers' liability insurance is taken out and that a copy of the certificate of insurance is displayed at the premises. Copies of certificates must be kept for at least 40 years. You should also consider taking out employers' legal indemnity insurance which provides cover against losses related to employment matters, such as legal expenses and compensation arising from employment tribunal awards. You can also insure against staff sickness, to cover the cost of sick pay.

### Fidelity insurance

This protects against any possible dishonesty by employees, volunteers and sometimes trustees.

### Professional indemnity insurance

This protects against claims for incorrect advice when staff or trustees of your charity give advice to the public or other organisations.

### Insuring for liability to members of the public

Public liability insurance is needed to cover for any injury, illness or damage to property incurred by members of the public as a result of the activities of the charity. 'Members of the public' may include the charity's volunteers as well as the trustees and you should see that volunteers are informed about the extent of cover provided for them by the charity. You should also make sure that volunteers are given advice about the insurance position if they drive their own vehicles in the course of their volunteering, and are properly protected while working on the charity's premises. Some policies exclude cover for volunteers over a certain age. Volunteers should be made aware of such exclusions, and of any alternative arrangements made to protect them.

### Trustee liability insurance

If you act prudently, lawfully and in accordance with your governing document, then any liabilities you incur as a trustee can be met out of the charity's resources.

However, if you do not act in this manner, for example if you make poor investment decisions, or unlawful payments to trustees, act outside of the charity's objects or engage in unlawful political activities, you may be in breach of trust and personally liable to make good any loss to the charity. As trustees act jointly in administering a charity, you and your fellow trustees are jointly liable to make good any loss. The Charity Commission has powers to take proceedings in court to recover from trustees personally any funds lost to the charity because of a breach of trust (see section 3.9 for more information on trustee liability).

There are no restrictions on trustees personally paying for insurance to protect their personal liability. The trustees may use the charity's funds to insure the charity against loss to its own funds resulting from the acts and defaults of trustees.

However, the Charity Commission will only allow the trustees to use the charity's funds to pay for liability insurance to protect trustees for two types of action:

- acts which are properly undertaken in the administration of the charity
- acts in breach of trust, but made as a result of an honest mistake.

The Commission does not allow cover for acts which trustees knew or ought to have known were wrong, or for acts or omissions made in reckless disregard of whether they were right or wrong.

There is a general power in the Charities Act 2006 to allow trustees to use the charity's funds to pay for insurance to protect their personal liability, unless there is an explicit prohibition in the charity's governing document.

For further information, see the Charity Commission publication CC49 Charities and Insurance.

If you are considering taking out trustee liability insurance you should identify the areas of your charity's activities where you may be at risk, assess how much cover you need, and balance this with the number of trustees and the size of premium quoted.

Remember that it is unusual for trustees who have behaved honestly to suffer financial loss as a result of their trusteeship. There are risks, but they should be kept in proportion. When breaches of trust have been committed as the result of an honest mistake, or when trustees have been found wanting in the degree of control they exercised over staff, the Charity Commission has rarely required trustees to make good any loss. Insurance would not protect you from liability incurred as a result of breaches of trust knowingly committed.

### How should trustees obtain insurance cover?

It is good practice to obtain up to three comparable quotes from insurers or brokers.

### Fulfilling conditions of insurance

It is essential that trustees understand the conditions of insurance policies and ensure that they are fulfilled. Failure to do so can be costly.

## Checklist

Does your board need to review its procedures for ensuring that the charity has adequate insurance cover?

Does your charity hold annual reviews of its insurance cover?

Has your charity taken appropriate advice on the sums insured?

Are you satisfied that all the important conditions of insurance have been fulfilled?

Does your charity inform volunteers about the insurance cover it provides for them? Are you satisfied that your charity fulfils its legal requirements in respect of employers' liability insurance?

Discuss the need for trustee liability insurance at a board meeting. Do you face a risk which justifies spending the charity's assets indemnifying the trustees, or are there better ways of protecting your personal liability?

If you plan to take out trustee liability insurance, have you checked your governing document to ensure there is not an express prohibition?

# 9.3

## Health and safety

The charity has ultimate responsibility for the health and safety of all employees and volunteers. Trustees should ensure that the charity has health and safety policies that comply with the law and that they are implemented and reviewed regularly.

### What are trustees' statutory responsibilities for health and safety?

There is a considerable amount of legislation governing health and safety. Obligations under these laws include requirements to:

- provide a written policy on health and safety (for organisations with five employees or more)
- appoint a competent person to help you meet your health and safety duties
- conduct a risk assessment in order that preventative and protective measures can be identified
- conduct a risk assessment for new and expectant mothers
- make arrangements for putting into practice the measures that follow from this assessment
- provide appropriate health surveillance
- provide basic welfare facilities (eg toilet and washing facilities and drinking water)
- set up emergency procedures, including fire drills and evacuation
- consult workers on health and safety
- provide information to employees and volunteers on health and safety
- display the health and safety law poster and current certificate of Employer's Liability Insurance if you employ any staff
- provide training opportunities for staff.
- register with the local enforcing authorities for health and safety, if appropriate.

Any risk assessment carried out should:

- be "suitable" and "sufficient"
- be carried out by a "competent" person; and
- enable you to set the charity's health and safety priorities.

Under the Workplace Regulations you are responsible for ensuring that your organisation adheres to requirements in the following areas:

- working environment – temperature, ventilation, lighting, room dimensions and the suitability of workstations and seating
- safety – safe passage of pedestrians and vehicles, windows and skylights, doors, gates, floors and falling objects
- facilities – toilets, washing, eating and changing facilities, clothing storage, drinking water, rest areas and rest facilities for pregnant mothers and nursing mothers
- housekeeping – maintenance of workplace, equipment and facilities, cleanliness and removal of waste materials.

There is a large, complex body of statutory regulation concerning health and safety and the Good Trustee Guide can only provide a very brief introduction.

Trustees are responsible for ensuring adherence to a wide range specific health and safety regulations. These regulations include – but are not restricted to – obligations with regard to fire safety in non-domestic premises; the ban on smoking in enclosed public places and workplaces; regulations relating to employees' working time, rest breaks and paid annual leave; regulations relating to the use of computer display equipment; regulations relating to first aid; manual handling; electricity; use of machines & equipment; protective clothing; hazardous substances; the reporting of certain accidents, diseases and dangerous occurences; and other specific regulations.

The list above is not exhaustive and trustees should take steps to check their obligations and ensure compliance with requirements specific to their charity.

### What can trustees do to promote good health and safety?

The Health and Safety Executive has published guidance specifically for board members and leaders. The guidance underlines the important role of the board in ensuring effective health and safety management and the importance of integrating health and safety into an organisation's governance arrangements (particularly around risk and internal controls). In particular, the HSE guidance covers:

- guidance on drawing up a health and safety policy, starting with an assessment of risks. The policy should confirm the board's commitment to leading on health and safety and set out a plan to communicate, promote, champion and monitor health and safety.
- a recommendation that trustees regularly include health and safety on board agendas and consider appointing a board health and safety champion.

The role of the board in relation to health and safety has also been highlighted by the coming into force of The Corporate Manslaughter and Corporate Homicide Act 2007. This Act came into force on 6 April 2008, creating a new statutory criminal offence of 'corporate manslaughter' for incorporated organisations (including charitable companies and other incorporated charities) causing death through gross negligence. The Act emphasises the involvement of senior management in a breach of duty as an important factor in a prosecution[13].

The new law serves as a further reminder to trustee boards to ensure they are fulfilling their health and safety duties and ensuring health and safety is an issue given attention at board level.

[13] See *Corporate Manslaughter and Corporate Homicide Act 2007* (Farrer and Co briefing note, 2007) available on the NCVO website.

## Checklist

Does your charity have a health and safety policy?

Are you satisfied that your board has adequate procedures for monitoring and overseeing your health and safety policies and practices?

Do trustees ever carry out spot checks in the charity's premises, for example, checking that fire exits are not blocked or locked?

Does your board need to check that a risk assessment has been carried out and that your charity's health and safety policies comply with recent legislation?

**Further information**

The Health and Safety Executive have 'businesses' and 'leadership' sections of their website setting out information about how organisations can manage health and safety and the role of the board – www.hse.gov.uk. The HSE have also published a guide specifically for charities entitled *Charity and voluntary workers: A guide to health and safety at work* (see part five).

# 10

# Data and ICT

## 10.1

## Information and communications technology

### ICT – trustees' responsibilities

What are trustees' responsibilities towards information and communications technology (ICT)?

The objective of ICT is to make a charity behave in a smarter and more productive manner – in "doing more" with less – or, alternatively, doing that which previously had been thought impossible.

ICT is a relatively new issue for trustees. It was developed within the last 40 years (originally as a method of controlling trading stocks and producing payrolls) and continues to develop at an ever increasing rate of change and impacts on all areas of a charity.

Trustees should note that there is little in the way of a legal framework for ICT to operate in.

The involvement of trustees in ICT will always depend on the size of an organisation, but, in essence, the trustee board's approach is like any other issue facing them – creating a supportive environment and asking probing questions about any ICT development, so that they are assured that what needs to be done is done.

### What does 'creating a supportive environment' mean?

It cannot be denied that ICT costs money. Neither can ICT always be viewed in strict terms of return on investment. A successful ICT project depends on spending what is necessary – not the least possible. Trustees need to be aware of this so that ICT proposals are not rejected out of hand. They must also constantly be aware of the benefits that change for the better can bring.

### What questions should trustees be asking about ICT?

The following list of questions can be used by trustees to help make decisions about ICT.

Questions to ask when considering a new ICT system

**About the overall proposal**

- In simple terms – what is proposed?
- Why do we want to do it?
- What will the benefits be?
- When will the project be completed by?
- How much will it cost and when will expenditure be incurred?
- How will the project be financed?
- Can any savings be quantified?
- Can any additional income be quantified?
- What will the benefits to our supporters be?
- What will the benefits to the beneficiaries of our charity be?
- What will the benefits to our stakeholders be?
- Who is making the proposal and what is in it for them?
- How will we know if we have succeeded? What are the success measures?
- Who will our in house project manager be?

**About the process involved**

If consultants are to be used

- Is it proposed to use consultants in the early stages of the project? If so why, what will their role be, how long will they be used for, what will they do, what is their track record? what will they cost and are they truly independent?

Purchases of software and hardware

- Projects may involve a mix of software and hardware. Who is the major vendor? Why have they been chosen? What is their track record? What is their financial strength? Are we dealing with industry standard names or very small enterprises? If a new software development is under discussion do we have sufficient existing computing power to make it run properly or do we have to invest in new hardware systems as well?

Installation and implementation

- How long will it take to get the project fully operational? Will existing and new systems have to be operated at the same time? How will the staffing implications be met? How will staff / volunteers be trained to operate the new systems and who will carry the training out?

About modifications and updates

- A software application is very similar to a living thing. It needs to grow to meet the challenges that are thrust upon it. The same applies to computer hardware. Has allowance for these been allowed for in the funding of the project? Will a management process be put in place which allows modifications and upgrades to be managed and installed on a regular and timely basis? Who will be responsible for the process?

Security of data

- What measures do we have in place to protect our information from unauthorised persons who may try to steal or misuse it? Do we have firewalls to limit outside access, do we have antivirus software, do we limit the use of our information to our own premises? Do we encrypt our data so that no one outside our organisation can read it? Do we limit our staff and volunteers' use of the internet? Are they able to install their own programmes? Do we audit our back up systems so that we check if all of the information we thought is secured actually is? Do we have multiple data security systems?

Maintenance

- Have we signed contracts so that essential maintenance can be carried out on our software and hardware? Do we have service level agreements that specify how fast this service will be provided? If we operate on a 24 hour 365 day basis are our contracts in the same time frame?

## Questions to ask about risk management

Insurance

- Have we increased our sums insured to take account of ICT expenditure? Do we have a technology risk policy that covers theft of data, disruption to our business, damage and reinstatement of our data and systems?

Disaster recovery

- Do we have strong and tested measures in place appropriate to the size of our organisation that will enable us to be back in business in case of disaster with the minimum of delay? Do we have a written disaster recovery plan? Is it regularly reviewed from time to time?

Location of data

- If we have a number of different server, do we concentrate all our file servers into one room or building or do we site them at differing locations so that a disaster could not strike them all at once?

Use of file servers

- Do we house more than one 'mission critical' software programme on a file server, or do we have a number of servers each with one function so that if one becomes inoperable only part of our system is affected?

Security of service

- What happens if our supplier ceases to support the system or goes out of business?

The life of a typical ICT project

| | Year 1 | Year 2 | Year 3 | Year 4 |
|---|---|---|---|---|
| Shortlisting | √ | | | |
| Purchase | √ | | | |
| Installation | √ | | | |
| Modifications | √ | √ | √ | √ |
| New Servers | √ | | | √ |
| Back Up Devices | √ | | | √ |
| Security Systems | √ | | | √ |
| UPS | √ | | | √ |
| Data warehouse | √ | | | √ |
| Workstations/Printers | √ | | | √ |
| Insurance | √ | √ | √ | √ |
| Depreciation | √ | √ | √ | √ |
| Training | √ | √ | √ | √ |
| Documentation | √ | √ | √ | √ |
| Stationery | √ | √ | √ | √ |
| Maintenance | √ | √ | √ | √ |
| Upgrades | | √ | √ | √ |
| Networking | √ | √ | √ | √ |
| Managing relationships | √ | √ | √ | √ |

## A glossary of commonly used ICT terms

**Electronic Computer** – a device to crunch large amounts of numbers very quickly. First invented by the British during World War 2.

**Hardware** – physical devices that make a sound if you tap them, usually a computer.

**Software** – instructions that make computers work for you.

**Installation, modifications and updates**. – It is a fact of life that software never does what you want it to and you have to spend more money to get it to do that. Updates come a little later to fix what the manufacturer promised it would do in the first place.

**Security of data** – keeping your information away from thieves.

**File server** – a large computer that holds data (information) and programmes (sets of instructions) that people can use.

**Desk top** – a small computer attached to a file server. It usually sits on top of some one's desk.

**Lap top** – a portable computer that can be attached to a file server when sitting on top of a desk or taken off site and used remotely.

**Note book, tablet** – same as a lap top but smaller.

**Mouse** – a device that lets you interact with computer programmes

**Key Board** – a device that lets you put letters and numbers into a computer

**Hacker** – some one who wants to get inside your computer for either profit or pleasure

**Virus** – an electronic illness that can infect computers

**Back up device** – a tape recorder that copies information from a file server onto a tape so that it can be stored off site

**UPS** – a car battery that is used to power a computer during a power cut so that it can be turned off properly

**Network** – a computer programme that connects a number of computers together so that they can share information, programmes and printers

**Internet** (the World Wide Web) – lets everybody in the world connect to everyone else.

**Extranet** – a way of sharing an organisation's information with a controlled number of people.

**Intranet** – a way of sharing an organisation's information with its staff and controlling their access to the internet

**Further information**
includes *From Nightmare to Nirvana – an ICT Survival Guide for Trustees* (ICT Hub, 2008) – free to download from NCVO's ICT development services website (www.icthub.org.uk ).

## Checklist

Does your organisation have an ICT strategy?

Do trustees feel confident when they are asked to consider new ICT proposals for the organisation?

# 10.2

## Data protection

As it becomes easier to manipulate and store data about individuals, so the need for protection over how that information is stored and used has increased. Every individual has the right to exert some control over how information he or she gives out about him or herself is used by organisations. The Data Protection Act provides individuals with that protection and sets out a framework around how organisations handle personal data.

When information from which a person can be identified is "processed" (i.e. used, stored, processed or transmitted) then the organisation doing the processing needs to comply with the provisions of the Data Protection Act. Special rules apply to "sensitive personal data" which relates, for instance, to racial or ethnic origin, political opinions, religious belief, health and sex life.

The Data Protection Act gives members of the public the right to find out what personal information is held by them. They do this by making a 'subject access request'. If a member of the public feel that they have been prevented from this access, they can contact the Information Commissioner's Office.

Do not assume that if your data about individuals is stored manually and not electronically the Act does not apply. Under the Act manually held as well as electronically held data are subject to the DPA.

Charities are likely to be processing data, and so need to comply with the Act, if, for instance, they hold any data about an individual in any kind of database (an example of a manual database would be a card index system). This might include:

- name and address lists
- donor databases
- fundraising databases
- records about employees.

Registration with the Information Commissioner (the UK government agency in charge of responsibility for monitoring data protection laws) is one of the first steps an organisation should take (not-for-profit organisations are exempt from registration if they use personal data only for certain specific purposes – such as membership records – but the exemption is quite limited and charities should check the guidance).

Trustees should be careful to ensure that compliance with data protection laws comprises part of their charity's internal systems and processes. They need to determine what information about individuals the charity gathers, how it uses it and whom it gives it to. It then needs to adopt a set of practices in relation to information which comply with the Act.

Generally, compliance with the Act requires compliance with what are known as the eight data protection principles. These include not using the information for purposes which are outside those for which the individual gave them the data, not transferring that data to other parties without the individual's consent, and keeping the information secure. Organisations also need to ensure that they only keep information for as long as is necessary for the purpose for which they have consent.

Any breach of the data protection laws can be punished by fines levied by the Information Commissioner. Individuals about whom data are held also have certain rights under the Act. The Information Commissioner's Office is a useful resource and starting point for understanding legal obligations relating to data (see Resources section).

## Checklist

Does your charity have a data protection policy?

Is the implementation of the policy reviewed to ensure the charity complies with data protection law?

# 11

# Staff and volunteers

## 11.1

## Employment responsibilities

Staff are a key resource for charities

- It can cost almost £8,000 to replace a member of staff[14]
- Voluntary organisations are over-represented at employment tribunals

A well managed and diverse staff group can help your organisation's public image and funding and improve the performance of staff.

[14] The Chartered Institute of Personnel and Development has estimated the average cost of filling a vacancy per employee is £4,333. This increases to £7,750, when associated costs, such as costs of training the new recruit, are added (CIPD Recruitment, Retention and Turnover Survey 2007).

## Overview of trustees' employment responsibilities

If the charity employs individuals, whether full-time, part-time, casual or temporary, the charity is likely to be their employer. Therefore, you will need to ensure that you understand and abide by current employment legislation.

Employment law is complex and changes frequently. Much of the detail of trustees' responsibilities as employers is beyond the scope of this section.

### Employed, self employed or worker?

Are you clear as to the employment status of people who are paid to carry out work for your charity? Are you clear whether they are employed, self-employed or in the category of 'worker'?

**Employees**
Employment rights extend both to full time employees and part time employees and employees on permanent, fixed term or annual hours contracts (see below).

**Self-employed**
Some individuals may carry out work for a charity on a self-employed basis. A self-employed person is not an employee of the charity and does not have any obligation beyond the specific piece of work for which they are contracted. There are a number of criteria to determine whether someone is self-employed. Self-employed people are responsible for their own tax and national insurance. Treating someone as self employed even if they say they are can have very serious tax and employment law risks if legally they are employed. Legal advice should be sought.

**Worker**
A 'worker' is an individual who works for a charity but is not employed on a contract of employment, but because of the nature of their work (usually on a flexible or casual basis) have some other contract that puts them in the middle ground between employee and self-employed. Workers have some rights under employment law, but not as many as for employees – for example, they do not have the right to claim unfair dismissal, notice pay or redundancy pay. However, they do have the right to receive the minimum wage, not suffer unlawful deductions from their wage and to receive paid holiday at working time regulation levels.

### Employment rights

In general, all employees have a right to certain benefits and conditions in the areas of equality, leave, pay and contracts/conditions. This is a complex area but, in broad terms the rights of employees include:

- not to be discriminated against or suffer detriment
- to equal pay
- rights relating to work on Sundays
- part time workers to be treated no less favourably
- employees on fixed term contracts to be treated no less favourably
- rights to take leave in certain circumstances, including maternity leave, and other entitlements, and rights around annual leave and working time limits
- pay – including the minimum wage, not to have unlawful deductions from pay and statutory pay (eg maternity pay, sick pay etc)
- a written statement of the main terms of the employment contract
- not to be unfairly dismissed
- apply for flexible working in certain circumstances
- notice of termination of employment
- a safe system of work
- trade union membership
- protected employment rights when a business transfers to a new employer
- written reasons for dismissal on request if they have one year's service
- be accompanied at disciplinary and grievance hearings
- protection when making disclosures of wrongdoing to the employer

Employers must

- register with HM Revenue and customs if they are taking on an employee
- adhere to data protection principles – some employee data is considered to be personal data (see section 10.2)
- check each employee's entitlement to work legally in the UK before employment commences under the Asylum and Immigration Act
- insure.

### Contract of employment

All employees have a contract once an offer of employment is made and accepted. This does not have to be in writing to constitute a legal contract. However, employees (including part-timers and those on fixed-term contracts) employed for more than one month have the statutory right to a written statement of terms and conditions of employment. Under the Employment Rights Act 1996 this must now be provided within two months of starting work. The statement must include certain information[15] and it is important that you ensure the statement of terms and conditions includes this information.

In addition to the statutory particulars which are required to be included in all employment contracts, it may be advisable for the charity to include additional clauses designed to give the charity further protection. For example, it would be advisable to include clauses dealing with payment of expenses, confidentiality, intellectual property rights, post-termination restrictions, the right to make deductions and so on.

## Employment policies and procedures

Trustees should ensure that the charity has policies for the recruitment of staff, ensuring that policies and practices are in place so that applicants are treated fairly and in accordance with equal opportunities practice at all stages of advertising, shortlisting and interviewing. They should establish policies for staff appraisal, support and supervision, probationary periods and remuneration that are proportional to the size of the charity.

Employers must follow certain statutory procedures, for example in relation to disputes at work such as disciplinary and grievance matters (although these are due to be repealed by the Employment Bill from April 2009 and replaced by an ACAS code of practice on discipline and grievance). If the charity has five employees or more it is required to prepare a written policy regarding health and safety.

Some employers, as a matter of good practice, adopt non-statutory policies, such as an email and internet policy. However, you should ensure that these policies do not form part of the employee/worker's contract. This is so that if you wish to amend the policies at a future date you do not need to obtain the employee/worker's consent before any amendments, additions or substitutions are made. You should, however, inform the employee/worker of any amendments as soon as is practicable.

All policies should be reviewed on a regular basis.

It is likely in small charities that the trustees will be personally involved in appointing all the staff. In larger charities they may appoint only the chief executive, or the most senior staff, delegating responsibility for appointing other staff to the chief executive or other senior managers. Similarly, trustees' personal involvement in staff appraisal or review will depend on the size of the charity.

[15] *The Good Guide to Employment: Managing and Developing People in Voluntary and Community Organisations* (NCVO) contains more information.

You should be aware that some staff may be bound by their own code of professional ethics, for example lawyers working for charities or medical staff working in charitable hospices or research institutes. You should respect the constraints which this may place on staff.

Trustees should be cautious about linking terms and conditions with that of local authorities (for example by placing salaries on the NJC – National Joint Council – pay scale). Although such an approach may be familiar to staff and funders, it risks tying the charity to a process over which they have no control. It is recommended that, if NJC scales are adopted, it is made clear that increments are not guaranteed but are dependent on affordability and at trustee discretion.

Employment issues and employment contracts are those areas most likely to give rise to a situation in which the charity will find itself liable. Employment law is a fast changing area of law and if the charity is in doubt about an employment issue it should seek expert advice.

## The chief executive

Where a staff structure is in place and a chief executive manages the staff team, then a direct responsibility of the board is to recruit and support the chief executive. The board takes overall responsibility for:

- setting the organisation's strategic direction and the boundaries within which staff operate
- recruiting and inducting the chief executive, setting remuneration, establishing a monitoring system
- managing and appraising the chief executive
- delegating authority, sometimes to the chair, for liaison and support to the chief executive in between board meetings
- respecting the boundaries between board and chief executive and reviewing these regularly (see chapter 8 for more guidance in this area).

This is an important area of board responsibility and other guides exist to inform the board in this area (listed in the Resources section).

## Dealing with conflict

Internal conflict in a charity is not uncommon. It can be time-consuming and costly and it distracts the trustees and any staff or volunteers from getting on with the work the charity was established to do. Moreover, the resulting bad publicity can damage the charity's public image.

Trustees should be aware that employers must follow certain statutory procedures in relation to disputes at work but that these are due to change in 2009 (see previous page).

**Further information**
*The Good Guide to Employment: Managing and Developing People in Voluntary and Community Organisations* (NCVO) 2008

# 11.2

## Checklist

Does your board need to review its procedures for ensuring that the charity is acting in accordance with employment law?

Does your board need to review its employment policy and practices, including its recruitment policy, and the grievance and disciplinary procedures?

Does your board regularly review the salaries, terms and conditions of service of the staff?

Does your board ensure that there is adequate support and supervision for staff?

Does a group of trustees agree an annual workplan for the chief executive officer and annually appraise his or her performance?

Do any of the trustees involved in appointing or appraising staff need support, for example, training in interviewing?

Does the charity have any fixed-term employees and, if so, should any of them be converted to permanent employees?

Should the board conduct an audit of employees on fixed-term contracts to ensure that their terms and conditions are not less favourable that for comparable permanent employees?

Should the board conduct an audit of part-time employees to ensure that they are not to be treated less favourably (unless it can be objectively justified)?

## Volunteers

Most organisations use volunteers to help carry out their work – indeed, trustees are volunteers, and many organisations rely entirely on volunteers. If your charity uses volunteers, trustees should be aware of their overall legal responsibility for their management and support and, through the board's leadership, create an environment that is a supportive and positive place to volunteer.

## What are the hallmarks of good volunteer management?

Like many aspects of a trustees' responsibility, the way in which the board support and manage volunteers will vary depending on the size of the organisation and the extent to which the organisation relies on volunteers. But all organisations should share the same principles of good volunteer management – and a good place to start is to review how your organisation compares to the ten principles of good volunteer management that make up the Investing in Volunteers quality standard (see box).

## Principles of good volunteer management

The Investing in Volunteers Standard comprises ten indicators:

1) There is an expressed commitment to the involvement of volunteers, and recognition throughout the organisation that volunteering is a two-way process, which benefits volunteers and the organisation.

2) The organisation commits appropriate resources to working with volunteers, such as money, management, staff time and materials.

3) The organisation is open to involving volunteers who reflect the diversity of the local community, in accordance with the organisation's stated aims, and operates procedures.

4) The organisation develops appropriate roles for volunteers in line with its aims and objectives, and which are of value to the volunteers and create an environment where they can develop.

5) The organisation is committed to ensuring that, as far as possible, volunteers are protected from physical, financial and emotional harm arising from volunteering.

6) The organisation is committed to using fair, efficient and consistent recruitment procedures for all potential volunteers.

7) The organisation takes a considered approach to taking up references and official checks which is consistent and equitable for all volunteers, bearing in mind the nature of the work.

8) Clear procedures are put into action for introducing new volunteers to the organisation, its work, policies, practices and relevant personnel.

9) Everybody in the organisation is aware of the need to give volunteers recognition.

10) The organisation takes account of the varying support needs of volunteers

**Further information**
Investing in Volunteers – www.investinginvolunteers.org.uk

## Volunteer management practice

How can our organisation put in place good volunteer management practices?

Volunteering England, the national volunteer support agency, has an online Good Practice Bank covering many aspects of volunteer management, including information sheets, case studies and links to other helpful guidance or external websites. Most sections include example and template documents to help you develop your own volunteer programme.

**Further information**
Volunteering England Good Practice Bank – www.volunteering.org.uk/goodpractice

## Keeping it legal

It is important to make a clear distinction between individuals who are paid to work for your organisation and individuals who volunteer. Blurring the boundaries between volunteers and paid staff risks placing volunteers in the category of employee or worker, bringing with it rights and responsibilities on the volunteer and organisation which may not be appropriate or desirable. You can help avoid this situation by:

- only reimbursing volunteers for genuine out of pocket expenses. Avoid flat rate expenses or payments over and above actual expenses, and avoid providing other material benefits that could be seen as constituting payment (for example, Volunteering England suggest that "training offered should be linked to the role that the person is carrying out, rather than a general perk or enticement to volunteer")[1]
- avoiding creating a relationship between a volunteer and an organisation that could be seen to be an employment or contractual relationship. Such a relationship need not have a written contract but includes consideration (the volunteer receiving something of value) and intent to create a legally binding relationship (an obligation for the volunteer to provide their services). This can be avoided by phrasing a volunteer agreement to avoid language that might suggest that an employment relationship could exist.[2]

[1] A summary of legal issues involving volunteers (Volunteering England Good Practice Bank)

[2] See Volunteering England's Good Practice Bank for further information

## Professional standards for volunteer managers

The UK Workforce Hub is the Standard Setting Body for the sector and has produced licensed standards in the Management of Volunteers which are available to use. These were updated in 2008.

**Further information**
To access the standards please visit www.ukworkforcehub.org.uk/mvnos08

## Checklist

Does trustees need to review the organisation's compliance with the law around volunteers?

Does your organisation have a volunteer policy?

Does your organisation regularly acknowledge and thank volunteers for the contribution they make – for example via awards or celebrations?

# 11.3

## Relations with staff and volunteers

As trustees you are collectively responsible, along with staff and volunteers, for ensuring that good relations exist between yourselves and any staff you employ or volunteers you manage.

All too often the board / staff / volunteer relationship in an organisation can be undermined because of a lack of clarity of roles. What are the boundaries between trustee and staff/volunteer roles? Where do roles overlap?

There is no 'right' or 'wrong' answer to any of these questions. An effective relationship is built on understanding the distinction between the roles and responsibilities of the board and those of the staff and volunteers, identifying where roles overlap and paying attention to building good working relationships.

## Clarifying the roles of the board and staff/ volunteers

It may help to begin by clarifying the formal aspect of the board – staff/ volunteer relationship – that is, the extent and nature by which authority is delegated from trustees to staff and volunteers. Are trustee role descriptions, staff job descriptions, volunteer role descriptions, policies and procedures and internal controls clear and up to date? Do they need to be reviewed?

Next, is there a clear and shared understanding between board, staff and volunteers as to their respective roles and areas of overlap? Has this been discussed by both parties? You could use an exercise like the one in the box as a starting point.

Remember that what is a board role in one organisation may be a staff or volunteer role in another. Where boundaries overlap – for example in the area of planning or budgeting – the respective duties of board members and staff/volunteers will vary between organisations. Even when a task is clearly the responsibility of the board, some organisations will involve staff or volunteers far more than others in helping trustees discharge their duties – for example by way of providing information, guidance or practical support.

Remember also that organisations are dynamic and change all the time. Your board should revisit the issue of board/staff/volunteer boundaries from time to time, particularly when your organisation reaches a new point in its development. It is important to take time out of the normal schedule of business to review roles (for example, by holding an away day).

## Exercise – Board, staff and volunteer roles

About this exercise:
This exercise explores the roles of the board and those of staff or volunteers. It should take about 45 minutes to complete.

**Learning objectives:** As a result of this exercise, participants should be able to list the complementary roles of the board and staff/volunteers and describe the areas of overlap.

**You need:** flipchart paper, pens

**Leader preparation:** Review the notes.

**How to:**

1) Prepare one or more flipcharts (depending on whether you need to divide participants into smaller groups) with three columns (as indicated): board, staff/volunteers, both.

| Board | Staff/volunteers | Both |
|---|---|---|
| | | |

2) Ask each group to identify the top five roles within each column (i.e. roles of the board; roles of staff/volunteers; roles of both).

3) Review the answers as a group. Is there anything participants would like to review or change, perhaps where roles overlap? Use the Good Trustee Guide to identify where practical changes may be needed (e.g. internal controls, induction of trustees).

## Relationships between the trustee board and the chief executive

Many staffed organisations employ a chief executive, manager or head of staff to manage the day to day running of the organisation.

An important way that the board exercises its power is through the appointment of the chief executive and the monitoring of their performance.

Both board and chief executive are dependent on each other: the chief executive needs the authority of the board to allow them to manage the organisation and the board needs the chief executive to exercise leadership by building a successful staff and volunteer team. The chief executive needs the collective wisdom that board members can bring to decisions about the organisation's mission and plans, and the board needs the support of the chief executive to ensure precious board time is used effectively.

Above all, the chief executive is a primary source of information and advice to enable board members to agree plans and priorities, monitor the organisation's work and make effective decisions.

For practical purposes, most chief executive have a closer day to day working relationship with one or more individual trustees:

- to ensure there is effective and efficient communication between the board and chief executive at and in between board meetings
- to ensure that board meeting agendas can be planned and papers drawn up to make best use of the board's time and most effectively utilise input from staff
- in order for the chief executive to be supervised and appraised
- in order that, in exceptional circumstances, decisions can be taken efficiently without always having to call a full board meeting

These day-to-day working relationships often take place between the chair and the chief executive – although not exclusively so. In some organisations responsibility for managing the chief executive is delegated to the vice chair or another trustee.

Furthermore, the chief executive may have some day to day contact with other trustees for particular purposes, such as with the treasurer for the purpose of financial oversight, or to utilise the skills or advice of a particular trustee in the area of, say, marketing or law.

### Developing board –chief executive relationships

The board – chief executive relationship will have a strong bearing on the way your board relates to staff and ultimately on the effectiveness of your organisation. It is important that both have a good working relationship based on a clear, agreed understanding of respective roles and responsibilities .

### When can the board-chief executive relationship break down?

Just as individual board members can engage in micromanaging the chief executive and interfering in the day to day running of the organisation, chief executives can be guilty of not helping board members engage in the oversight of the organisation and fulfilling their responsibilities. What might be the indicators of a poor board-chief executive relationship?

- Where the board is unaware of the true financial condition of the organisation, perhaps because they do not understand financial information given to them, do not receive adequate financial information or do not take the time to read information
- Where the board is not kept informed by the chief executive about important news – and where board members find out about important news informally from staff, or even from the media
- board members that are reluctant to evaluate the performance of a strong and charismatic chief executive
- chairs acting as a 'second chief executive', heavily involved in the day to day running of the organisation, with trustees and staff unclear as to who holds authority in different areas of organisational activity
- where there is little or no contact between the board and chief executive, even via an individual such as the chair.

### Building healthy relationships

A healthy relationship between the board/chair and chief executive might best be described by the following two quotes:

*"Close but critical, co-operative but never cosy"*[16]

or

*"Constructive tension tempered by mutual respect."*[17]

[16] from *Lost in translation – a complete guide to Chair/Chief Executive partnerships* (Tesse Akpeki – NCVO, 2006)

[17] from *Your Chair and Board – a survival guide and toolkit for CEOs* (acevo – 2008)

### What can help build good relationships between the board and chief executive?

- Clear boundaries between the roles of chief executive, board and individual trustees (particularly those that have specific roles on the board)
- Role descriptions and guidelines for board members and chief executive
- A recognition that individual board members only act on the specific authority of the board
- Clear communication between the chief executive and the board
- Regular meeting times and agreed methods of communication between the chief executive and the chair (or other board members with specific roles)
- Agreement on the level of contact that the chair and individual trustees have with the chief executive and individual members of staff
- Where board members have contact with individual members of staff, to respect the agreed boundaries between staff and board roles
- Recognition from the chief executive that, if a decision is required between board meetings, the chair or other board members with specific roles will need to consult with other board members. This means allowing time for this in the decision-making process
- Clear systems of internal control, so that levels of authority are clear and unambiguous
- Annual appraisal of the chief executive
- Taking time out to review relationships.

### What can be unhelpful?

- Over-involvement or interference by trustees in the day-to-day management of the organisation
- Chief executives seeking to make decisions which properly belong to board members and vice versa
- Poor judgement by the chief executive or board about what falls within their delegated powers
- The chief executive concealing information from the board
- Board members or chief executive seeking independent publicity
- The chief executive seeking to manipulate individual board members against each other.

Trustees should be aware that the chief executive is (usually) an employee of the charity. If the relationship between trustees and chief executive does reach a serious point, it for example with regard to a grievance or disciplinary issue, trustees should be aware of their responsibilities with regard to employees (see section 11.1). This is a complex area and if this situation occurs it is recommended trustees take appropriate professional advice.

## Case study

The trustees of a patient support group have all been involved from the beginning. Despite recruiting a chief executive all the trustees still regularly work in the office carrying out a variety of tasks including managing some of the other staff. Board meetings are monthly and typically still involve all purchasing decisions, recruiting decisions and decisions on many other day-to-day matters.

**The lessons**

The new chief executive is unclear whether they were really recruited as a head of staff or as a glorified administrator. The board must decide if it is ready to let go of the day-to-day management and set remits, limits of authority and line management structures so that the chief executive can effectively become the head of staff and relieve them of some of the burden of the day-to-day running of the organisation.

## What helps build relationships between staff and board?

- Creating an environment in which the chief executive can comfortably raise issues that concern him or her.
- The board receiving an overview of organisational activities, progress, challenges and strategies from the chief executive's report.
- Co-ordinating strategy sessions for the board and senior managers
- Appropriate level of attendance at board and committee meetings by senior managers
- Investing in a trustee and board development, including an induction programme for new board members and ongoing briefings / support for all board members
- Inviting board members to informal and formal events, where they can be ambassadors for the organisation, get to meet staff and learn more about the organisation's activities
- The chair being prepared to deal with board members who step out of line
- service user involvement at board level.

## Relations with staff and volunteers in small organisations

If your organisation is a small one, you may find that it is much more difficult than the above guidance suggests to distinguish between 'governance' activities undertaken by trustees and operational, or 'day to day' activities.

In organisations without a chief executive and where few or no staff are employed, trustees will inevitably find it tricky to separate their strategic, governance roles and their operational roles, because much of the attention of board members will be concentrated on the day to day running of the organisation. Individual trustees may be involved in managing specific projects, running the organisation's services, fundraising or book-keeping. If a very small number of staff are employed, and no overall chief executive, individual trustees may 'manage' specific areas of the organisation's work on a day to day basis. Trustees may act as board members, managers and volunteers.

However, the distinction between strategic and operational roles is still important, for three reasons:

- as an organisation grows, the activities of the board may change but the fundamental duties and responsibilities of the board – as set out in the twelve responsibilities in section 1.5 – remain the same
- all trustee boards should be able to distinguish between governance matters – issues that trustees must deal with collectively as a board and matters relating to the long term future or strategic direction of the organisation – and operational matters – issues relating to day-to-day operations that may in a larger organisation be delegated to staff but in small organisations may be carried out by individual board members.
- The more complex the relationships between a trustee's strategic role and the day to day roles of trustees, staff, and volunteers, so it becomes more important to ensure that respective roles are clearly understood, to avoid confusion and tension

If the distinction between strategic and operational roles is made, even in small organisations with few or no staff and where trustee agendas tend to be dominated by operational issues, it can help trustees to keep abreast of their duty to guard the charity's long-term future as well as to deal with short-term crises. The 'hats' exercise (see box) may help trustees in understanding the different roles they may take in a small organisation.

## The 'hats' exercise

As a trustee you may have several 'roles' or 'hats' in your organisations. Which of the following hats do you wear?

- the governance hat: worn when attending formal board meetings and taking board decisions. This is a collective responsibility, working with other trustees.
- the 'specific role' hat: when you are authorised to implement a particular decision the board has made. Your individual responsibility will be specifically delegated to you by the board.
- the management hat: when you are managing a specific project (usually in a small organisation where no chief executive is employed). You will be wearing the hat of an unpaid manager, distinct from your role as trustee. You may be accountable to the board or sometimes to another member of staff. Your authority only extends to that which has been specifically delegated to you.
- the volunteer hat: for other times when involved with the organisation (for example, volunteering in the organisation's office). You will be wearing the hat of a volunteer, distinct from your role as a trustee. You may be accountable to an individual member of staff, who will be responsible for managing your work even though staff are ultimately accountable to the board.

Trustees in small organisations can wear many hats and the roles and relationships between the board, individual trustees, staff and volunteers can be complex and less clear cut than in larger organisations. Identifying different 'hats' can help to distinguish between when you are involved in the 'governance' matters of the trustee board and when you are instead involved in the day-to-day running of the organisation.

## Issues to consider

Staff, volunteers and trustees have distinct roles that each should acknowledge, respect and avoid undermining. Ultimately it is the way your board, staff and volunteers treat each other that does more to affect the quality of leadership and governance in your organisation than any iron-clad agreement on proper boundaries.

The relationship between trustees, staff and volunteers is a factor you should consider when assessing the effectiveness of your board (see chapter 22).

There are many ways to encourage good working relationships. Some charities hold annual conferences to which both trustees and staff/volunteers are invited; others encourage staff to form a staff association or belong to a trade union, representatives of which are invited to attend board meetings as observers.

If you are not satisfied with this relationship, you could consider holding a meeting of trustees and staff/volunteers to review your roles and responsibilities. If agreement is not reached, you could consider inviting a consultant or facilitator to work with the board, staff and volunteers. (For further information about dealing with differences, see section 16.2)

## Checklist

Has your board and staff/executive/volunteers carried out an exercise to review respective roles?

Does your organisation have written agreements, procedures or documents regarding the respective roles of board and staff/volunteers?

Do board members recognise the distinction between their role as a board member, with collective responsibility, their role when they act on the express authority of the board, and their role when they act in some other voluntary role for the organisation?

Are you confident that the relationship between board and staff/volunteers is positive?

# 12

# Equalities

## 12.1

### Equality and diversity

The principle of equality is fundamental to the work of charities and should be an underlying principle of good governance.

What does equality mean?
In charities equality can be defined as meaning ensuring equity, diversity and equality of treatment for all sections of the community.

## What is the board's role in upholding equality and diversity?

One of the principles of the Code of Governance is that "the board should ensure that it upholds and applies the principles of equality and diversity, and that the organisation is fair and open to all sections of the community in all of its activities." [1]

### How can the board uphold equality and diversity in practice?

In practice, boards can follow equality and diversity principles in many practical areas of their responsibility. Here are some examples:

- agreeing organisation-wide policies that set out equality and diversity principles. These can include:
  - a diversity strategy – setting out an approach to diversity and equality across the organisation, including clear plans, targets (where appropriate) and reporting arrangements
  - an equal opportunities and diversity policy – setting out the principles and practice by which the charity can ensure it is open and fair to all
- as part of the strategic planning process – including the identification of needs and priorities
- making decisions on the use of resources, grants or services
- the accessibility of services, activities and premises
- policies around the purchasing goods and services
- monitoring and evaluating services and activities
- staff and volunteers – recruitment, training and management
- accessibility of meetings and communications within the organisation
- communicating with stakeholders and the public

## Equality and diversity – legal responsibilities

### What are trustees' legal responsibilities with regard to equality and diversity?

All trustees are required to observe equal opportunities legislation. Much of this is concerned with discrimination in employment and trustees must always take expert advice.

The duty to avoid discrimination also extends to the provision of services, although there are some exceptions – for example, the provision of single sex schools.

In the case of disability, trustees are required to make reasonable steps to adapt their services and premises.

Some charities are treated as public bodies and have a stricter duty to promote racial equality. Many other charities adopt this principle as a matter of good practice.

This is a very complex area and advice will often be required.

For further information see the NCVO publication *Managing Diversity in the workplace*.

[1] Good Governance: A Code for the Voluntary and Community Sector

# 12.2

## Equality, diversity and the board's role

The board can also follow equality and diversity principles within its own role and functioning – for example with regard to:

- board recruitment practices – creating an inclusive board, for example by encouraging user involvement at board level
- board codes of conduct – ensuring that equity and fairness are part of the values and behaviours expected of trustees
- attention to board meetings – including the timing, location and accessibility of meetings, the format of board papers and language and jargon used in papers and during meetings
- creating an inclusive wider decision making process – for example, ensuring board business is open and accountable (unless confidentiality restricts this); creating opportunities for user involvement in advisory groups or working groups; and making Annual General Meetings inclusive and accessible

What if our charity serves a specific section of the community?
The Code of Governance recommends that, where an organisation is set up to serve a specific section of the community, this should be clear and the principles and practices around equality and diversity should be interpreted and applied as appropriate.

## Checklist

Does your charity have an equal opportunities and diversity policy?

Does your charity have a diversity strategy or plan that is regularly monitored and reviewed?

Are you trustees aware of their legal duties with regard to discrimination?

Have trustees considered how the functioning of the board can be made more inclusive and diverse?

## Involving users

Whatever the purpose of your charity, it is quite likely to benefit a group of people: your 'users' or beneficiaries. Depending on your charity's purpose, users[18] may be a specified group or groups of individuals who benefit from a service, set out in the objects clause of your governing document. You may also have a range of 'secondary users' who benefit indirectly from your work.

Many charities involve users in the planning or delivery of their work, as a way of better meeting their mission. Indeed, the benefits of involving service users in activities are increasingly being recognised by organisations as a way of being more effective and more 'inclusive'. Government, regulators, charitable trusts and corporate funders also recognise the importance of user involvement. For example, the National Lottery emphasises the need to "extend access and participation" in the projects it will fund, and the Charity Commission "welcome user involvement as a way of helping a charity achieve its aims more effectively"[19].

[18] The term 'users' will be adopted in this section to describe those who benefit from a charity's work.

[19] Charity Commission publication *Users on Board: Beneficiaries who become trustees* (CC24). Crown Copyright.

## Why involve your users?

Instead of having a one-way relationship with users – in which a charity provides services or activities 'for' users – it is possible – and increasingly common – for organisations to develop a two-way relationship with users, in which users take an active part in decision-making, planning and evaluation. Involving users in this way can generate new ideas, challenge the assumptions of the trustees board and ensure an organisation's services are as relevant as possible to the needs of users. Involving users can also empower them, use their expertise, and allow them to better 'own' the organisation.

Many charities see the involvement of users as an essential element of their value, but it is important to remember some key principles.

## Principles for involving users

Involving users

- should lead to improvement and not be an end in itself

  If users are involved as part of a 'tick box' exercise to satisfy government recommendations or improve funding opportunities it is unlikely to result in genuine improvement for either the organisation or its users.

- is not right for every organisation in every circumstance

  User involvement can be costly, and if done for the wrong reasons or for no reason at all, can be distracting and unnecessary.

- can meet both your organisation's and service users' needs

  Done well, it can help improve performance, by using limited resources more effectively to meet users' needs and delivering greater changes for the people, causes and issues you work for.

- is something you learn by doing

  Test out a range of approaches and techniques. You will improve with practice and can build on your efforts.

- may be something you're doing already

  You may already be involving service users informally without recognising it. Any kind of dialogue with your service users could be the beginning of user involvement. You need to recognise the value of these conversations, capture what is said and turn it into something useful.

- can happen in a variety of ways

  The way in which you involve users in your organisation's work can vary, from board membership to consultation to informal input. Don't assume that one particular method is the only way to involve users. Start by considering what you want to achieve by involving users.

## Steps to user involvement

### Your organisation's needs

First, consider what your organisation needs from user involvement. It could be in order for example

- to improve communications
- to evaluate services
- to develop and deliver better services
- to empower service users and/or include them in governance.

### The degree of involvement

Next, what degree of involvement will help you meet these needs?

**Inform:** To provide full information to enable people to make informed choices about the services or activities your organisation provides

**Consult:** To get feedback on people's needs and views to inform decision-making

**Engage:** To collaborate with people in developing and delivering services

**Empower:** To enable people to play an equal part in making key decisions about services

### How to involve users

Next, decide when you want to involve users, for example:

- As they receive services
- As you are planning and evaluating service provision
- At a "high level", where the organisation makes strategic decisions

## Examples of user involvement

### Involving users as they receive services

You could consider:

- giving clearer information about what each individual can expect from the organisation
- giving more and clearer individual choice on the services available
- engaging individuals more in putting together the package of services they receive
- empowering people as individuals to deliver their own services to peers.

### Involving users in planning and evaluating service provision

Possibilities include:

- providing better and more accessible information about your plans for your services
- getting their feedback on current services, or consulting on plans for the future
- engaging with service users as advisers or partners in service development
- empowering service users to take part in decision-making about services.

### Involving users at board level

This could include:

- a trustee board entirely consisting of users
- some trustees as users, some non-users
- user input directly to the board in an advisory capacity
- user input indirectly to the board via an advisory group, council or committee

Your approach may be set out formally in your governing document or a policy; or it may be informal, based on the needs of the organisation as they change.

There is no right or wrong approach to involving users at board level. Some organisations see it as part of their mission and values that they are user led and hence have a trustee board comprising entirely of users. Others seek to involve some users as trustees, either informally, through encouraging user involvement, or more formally by reserving a number of vacancies on the board for users. Some organisations instead involve users in a more indirect way – for example, where a user is nominated to attend part of a board meeting in an observer capacity, or where an advisory group is set up to feed back to the board user issues.

### Users on board – issues to consider

- User involvement vs. representation – don't confuse user involvement at board level with 'representing' user interests. Trustees act in the best interests of the organisation as a whole – they don't just 'represent' the people who elected them. In recent years, some mainly large national organisations have restructured their governance arrangements away from a large board 'representing' many users interests to a smaller board and a larger representative advisory council (see section 21.10).
- Conflicts of interest – there may be occasions when there is a potential conflict of interest between the user's role as trustee and their role as beneficiary. It is recommend you read section 3.6 on conflicts of interest and refer to the Charity Commission's useful guidance CC24 – *Users on Board: Beneficiaries who become trustees.*
- Capacity – trustees have legal duties which all trustees are legally responsible for. Will users have or be able to rapidly acquire the necessary knowledge, experience and skills?

## Case study: user involvement at board level

### Warwickshire Association of Youth Clubs

Warwickshire Association of Youth Clubs has six young people elected onto their Council of Management (board of trustees) as well as inviting young people to participate in a number of youth forums. The Association supports 130 volunteer youth groups and works alongside young people in Warwickshire, Coventry and Solihull. William Clemmey, Director of the Association, says,

"We believe that young people should have an equal say in society so if on a day-to-day basis we're working with young people then we have a duty to ensure that they have a say in the running of the organisation."

William explains how it can be extremely useful to have young people on the Board when you're talking about youth services:

"A youth officer came to a meeting to talk about changes being planned to youth services and it was the young people who asked the most pertinent questions that the other trustees wouldn't have thought of. The other trustees were very impressed. The young people know what's relevant because they are the users of the service. It is they who are taking the organisation forward. The fact that the ideas are coming from them gives them more authenticity in the eyes of the youth workers and keeps the trustees closer to the work we do."

## User involvement – issues to consider

### What do your users need from involvement?

Consider what your users might need and expect from getting involved in your organisation. Think about which users should be included and others that might want to. Explore what their needs and motivations might be and whether there are any barriers which might be preventing them from actually taking part. You will also need to be prepared to encourage your users once they are engaged, and have strategies in place for sustaining their involvement. Service users often get involved gradually and you should be prepared for this.

### Are you really committed?

There is no point in inviting users to be involved if your organisation is not committed to responding to what they have to say, and to making changes as a result. Before you approach any service users, it is vital that you know how far your organisation is committed to taking on users' views so you can communicate this accurately. It is worth checking this at the start, because a lack of genuine commitment will eventually become obvious to the people you are trying to involve, and may undermine your efforts in future.

Other factors to consider could include:

- taking into account any previous initiatives your organisation has undertaken and the reaction from users
- other activities happening outside your organisation which might impact on the availability or attitudes of your users
- the resources you have available for your plans
- timing.

Remember to record your involvement activity so that you can easily

- feed back to service users
- act on the information you've gained
- evaluate your work in this area
- demonstrate your commitment to involving users to external stakeholders.

# 13

# Making a difference

## 13.1

### Introduction

So your policies and plans are in place, but how do you know whether your charity is making a positive difference? Only by tracking and evaluating its progress can you understand how effective your charity has been in achieving the changes you were aiming for.

Charities use a range of terms to describe the different elements involved in measuring the difference their work makes.

- Outputs are the products or services a charity delivers – for example training courses, advice sessions, publications, a user survey, a helpline, or a website.
- Outcomes are the benefits, changes and other effects that happen as a result of your work. Your planned outcomes should relate to your charity's strategic plan (see chapter 6). Often, they can be less tangible and therefore less countable than outputs, but there are a range of tools and techniques to help you capture evidence of these 'soft' outcomes.
- Impact is more tricky to define. Some take it to mean summing up all the changes resulting from an output, including intended as well as unintended effects, negative as well as positive, and short-term or interim outcomes. But 'impact' is also often used more generally and inter-changeably with 'outcomes'. Others, meanwhile, understand it as the wider, more long-term, cumulative effects of your outcomes. You'll need to decide what it means to you – or you may feel that it's wise to simply avoid the term.

## Full Value

NCVO recommends that organisations adopt a comprehensive approach to assessing their effectiveness, by exploring the full range of their value, much of which is often hidden. An organisation's full value includes:

- all the outcomes you bring about for your users or cause and for other stakeholders and your operating environment – such as staff, the neighbours of users, the tenants in your building, the local economy or sector policy development
- the satisfaction your services bring – the 'feel good' factor which your users and other stakeholders get through their contact with you.

This approach is introduced in the NCVO guide True Colours: Uncovering the full value of your third sector organisation. The approach has been developed as an alternative to two other concepts: full cost recovery, which focuses boards and staff on the costs of their work rather than its impact; and the idea of the voluntary sector's 'added value', which has no clear meaning and has been criticised for being too crude to be really useful.

Other elements of your work include:

- Inputs – the resources that contribute to a programme or activity, such as income, staff, volunteers and equipment
- Activities – what an organisation does with its inputs in order to deliver its outputs – HR procedures, running an office devising a service and so on – as well as the other activities you need to do to deliver that service, such as promotional work.

| Inputs | Activities | Outputs | Outcomes |
|---|---|---|---|
| people, income, assets, materials etc | the actual work that happens, using the inputs | the products, services etc, resulting from activities | the benefits to users resulting from outputs |

The process of actually measuring your work requires:

- Indicators – signs that tell you if the planned outputs and outcomes are actually happening, often described in terms of quantity, proportions, frequency or quality. Indicators could include, for example, the number and frequency of courses, the number of participants or the percentage of students achieving accreditation. You could also include satisfaction levels too.
- Targets– a particular level of output, outcome or satisfaction an organisation aims to achieve over a set period – for example, six courses every quarter, 20 participants on each course, 50% of participants achieve level 2, 75% of tutors are satisfied with the level of administrative support and so on
- Data – both countable information (quantitative) and descriptive information (qualitative)
- Monitoring – the systematic process of collecting and recording your indicator data
- Evaluation – the process of drawing together your data and making judgements about progress against targets, either at the end of a project or at certain points along the way. It can be useful to collect baseline information early in a project to help you make before-and-after comparisons.

# 13.2

## Deciding what caused a change

Establishing cause and effect can be difficult: how do you know that a particular activity and output was the cause of the change? For example, how do you know that the recent governance review carried out by the board was the cause of the improvement in your charity's services?

Three things can help with this:

- Firstly, don't worry too much about 'proof'. 'Reasonable evidence' is what you need. After all, there is no burden of absolute proof in the legal system; people are sent to prison for life on the basis of 'reasonable evidence'.
- Secondly, you can sometimes track the cause from the effect. For example, you could ask the staff and managers who improved the charity's services about the role that the governance review played in these improvements. It might have been the staff that actually made the changes, but perhaps it was the board that saw the need for them and insisted upon them happening.
- Finally, it's sufficient to say you contributed to the outcome and to identify the other factors you think have played a part.

## How boards should monitor and evaluate

Boards should have a good idea of what the charity is achieving and how this compares with the strategic or operational plan (see chapter 6). This means ensuring that the charity has in place a system to collect data regularly about its achievements (both outputs and outcomes) and for providing summary information to the board so it can assess progress.

As a board, you need to decide what information you require to form judgements about progress, rather than relying on the chief executive or staff, if you employ them, to put forward the information they think you need. If you have a staff team, you should delegate to them the actual design and implementation of the monitoring system.

You should also ensure that the monitoring and reporting requirements of any funders are built into your system to avoid duplicating work by creating different data for different people. Where duplication seems to be happening it may be worth negotiating with funders to ask them if you can streamline reporting requirements, for example by offering to provide them with reports in the same format as the report to the board, rather than creating multiple reports.

**Further information:**
NCVO's publication *Funding Better Performance* provides examples of how a range of organisations have done this successfully.

### How much activity should trustees monitor?

You are responsible for monitoring all areas of the charity's activity. However, in larger charities, it is worth taking time to consider the level of detail that should be reported on your charity and how much operational monitoring is best left to staff.

Too many detailed reports of activity will weigh down your board or tempt it to interfere with the management role of staff; too few could lead to the charity's programme going seriously off course before action can be taken.

In larger charities, an audit committee and internal audit reports can play a useful role in helping you to execute your responsibilities for monitoring (see pages 96-7).

### Key indicators

Identifying a list of the key indicators across the most important areas of your charity's work is crucial. This should certainly cover your services – for example. a key indicator about the number of counseling sessions run – and could also include some that trigger alarm bells about the health of the charity – for example, the number of staff resignations (see also section 9.1 on risk).

Taylor Reveley, a writer on governance, observes that key indicators are an opportunity for the board to "think seriously about what really matters to the organisation... determined efforts must be made to find simple, intelligible methods of tracking performance, watching closely for warning signs, and then utilising the information needed to make decisions in a timely way".

### Evaluation

Evaluating the work of your organisation encourages you to question whether you are:

- carrying out your aims and objectives
- meeting the needs of your beneficiaries
- providing the appropriate quantity and quality of service
- using the resources you have to the greatest effect, or in the most efficient manner
- working within the organisation's policy framework.

There are four principal areas the board should evaluate:

1) The organisation's outputs and outcomes

2) The organisation's internal functioning

3) The chief executive's performance (if one is appointed)

4) The board's own performance

At the planning stage, your board needs to make sure that you or your staff decide on indicators and, where appropriate, set targets. There should be processes in place to collect information about both these, so that when it comes to the stage of evaluation, the necessary data are available.

Evaluation of the organisation's outputs and outcomes will usually take place fairly regularly, say every quarter or every six months. It can also take place at key stages in a project and after work has been carried out.

Evaluation of the chief executive and board's performance usually takes place at period intervals – as part of the annual appraisal of the chief executive (see section 11.1) and as part of a periodic board or governance review (see chapter 22).

There are a huge range of tools and techniques to help charities evaluate their work. If your board of trustees is having difficulty in evaluating your charity's work, you should seek advice.

## The impact of campaigning

*Is your campaign making a difference?* (Jim Coe and Ruth Mayne – NCVO, 2008) provides practical tools that organisations can use to assess the extent to which their campaigning or advocacy work is making a longer-term impact. This might include changes to policy, practice and behaviour, or empowering people and communities.

## Checklist

Do you regularly evaluate your charity's progress in delivering its outputs and outcomes?

Do you need to improve the way in which information is presented to the board?

Are planning, monitoring and evaluation integrated with each other?

Do you need to seek advice on monitoring or evaluation methods?

Once you have evaluated your charity's work, you need to make use of the findings in two distinct ways: feeding your learning into future planning to make improvements, and communicating your impact. We cover both of these approaches below.

# 13.3

## An improvement culture

Unfortunately, not everyone will be receptive to the idea of measuring your progress. For instance, it may be difficult to convince some funders that assessing outcomes is a worthwhile (and fundable) activity. You may also encounter internal resistance: staff may see outcome measurement as a waste of resources which should be spent on frontline services.

However, creating a culture of continuous improvement is an essential element of all truly successful organisations. Introducing and then fostering this attitude is a crucial role for the board. An endless process of striving to be better can sound like hard work, but many would argue that's exactly what our sector is all about: achieving the best possible outcomes for our users or cause. Embedding a culture of continuous improvement is at the core of these aspirations and, over time, by staying open to new ideas and possibilities and honing our practices, it should also allow us to achieve more, without necessarily doing more.

## The role of monitoring and evaluation

There are various ways to encourage an improvement culture, but ensuring that there is a sound monitoring and evaluation process in place is a key starting point. The board can help to ensure that insights and learning are drawn out of the review process and fed into future strategic planning, by prompting, asking questions and acting as a 'critical friend'. It's important to show how the findings from evaluation ultimately lead to better services for users, and to make sure that the results of this cycle of improvement are clearly evident to everyone contributing to your organisation.

## Benchmarking

Benchmarking is the process of comparing your organisation's performance with other organisations. By taking a look at how other people do things and the results they achieve, benchmarking can save you from re-inventing the wheel. It also shows what is possible and can help to promote an organisational culture that is open to new ideas. Benchmarking provides organisations with reassurance and enables them to celebrate by showing where they perform well.

You can benchmark any aspect of your charity's operations, for instance, comparing numerical information such as the cost per user of providing a service or the average length of time served by trustees. Alternatively, you can compare how things are done, for example, the way an organisation plans strategically or the way its accounts are presented.

## Quality

You can use the concept of 'quality' to improve the way you do things. A quality service means doing something that is:

- needed by users, to a standard they require
- well run
- assessed and improved
- shown to make a positive and measurable difference to users, and
- continuously improved again and again in order to achieve the very best results.

It is an excellent mechanism for embedding an improvement culture.

Since the 1990s there has been a significant increase in interest amongst voluntary and community organisations in using the concept of quality. Many funders are now keen to see organisations adopt quality systems and the implementation of certain quality standards or frameworks has in fact become a requirement of some funders and statutory commissioners.

### Quality assurance systems

A quality assurance system is a systematic way of ensuring your organisation undertakes a continuous process of learning, developing and reviewing, usually by aiming to meet an agreed level of performance. It's possible to devise your own quality system with your own standards and to do your own self-assessment but there are also a range of ready-made standards or frameworks available, with or without kitemarked assessment, such as:

- PQASSO – the Practical Quality Assurance System for Small Organisations
- Investors in People
- EFQM Excellence Model
- Social auditing and accounting
- Investing in Volunteers
- Quality Mark

### What is the board's role in quality improvement?

Because your board is able to step back and take a more strategic overview of its organisation, it is in an ideal position to take the lead in choosing and committing to a quality assurance system. Indeed, the decision to implement a particular quality assurance system is one that should be made by trustees. The board is also able to ensure the overall process is balanced across the organisation and the priorities for quality improvement are the 'right' ones for the charity's long-term future.

### Engaging in quality improvement

Your first step is to consider which areas of your charity you want to quality assess. You may have particular priorities such as the management of your volunteers or your human resources processes, or you may want to take a holistic approach initially, to help you identify the areas of your organisation which most need improvement.

Once you have a list of topics or areas, you then need to decide on an approach to quality improvement. NCVO suggests three possibilities:

**Devolved approach:** this involves giving responsibility for each area to people with specific roles within your organisation. Individuals would be expected to check and compare their practices against any identified standards. In small charities, many of the core topics such as strategic planning, recruitment and external relationships can fall to the chief executive or to individual trustee(s) who may need support from the rest of the board to assess current practice and suggest improvements.

**Centralised approach:** this involves establishing a working group to take forward quality improvement. Depending on the size of your charity, the working group may consist of, say, a few managers, frontline staff and board members and is typically led by a named individual. The group considers all areas in turn, talking to those who have a particular stake in each area. Improvements are identified by the working group and reported to the board, although sometimes working groups have decision-making and reviewing powers. This approach introduces a stronger element of 'challenge' which can be useful where some topic areas have been neglected or where the culture of improvement needs strengthening.

**External approach:** this involves getting an external agency to assess your practices, to rate them, and to suggest alternatives. This external validation of the way your charity is run, perhaps with a kitemark for the successful, can be useful with funders or potential partners. However, it focuses more attention on assessing and recognising your existing standards rather than on improving them. You may still need a working group to facilitate the process, especially the collection of data for the assessor.

The process you adopt will need to reflect your charity's existing culture and attitude to improvement, as well as the state of your existing practices. It will also be dependent on the time you have available and the financial costs involved, for example, purchasing an off-the-shelf system or buying in advice or external assessment and/or accreditation.

Both the centralised and external approach require investment of considerable energy over a sustained period.

Some would argue that the devolved approach is the ideal that you should aim for, because it is sustainable and involves a self-generating culture in which people across the organisation enjoy taking responsibility for continuous improvement, albeit with the support and encouragement of their managers and the board. However, in order to get to the devolved approach to quality improvement, you may need to use the centralised or external approach at least once, and work hard to ensure that both the specific learning and the broader attitude of improvement 'sticks' within the organisation.

Useful tips:

- If you employ a chief executive, they can support the board to ensure that it is ready to take on quality improvement. This can involve skills development, recruitment, communication and information and clarifying boundaries between the board and staff.
- Be sensitive to workloads if you are expecting a large investment of time from staff or, in smaller charities, from individual board members
- Decide who on the board will be involved and how you will monitor and review the process
- Communicate across the organisation. A quality improvement system will only work if people within the organisation are committed – which means raising awareness of what you want to achieve and feeding back on progress and outcomes.

How can quality improvement help trustees?

- Structured checking mechanism

  A quality system helps you to make sure your organisation is performing as well as possible and meeting the right needs in the right ways
- Improving board–staff communication

  If boards are involved in a quality improvement initiative it can help to develop a shared understanding about the organisation's current and future position – what is working well, what can be improved and what role the board can take in leading the process and setting direction.
- Board performance

  The performance of the board itself is a vital stepping stone to continuous improvement. The quality improvement process can include evaluating the board's own role in the organisation – some approaches, like The Code of Governance, focus specifically on the role of the board (see chapter 22).

# 13.4

## Reporting your impact

### What is impact reporting?

'Impact reporting' basically means communicating your achievements. Few charities will thrive if they fail to do this.

Large charities are already required to report on their achievements (see SIR box below), but there are many reasons why an organisation of any shape or size might want to demonstrate its impact to various audiences:

- The changing role of the voluntary sector in the delivery of public services means that voluntary organisations are keen to demonstrate their value (see Full Value above)
- Funders and commissioners are increasingly asking for evidence that a programme has achieved its outcomes
- Donors are becoming more discerning in their choice of causes to give to and organisations are keen to demonstrate that they are using funds in an efficient and effective way to bring about a positive impact on their cause or the lives of beneficiaries
- Measuring and communicating impact can be a very powerful way to motivate staff and volunteers – and your own board – by showing that their work is making a difference and to encourage the whole team to build on successes to achieve even more for users or the cause.

### Summary Information Return

The Charity Commission requires charities with an income over £1m to complete an annual Standard Information Return to help the general public understand what your charity does and how it has performed.

**Further information**
Charity Commission website – Meeting our requirements – Annual returns.

Three things are crucial in impact reporting:

**Clarity:** Do not underestimate the power of being specific. It is as important to be accurate about your achievements as it is to be accurate about your organisation's finances.

**Success:** To make the most of opportunities to sell your organisation's achievements, consider its full value (see box above)

**Honesty:** To give credibility to your organisation's communications you must display real humility about what you don't know and straight honesty about things that haven't gone to plan and that will be improved.

## Five steps to successful impact reporting

1) Identify why your charity wants to engage in or improve its impact communications.
2) Decide the priority audiences for your impact communications, what you want them to know, and how you want this knowledge to influence their behaviour. Don't forget your internal audiences, including the board itself!
3) Agree the general formats, content and channels for the different impact communications you will produce.
4) Check what information you will need, consider what you already collect and where necessary, fill in the gaps in your monitoring systems.
5) Create and communicate your messages.

## Checklist

Is your charity committed to a culture of improvement?

Have you considered implementing a quality assurance system in your charity?

How do you report on your charity's impact?

Is your charity required to complete a Summary Information Return?

14

# Accountability

Trustees are accountable for the way in which they carry out their responsibilities and for the decisions they take. 'Accountability' takes place in a number of different ways:

- being held "to account" for decisions taken and work carried out – this might take place, for example, at an Annual General Meeting when members question the activities of the charity or in the way an organisation reports back to a funder on money spent.
- "giving an account" – this might take place in an Annual Report, where trustees set out an account of their work over the previous year.
- it can also mean "holding others to account" – to be accountable, trustees will need to hold to account those to whom they delegate the work of the charity, like staff, volunteers, committees or other trustees.

# 14.1

## To whom are the trustees of a charity accountable?

For almost all charities there is a need to be accountable to multiple parties. These parties are sometimes known as 'stakeholders' because they are thought to have a stake or interest in the charity, either a formal or informal interest. They include:

- those who give the charity money – private donors, other funders such as government, local authorities, trusts, foundations or corporate donors
- regulators – for example, the Charity Commission and Companies House
- members in membership organisations
- beneficiaries, clients or service users
- partner organisations
- staff and volunteers and
- the general public.

# 14.2

## Accountability in practice

The Code of Governance recommends that "the board should be open, responsive and accountable to its users, beneficiaries, members, partners and others with an interest in its work".

In practice, trustees can be accountable in a number of different ways:

- regular communication with private donors on the use of the charity's funds
- formal reporting to a funder – such as a trust or foundation – in line with terms and conditions. This may involve the completion of monitoring reports setting out how the money has been spent and the benefits of the funding. Remember that if such reporting is delegated to staff, trustees remain ultimately responsible and hence should have a system of reporting to ensure that staff and volunteers are accountable (in the 'holding to account' sense) to their managers and ultimately to the board of trustees
- complying with regulatory requirements:
  - Charities must comply with their requirements to report to the Charity Commission. The requirements vary depending on the size and status of a charity (see pages 83-4).
  - Companies limited by guarantee and industrial provident societies must comply with their requirements to report to Companies House with regard to an annual return, reports and accounts (see page 84), along with other requirements including registering ongoing changes to the company's directors, secretary and registered office

  you may be required to report to other regulatory bodies, depending on your activities, services or legal structure
- involving members – in a membership organisation, your Annual General Meeting is an opportunity for members to receive a report on the charity's work, formally consider specific issues (motions or resolutions) and elect the trustee board
- your annual report and accounts – your annual report and accounts is a key method by which you can inform stakeholders about your charity's work and achievements. An annual report is often a regulatory requirement. Often charities produce a formal trustees annual report and accounts and then a shorter or more accessible version for wider public distribution (see page 81).

- being open and responsive to beneficiaries or service users – this could take place in a variety of ways: for example, involving service users at board level and ensuring communications are accessible and available in a variety of forms and languages (see chapter 12)
- consultation with stakeholders as part of planning, decision making and evaluation. Stakeholder representation on trustee boards has been seen as a useful mechanism for accountability. However, muddling the 'holding to account' role of a stakeholder with that of a trustee can lead to both being handled badly (see section 12.2)
- being open and responsive to feedback and criticism via a proper complaints procedure. All charities should have a complaints procedure in place (see box).

## Dealing with feedback and complaints

In recent years, attention has focused on how charities deal with complaints and feedback. A 2005 Charity Commission survey found that only 30% of charities surveyed had a complaints procedure in place. The Commission's regulatory study on charity complaints highlighted the importance of charities having in place a complaints procedure that is understood by everyone working in the charity. The study found that "an effective complaints management system is a proven way of maintaining and building relationships with the people on whom the charity depends". The Commission's report uses best practice examples to illustrate the benefits of a complaints procedure. The Code of Governance also recommends that charities should have a procedure to deal with feedback and complaints.

**More information:** Charity Commission publication *Cause for complaint: how charities manage complaints about their service* (RS11)

## Checklist

Have you taken stock of all the stakeholders you are accountable to?

Does your board comply with the statutory obligations to account to the Charity Commission?

Does your board comply with the statutory obligations to account to Companies House?

Does your board need to review how you account to donors, funders, staff and

volunteers, perhaps by producing more popular versions of reports prepared to meet statutory requirements?

Does your board need to review how staff and volunteers are held accountable?

## Public relations

Raising the profile of your charity and creating a positive public image is a prerequisite for raising the necessary funds to develop and grow. This is just as important for small, local charities as it is for large, national ones.

As trustees, you are responsible for ensuring that your charity develops an effective public relations strategy. You are uniquely placed to bring perspective or spot media opportunities when they arise.

### A media policy

An organisational media policy should spell out how media enquiries will be handled, who may speak to the media and how an organisation's position is decided.

As part of your public relations strategy you may wish to create or review your charity's logo, house style and the way you present yourself to your members, funders and the outside world. Some organisations even change their name to update their image or to reflect more clearly the nature of their work. Relate (formerly the Marriage Guidance Council) and Scope (formerly the Spastics Society) have both done this.

If you represent the charity in public or in the media you must follow the public relations strategy agreed by the board and you should be given any necessary training. An effective public relations strategy will also include procedures to limit damage should the charity ever come under public criticism, and you should be aware of this. When speaking to the press, always give the charity's agreed position rather than your personal opinion.

Getting celebrities and famous or influential people to acknowledge publicly their support for a charity can support your public relations strategy. Such people are unlikely to have sufficient time to act as trustees, but you could ask them to act as patrons. It may be best to ask them to act as patron for a fixed period, say five years, in case they fade from the public eye or their own reputation becomes tarnished.

## Checklist

Do you have an agreed public relations strategy?

Does the name of your charity adequately reflect the work you do?

Does your board need to review your logo and house style?

If certain trustees speak to the media, do they have proper training?

Does the strategy:

state who is authorised to make public statements?

outline the process for agreeing press releases?

explain on what occasion staff should contact the trustees about PR?

# 15

# Collaborative working

"All charities should consider seriously and imaginatively whether there are ways in which they could do more and better for their users by working together. Examples of good practice in this area range from shared helplines, shared service delivery, combined grant administration and joint marketing or purchasing initiatives, to partial or full mergers."[20]

[20] Charity Commission publication *Collaborative Working and Mergers* (RS4). Crown Copyright.

# 15.1

## Introduction

In recent years charities have increasingly explored collaborative working as a way to improve organisational efficiency and effectiveness. As a trustee, examining how to further the charity's objects, and assessing the environment in which the organisation operates, may involve looking at working with other charities.

Working in partnership can bring substantial benefits, including cost savings, greater credibility, sharing good practice and improved services for beneficiaries.

However, it is also important to understand the risks involved. Will the work still be within your charity's objects? Will it enable you to further your mission? What are the legal implications arising from joint ventures? Is the organisation ready for joint working or will it cause disruption? How will it be perceived by stakeholders?

The final decision on any collaborative working arrangement rests with trustees. It is the trustees' role to see that the decision-making process covers all angles to make the most effective use of funds. Trustees must ensure their organisation acts legally and that professional advice is taken where relevant. The key question should be: will engaging in joint working provide greater outcomes for users?

# 15.2

## Types of partnership

The term 'joint working' covers a wide spectrum of activities. These include:

- networks and alliances
- partnerships
- joint ventures
- mergers

### Informal networking
Attending events and conferences can be worthwhile in keeping your charity 'visible' and sharing information. Joining a membership organisation can be a valuable way of accessing information and support.

### Committee links
Some charities pool their knowledge and share information. One approach is to have trustees who are nominated by outside organisations. Alternatively you may want specifically to co-opt a trustee from a charity you wish to build closer links with.

### Resource sharing
Staff, services (e.g. payroll or ICT support) or office space can be shared between charities to reduce duplication and save costs and time. One of the key considerations is whether there are VAT implications to sharing services. Further information is listed in NCVO's publication Sharing back office services.

### Outsourcing services
Here a charity's service or services are provided by another charity (or non-charitable organisation) in an outsourcing agreement.

### Providing joint services
Many charities work in partnership to provide services jointly. Sometimes one organisation is a lead partner who takes overall responsibility, backed up with an agreement between the other partners.

As a trustee, it is essential to clarify where overall accountability lies. If it is with your organisation as lead partner then your board will take overall responsibility. Are there proper procedures in place to ensure that this does not become too big a risk? If it is with another organisation, what agreement is in place with the lead partner? For more information see NCVO's Joint working agreements.

### Federal and branch structures
Organisations with a national body and local groups can work together in a variety of ways, providing a balance between national presence and grassroots involvement. A federal structure involves a national body and a number of independently constituted local groups. Organisations in a branch structure constitutionally form one legal entity, with local branches sharing the national body's governance and charitable purposes. For more information see NCVO's *National organisations with local groups.*

### Group structure

A group structure normally consists of a parent body and one or more subsidiary bodies in which the parent has a controlling interest. Group structures can be complex because they do not form a legal entity of their own. Rather they are a collection of bodies which enter into a legally binding agreement to work together that, usually, is not time limited. Groups can be formed with the parent body, which has overall control, providing a strategic role and in many cases having a central servicing function for other members of the group. The group can involve a charitable or non-charitable body becoming a subsidiary of another organisation (for example, a non-charitable trading subsidiary).

One of the advantages of a group structure is that a subsidiary organisation can retain its existing legal structure, avoiding some of the issues involved in the process of full merger. With a non-charitable trading subsidiary it can allow commercial trading to take place (see section 2.2). It can also allow a struggling organisation to be sustained whilst retaining its own structure.

### Mergers

A full merger involves two or more charities becoming one organisation. This could involve two equal charities merging to set up a new body (for example, the merger of Cancer Research Campaign with Imperial Cancer Research Fund to form Cancer Research UK). Alternatively it can involve an organisation transferring its staff, assets and activities to another organisation, and then winding up.

Mergers can bring advantages but can be time-consuming and have legal implications. Transferring staff or assets may bring problems because of the restrictions placed on sources of income or TUPE. It is important to take the time to consider the pros and cons of such a venture, and is very essential to take professional advice if your charity is considering this route.

There will be governance and management implications. What form will the board of the new organisation take? Who will sit on the board? Will the new organisation be able to develop an effective governance and management relationship? For more information see NCVO's *Merger*, and *Due Diligence Demystified*.

## Checklist

Is collaborative working permitted in your charity's governing document (objects and powers)?

What are the legal implications?

Is there a danger of 'mission drift' (losing sight of your mission because, for example, of an attractive funding opportunity)?

Is it cost-effective?

Who is liable for the partnership if things go wrong?

If a trustee of your organisation is sitting on the board of a partnership, however constituted, have you considered the difference in roles (between being a trustee and being a member of the partnership) and any potential conflicts of interest?

Are there VAT implications?

Can you afford the initial costs of setting up joint work or merger?

If the work involves transfer of staff, there will be TUPE implications – Transfer of Undertaking (Protection of Employees)

# 16

# Handling change and conflict

## 16.1

### Managing change

Every charity will face change at one time or another. The question is whether trustees will steer the charity to a desired future, or let the pace and direction of change go unmanaged.

## Reasons for change

There are a number of reasons why your charity may be changing or will need to change. The causes of change can come from within or outside your charity.

External causes of change might include changes to the law, new funding opportunities, changes in government policy or increased competition from other organisations. To help identify these causes before they happen, you could use a tool such as a PEST (Political, Economic, Social, Technological) analysis.

The need for change can also come from within. You may have carried out a review of your performance, such as assessing your progress against plans and targets, or comparing performance and practice with other charities or against an established quality standard (see section 13.3).

You may have experienced changes in key individuals, such as the departure of a chief executive or chair of the trustee board, or undergone a sudden crisis such as a disaster or dispute.

## Types of change

Changes may be planned or unplanned, major or minor, fast or slow. You may be looking at a long term office move, a short term restructuring, a loss of premises or sudden departure of a key person.

All these factors will affect how you will respond to change. Obviously, the sooner the change or the need for it is identified, the earlier you can start managing it. The size of the change will affect the timescales and resources you will need, and decisions about who to involve and to what extent. The nature of the change will determine how it will affect different elements of your organisation such as its purpose, its relationship with key stakeholders, its ways of working or culture. Remember that changes in one area will often mean changes in another.

## Key principles for managing change

The role of a trustee can involve making difficult decisions. Remember that the charity's overall purpose (as ultimately set out in its charitable objects – see section 2.3) should be at the forefront of the decision making process.

In managing a process of change, bear in mind the following principles:

### Lead, but don't go it alone

Above all, managing change requires clear leadership from the board. This includes creating and communicating a clear vision for the change by answering some key questions: Why does this change need to happen now? What will the organisation look like afterwards? And who will it affect and how?

But this doesn't mean the board should try to manage change on its own. You should involve others in your organisation to help you manage a process of change – this could include your chief executive, if you employ one, and perhaps advisors and other external stakeholders.

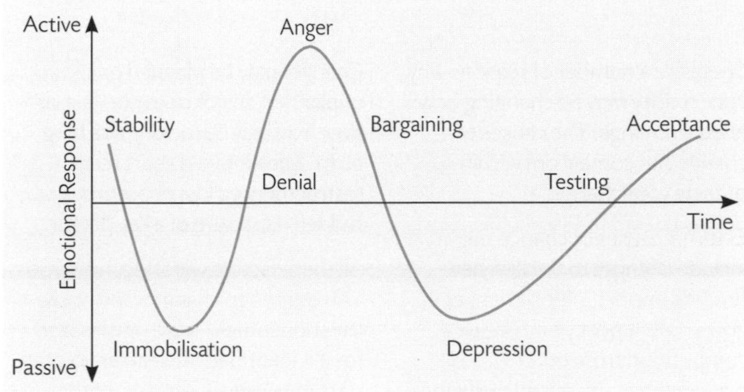


### Choose the right approach

Reflect on your organisational culture – the way things usually happen in your organisation and way the people behave and interact with each other. Managing change will be more successful if you choose an approach that fits with the way you do things generally. For example, a change approach in which the board makes decisions without much consultation may work if that's how things usually happen, but is less likely to work if your organisational culture is more democratic, involving staff at all levels in decision-making.

Also, certain approaches to change might be more appropriate to particular situations. For example, it may be difficult to involve a range of stakeholders if change needs to happen rapidly.

### Anticipate how people might respond

Understanding and anticipating people's reactions to change can help you support them to accept and adapt to new circumstances. Organisational change can be very stressful for people for a number of reasons. Some may be reluctant to shift from their comfort zone. They may fear that their job is at risk, or that their role or working environment will become unfamiliar. Others may worry that they lack skills or expertise needed for new systems or ways of working.

You might find it helpful to think about the stages people go through when experiencing change.

The Kubler-Ross Coping Cycle states that people go through the following stages:

**Shock:** initial paralysis on hearing the news

**Denial:** trying to avoid the inevitable

**Anger:** venting frustration

**Bargaining:** seeking to negotiate an alternative outcome

**Depression:** realisation of the inevitable

**Testing:** seeking realistic solutions

**Acceptance:** finding the way forward

To overcome resistance, you can use allies in different parts of the organisation, engage with people to address their objections, and provide third party support. This support could include training to help people learn new skills or ways of working, or opportunities to talk about their feelings and experiences.

### Communicate consistently and honestly

It is vital to communicate clearly and honestly during a period of change. This does not mean telling everyone everything all of the time – use your judgement to decide what's useful to say to who and when – and who should say it. If there are legal implications, particularly employment ones, take early advice.

Planning your communications can ensure you give the right messages to the right people, in the right format, at the right time. First identify your stakeholders, then think about what they need to know or understand and when. For each group, think about specific messages and which communication channel will best meet their needs. For staff and volunteers options might include face-to-face meetings or briefings, emails, staff newsletters or extranets. For external communication, you could use newsletters, events, emails, websites and press releases. Make sure your communications are two-way, giving people an opportunity to speak to you and ask questions.

# 16.2

### Embed the change

It is important to ensure that changes are sustained and become part of the lifeblood of the organisation. A model that can help with this uses the idea of unfreezing, moving and re-freezing. The idea is that, in order to change, people need to:

- Unfreeze – give up old ways of doing things
- Move – accept the need for change and use the support offered to them to learn new ways of doing things
- Re-freeze – adopt and become comfortable with new ways of working.

Refreezing tactics could include removing old ways of working, rewarding people for embracing new working practices and building change into existing management systems and structures.

**Further information**
*From Here to There: Managing change in third sector organisations* (Jake Eliot and Julie Pottinger – NCVO, 2008)

## Handling conflict

## When things go wrong

Every board will face periods of conflict from time to time – between trustees and staff, between individual trustees or between factions or cliques on the board.

The first thing to acknowledge is that conflict is not inherently unhealthy; it can be a source of creativity and can revitalise the work of the board. Many community organisations function as a forum in which tensions and disagreements are addressed and resolved. However, there is a difference between this situation and the type of conflict which negatively affects the ability of the organisation to fulfil its mission.

Whatever the cause, it is important that disagreements are acknowledged and addressed before they become serious disputes and cause damage not only to internal relationships but also to the external reputation of the organisation.

## Conflict on the board

Working collectively is what boards are about – but it is not always easy. Human nature means that we can be ambitious or energetic – strong characteristics in many walks of life but which can lead to tension in the boardroom. Common scenarios include:

- ignoring boundaries (see case study below)
- monopolising meetings
- reticent or 'sleeping' trustees
- the loose cannon trustee
- belittling others
- withholding information
- hogging the credit
- factions and inner circles
- outside agendas
- the 'founder syndrome' (see case study).

## Case study – ignoring boundaries

A new trustee who was previously a volunteer has been upsetting staff by coming into the office unannounced, bossing staff around, countermanding the Director's orders, demanding confidential information and generally meddling in day-to-day affairs.

**The lessons**

Boundaries have clearly been stepped over in several ways. This is an example of someone not only confusing which hat they are wearing and when, but also disregarding what is acceptable behaviour in terms of respect for others. Have a board development session and do the "hats" exercise (see section 11.3) during which attention can be drawn to the importance of the board acting jointly. A trustee has no power individually except that which is specifically given to them by the trustee board. Remind the trustees of the organisation's values and of the trustees' code of conduct, the employment law risks of upset staff, and clarify what responsibilities have been delegated by the board to the chief executive. In addition, a one-to-one between the Chair and the new trustee will provide an opportunity to explore these issues in more depth.

## Case study – conflict with founders

The founder of a prominent charity effectively runs the organisation by chairing the executive committee (a sub committee of the board), which takes all of the important decisions. The remit for the executive committee was minuted but no one is sure where and its wording is not precisely known. It is believed that the remit contains the phrase "an open door to trustees who wish to attend" so none of them feels obliged or even particularly encouraged to attend. Consequently the founder is the only trustee to regularly attend as well as chairing the committee (the chief executive and senior manager also attend). The chair of the board was selected by the founder, and is a prominent and busy person who was given to understand that the role was almost one of president who merely chaired the once or twice yearly trustee board meetings and the AGM. The other trustees selected are similarly high powered and busy people who understand their role to be largely as figureheads.

**The lessons**

Such situations can be difficult to tackle. The chief executive could put an "update" session on the agenda of the next trustee board meeting or AGM. Using the Code of Good Governance, trustees could then be sensitively but firmly reminded that they have a duty to be active, and that they must act jointly, reasonably and in accordance with the constitution, acknowledging their ultimate responsibility for the organisation's policies and strategic direction. A governance audit would reveal the true remit of the executive committee and the lack of involvement of the other trustees, and identify the skills the board needs to be effective. It would also be an opportunity to look at the values of the organisation and to consider a role description for the chair. Third party facilitators and legal advisors can help in the process.

## Conflict between board and staff

Conflict between the head of staff (chief executive/director) and the head of the trustees (chair) arises all too frequently, often because of a lack of clarity about their respective roles and boundaries.

A key question at the root of the conflict is who leads? (and consequently who follows?). There are many models of board/staff relations but it is vital to remember that the distinction between governance and management is a dynamic one.

A chief executive who has become used to taking the lead and even expects their board to simply act as a rubber stamp to their ideas will resist the efforts of a new chair who starts to set the agenda. Conversely, a board that is passive and allows staff to lead the organisation may feel uncomfortable with a new chief executive who expects the board to take a more active role in leading the organisation and setting policy.

A founder who becomes chief executive needs to accept that at some point the board may set the organisation in a new direction. That is the role of the board and, provided the decision is reached in a considered way, then the founder must respect the board's decision.

### Practical steps to avoid staff/board conflict

Clarify roles: Who is responsible for taking which decisions? Tempers can flare when the board treads on what staff regard as their territory or vice versa. Board policies and a code of conduct can help.

Induction of staff and board members: When recruiting a new chief officer be clear and realistic about what they will be able to achieve and ensure that their assumptions of their role are the same as the board's. Introduce new trustees to the management team and encourage them to ask questions.

Foster good personal relationships: build in time for social interaction.

The chair/chief officer relationship is key – if they don't get on, the whole organisation is affected. They should commit to regular contact including one-to-one meetings to share information and to identify and address any potential conflict.

The board should also get to know the staff and volunteers – no one likes the idea of being ruled by a distant, faceless entity! For example, you could include site visits in your induction, invite staff to board meetings or hold open house where staff members and volunteers can meet and mingle with board members.

Turn to section 11.3 to find out more about board/staff/chief executive/volunteer relationships.

## Disagreements between trustees

A board of trustees will often be made up of people from diverse backgrounds who may have different reasons for being on the board, and be either new or long-serving. They may have been nominated by another organisation, or by a local branch of the national organisation. They may be a service user, or be a specialist in their daytime profession. This mix can provide valuable knowledge and expertise, but can also lead to individuals taking entrenched positions on matters being discussed.

Firm leadership from an experienced chair will ensure that there is consensus, but if there is a personality clash between the chair and another trustee, this may require the intervention of a neutral person respected by both the board members.

In some circumstances the vice chair can be the facilitator, in others it may be the president or a patron. It is not appropriate for a staff member to play this role. In extreme situations an external mediator may be needed. Having a grievance procedure in place for the trustees will go some way to preventing disagreement resolution requiring external help.

## Dealing with internal conflict: hints and tips

Understanding motivations and being clear about expectations on both sides from the beginning can help lessen conflict or prepare for when it happens.

You should:

- ensure that staff and trustees have a proper induction process from the beginning
- ensure that the boundaries between different roles – board, individual trustee, staff and volunteer – are defined, clearly communicated and understood by everyone
- rely on a strong, perceptive chair to make sure that factions or individual disruptions are not detrimental to the work of the board
- make sure that the chief officer understands the particular board/ staff relationships that exist in your organisation.
- focus on the organization and its mission, not personalities
- refer to your board's code of conduct, which sets out the values which trustees need to adhere to in order to fulfil their duty (an agreement for board members can also set out the procedure if the code of conduct is breached)
- bring in outside help (to mediate or inform) if conflict cannot be resolved internally: the involvement of someone neutral from outside may help people to communicate more freely and to find a resolution
- consider mentoring for the chair and for the chief executive: finding that others may have had similar problems and hearing how they dealt with them can diffuse tense situations
- be prepared to remove trustees. Check your governing document to see what it says about disqualification or removal. There are certain statutory disqualifications in law, and governing documents sometimes also include clauses such as failure to attend meetings.

## Conflicts in membership organisations

Many charities have a formal membership. Usually, relations between members and trustees are positive. However, tensions can sometimes occur which can, if unchecked or poorly handled, lead to dispute and affect the charity's ability to govern well.

The relationship between trustees and members can be positive if members feel their views are represented and if they feel they can exert their influence. But a perception amongst members that they are ignored or undervalued can risk leading to conflict and dispute. Often the breakdown in relationships can result from inappropriate governance structures combined with a lack of communication and consultation with members. NCVO's Good Membership Guide talks about tensions between trustees and members originating in a distinction between governance (the control of strategy and policy by trustees) and representation (the influence members exert on strategy and policies and how trustees take account of this).

Attention to good governance practice can, then, help create good member relationships – in particular: attention to board election / appointment methods (chapter 1), decision-making structures (chapter 21), accountability (chapter 14), conduct of annual general meetings (chapter 21) and periodic governance reviews (chapter 22).

Sometimes, changes to governance structures can be the most effective way of improving trustee-member relations – see chapter 21 for examples. Remember that change can be controversial in itself and restructuring governance arrangements should have the support of members and involve good consultation and communication with members.

**Further information**
See NCVO's *Good Membership Guide* (see resources section).

## Dealing with external conflict

Trustees have a responsibility for ensuring that conflicts between the organisation and its beneficiaries, partners or service providers are dealt with efficiently to protect the reputation of the organisation. A dispute may involve one of the trustees, but not in their role as trustee.

Reference to the organisation's complaints policy, a contract or service agreement may provide the answer, but trustees must ensure they obtain the best possible advice to resolve the matter, possibly from a lawyer or an accountant, and identify when neutral external mediation is necessary.

## Preventing conflict

Whether internal or external, disputes can be avoided by:

- Clarifying areas of responsibility
- Ensuring expectations are mutually understood
- Avoiding making assumptions
- Being aware of personal perceptions and prejudices
- Respecting the views of others
- Making time for informal discussion
- Obtaining the best possible advice where professional expertise is needed
- Setting achievable targets and timeframes
- and, above all – listening, and asking questions when a situation is not clear.

## Conflict and the role of the Charity Commission

The Charity Commission will not get involved in a dispute or conflict if there are properly appointed trustees in place. It is the responsibility of the trustees to ensure any complaints are addressed. The Commission will become involved in a dispute or conflict if there are no validly appointed trustees and all other methods of resolving the dispute have failed.

The Charity Commission will take regulatory action about a dispute or conflict "When there is evidence of misconduct or mismanagement which puts the charity's assets, beneficiaries, integrity and reputation at risk; when the charities is being run by individuals who are not entitled to run it and are unwilling to put the situation right; or when the charity can no longer operate."[21]

If there are serious regulatory concerns, the Commission may open a formal inquiry (under section 8 of the Charities Act 1993, as amended by the Charities Act 2006).

## Further information

There are a number of sources of support and advice listed in part five.

[21] Charity Commission *Conflicts in your charity: a statement of approach by the Charity Commission* (June 2008 – under Meeting our Requirements on the Charity Commission website). Crown Copyright.

Part Three:

# Developing the Board

# Developing the Board

## Introduction

The board of trustees is ultimately responsible for everything your charity does. Good governance demands that trustees set clear aims and objectives, establish priorities, safeguard the charity's assets and use them effectively and exclusively for the benefit of the charity's beneficiaries.

The changing environment within which charities operate requires organisations to have in place a knowledgeable and committed board, which is sufficiently aware of these developments to respond to change.

As trustees it is essential that you feel confident that you can direct your organisation as well as possible. This involving using and developing your existing skills and acquiring new skills as appropriate. It is your knowledge and experience that makes you uniquely capable and valuable as a trustee.

Remember that the role of a board member is a collective one – you are not expected, individually, to have expertise in all areas – but it is important to ensure that the combined skills, qualities and knowledge of your board meet the organisation's needs, or that you know where the gaps are and where to access advice.

So how can your board achieve this ideal balance? The first ingredient is to have a group of trustees with the right mix of skills, experiences and backgrounds. Add to this the support and development they need to carry out their responsibilities.

Next, ensure that your board has in place the processes and decision-making structures to enable trustees to perform effectively. Finally, examine the personal and professional motivations of trustees – are your board members engaged in their work? If not, what can be done to harness their potential and tap into their experience?

And throughout this journey, keep a focus on the big picture. What does your board need to support and develop your organisation in an ever-changing environment?

# 17

# What makes a good trustee and an effective board?

## 17.1

### What makes an effective trustee?

The UK Workforce Hub, working with the Governance Hub and a steering group of trustees and experts, have developed a set of National Occupational Standards for Trustee and Management Committees. These standards (see box) set out the competencies that all trustees should develop to ensure that they are able to carry out their role. The standards are not compulsory, but they do refer to both the legal responsibilities of trustees and good practice.

It is recommended that you use the standards as a starting point in looking at the skills, qualities and knowledge of trustees. There are accompanying resources (see resources section) that can help you use the standards as a way of improving your board's performance.

# 17.2

## What skills and competencies do trustees need?

The National Occupational Standards set out a list of 'competencies' that it is felt all trustees should be able to demonstrate. These are:

- be committed to the purpose, objects and values of the organisation
- be constructive about other trustees' opinions in discussions, and in response to staff members' contributions at meetings
- be able to act reasonably and responsibly when undertaking such duties and performing tasks
- be able to maintain confidentiality on sensitive and confidential information
- be supportive of the values (and ethics) of the organisation
- understand the importance and purpose of meetings, and be committed to preparing for them adequately and attending them regularly
- be able to analyse information and, when necessary, challenge constructively
- be able to make collective decisions and stand by them
- be able to respect boundaries between executive (staff or day to day) and governance functions

### National Occupational Standards for Trustees and Management Committee Members

The National Occupational Standards cover four units:

- Safeguard and promote the values and mission of the voluntary or community organisation
- Determine the strategy and structure of the voluntary or community organisation
- Ensure the voluntary or community organisation operates in an effective, responsible and accountable manner
- Ensure the effective functioning of the voluntary or community organisation's board of trustees

**Further information**
National Occupational Standards for Trustees and Management Committee Members (available from the UK Workforce Hub website – see resources section).

# 17.3

What specialist skills might trustees need?

As well as having the competencies that are set out in the National Occupational Standards, it is important that an effective board of trustees should be able to draw on a diverse range of skills and knowledge. These may well include:

**The 'hard' skills such as**

- management
- financial management,
- recruitment and personnel management (including a knowledge of employment legislation),
- public relations
- marketing
- legal
- information technology
- fundraising
- campaigning and advocacy
- setting targets,
- monitoring and evaluating performance

**The 'soft' skills such as:**

- team working,
- problem-solving,
- asking difficult questions,
- decision-making
- negotiation skills
- listening skills

– and making people laugh!

The lists are not exhaustive and the level of knowledge and understanding will be different for different organisations. If you are a trustee of a small community organisation your financial knowledge will not need to be as high as if you are a trustee of, say, a large housing association.

Remember – each trustee does not need all of the above skills and knowledge. It is, however, important to identify what skills at what level are required by the board as a whole to ensure your organisation works well, and then to identify which trustees have which skills and where any gaps may be.

## What are the collective skills and competencies needed by a board?

Good governance is a collective responsibility – so any consideration of the skills and qualities needed by trustees should consider what the board as a whole needs to be effective.

What are the specific skills that make trustee boards effective? Researchers Richard Chait, Thomas Holland and Barbara Taylor[1] suggest six key areas – or dimensions – where board competence made a measurable difference to organisational performance.

1) Contextual
You need a profound understanding of your organisation's mission – coupled with an up-to-date knowledge of the threats and opportunities posed by the organisation's environment.

2) Educational
You should continue to learn and train, assess and evaluate your own performance, and identify your strengths and weaknesses.

3) Interpersonal
You shouldn't let individual personalities, no matter how brilliant, dominate the governance process. Instead, encourage group decision-making, teamwork, and a sense of shared purpose.

[1] Taylor, Barbara E, Chait, Richard P, and Holland, Thomas P (1996) 'New Work of the Nonprofit Board', Harvard Business Review, September/October 1996

# 17.4

4) Analytical
Cultivate your analytical skills so you can stand back, take the long view of difficult situations and suggest appropriate actions to better serve the overall mission.

5) Political
One of your primary responsibilities to the organisation is to develop and maintain healthy relationships among key constituencies such as members, volunteers, clients, government agencies and community groups.

6) Strategic
As a board member, you are part of the strategic engine behind the organisation. As such, you must eventually take responsibility for the organisation's long-term success or failure.

## How can our board identify its skills needs?

Your board was set up when your organisation was at the start of its life. As the organisation has grown or developed, it is inevitable that different skills will be required from board members. A good starting point is to conduct a skills audit or training needs analysis of your current board.

This will identify:

- The skills needed by the board
- the skills of current trustees
- what gaps exist on the board
- what training needs to be arranged for board members.
- what new or prospective new trustees can offer.

A skills audit also avoids assumptions that one can make about why a trustee has joined the board and what they can offer. Some join out of commitment to the organisation's work and its beneficiaries, others bring a particular technical or professional skill and others may see board membership as a way of gaining valuable work experience.

The Charity Commission recommends that all charities undertake a skills audit of their board to identify the skills required and the gaps. The form the skills audit takes will vary depending on the size of your organisation. This process should be carried out regularly as your trustee board and your organisation changes – remember to ask all new board members to complete a skills audit when they join the board.

## What role can I play on the board?

As trustees, you can add value to the board in many different ways. These can be considered when identifying skills and attributes. A trustee may act in one or more of the following capacities:

**Advisory** – providing free expert advice/management expertise

**Regulatory** – ensuring probity

**Democratic** – contributing to the resolution of various stakeholder interests

**Educational** – providing opportunities for debate, learning and sharing of expertise

**Participatory** – engaging users/consumers of services

**Networking** – being ambassadors, linking to contacts, shaping and influencing others

**Involving** – motivating skilled volunteers

**Visionary** – adding missionary zeal, bringing passion to the mission

**Leadership** – steering the organisation in the right direction

**Supportive** – supporting, valuing and rewarding the chief executive.

## Example Trustee Skills Audit

Name: ______________________________ Date: ____________

1) What kind of expertise do you consider you bring to the board? (please tick all that apply)

☐ Administration
☐ History of the voluntary sector
☐ Campaigning/advocacy
☐ Human Resources/Training
☐ Change Management/Restructuring
☐ Information Technology
☐ Consultancy
☐ Legal
☐ General
☐ Strategic Planning and Training
☐ Governance
☐ Property
☐ Neighbourhood Renewal
☐ Conflict Resolution
☐ Knowledge of the Community
☐ Other

Please give further details:

2) What other experience or skills do you feel you can offer?

3) Are there any areas of the charity's work you have a particular interest in and/or would like to become more involved in?

4) What motivated you to become a trustee of the charity?

# 18

# Learning and development

A skills audit of your board can help identify learning and development needs. All board members should be encouraged to keep their existing skills and knowledge up to date and develop new ones where appropriate.

## Learning methods

Trustees come from all walks of life so everyone will have different support and development needs, and will want to meet these needs in different ways.

In addition to formal and informal training, there is a wealth of practical and up-to-date information available to trustees. These include books and magazines, email newsletters and websites. A selection of the most useful sources of information is included in the Resources section.

Here are ten suggested learning methods for trustees. The ten methods are based on The Third Sector Leadership Centre's list 'Learning to Lead':

1) Join an action learning set or network: become part of a small group of other trustees to address real life problems, develop solutions and take action (see case study overleaf). Alternatively, is there a trustee network in your area, or nationally, that you can join to meet other trustees, access mutual support and share experiences? Visit www.trusteenet.org.uk to find out about the work of Charity Trustee Networks and access online networking (see part five).

2) Undertake an assessment of skills: many questionnaires help gain insights into strengths, abilities, and the identification of development needs

3) Access a coach: an individual development relationship between trustee and coach can support a board member in recognising their potential, identifying their goals and overcoming barriers.

4) Benchmark yourself against a competency framework: will help to establish a frame of reference for organisational good practice and individuals' competence. See Part Four for ideas on how your organisation's governance and your individual role as a trustee can be reviewed.

5) Seek guidance from a mentor: can help trustees to think through their ideas and support their professional development. Some organisations offer new trustees the opportunity to be mentored by existing trustees, or a trustee network may offer mentoring opportunities between trustees from different organisations.

6) Consider a qualifications route: accredited certificates of competence and achievement can aid career progression and establish a sound knowledge base. The National Occupational Standards for Trustees and Management Committee Members can form a route towards qualifications for trustees.

7) Take time to reflect on a residential programme: offers dedicated time away from ongoing work to learn, reflect and network. Many boards take time out at away days to reflect and plan, away from board business.

8) Challenge yourself in a new environment: trustees can learn insights from finding out how other boards operate. Is there a trustee network in your area, or a national network, that you can join to meet other trustees, share experiences and provide mutual support?

9) Research your needs and direct your own learning: taking responsibility for finding, managing and assessing your own learning builds confidence. Trustees can, for example, benefit from free online learning opportunities like the trustee e-learning initiative (see resources section).

10) Attend a workshop or masterclass: allows trustees to learn specific topics and provide opportunities to get information, develop skills and learn from others. These could be small or large scale: for example, NCVO holds an annual Trustee Conference; or workshops could be provided in-house if there is a particular need across the board.

It is important that you also remember that you have much to learn from other trustees, volunteers and staff.

## **Case Study** – Hundred Houses Society

A housing association offers all board members access to traditional training and opportunities to attend conferences . In addition, a 30-60 minute update session is organised before each board and sub committee meeting. The update sessions cover either issues that affect the organisation – changes in legislation, for example – or provide an opportunity for trustees who have been on a course/ conference to pass on their learning.

## **Case Study** – Helen Rollason

"I had been chairing my village hall for 3 years and I was beginning to lose heart. Despite having very committed colleagues on the committee, I felt the onus was on me, especially as many of them are older or have other commitments. And I didn't really know where to go for help."

Then came a timely offer. Helen was invited to join an action learning set of chairs of local village halls, who would come together to share and learn from each other's experiences.

The group of six chairs was led by a facilitator and met three times. The group used an 'action learning' approach. People take it in turns to share an issue and, with the help of targeted questions by the rest of the group, take a fresh look at the issue and the options they have to deal with it.

Helen used her turn to explore how to get more people to use the village hall. 'I got so many good ideas. What really surprised me was that I wasn't alone, other people were dealing with the same challenge.'

Helen suggests: "Be open-minded. Action learning helps you challenge not just your own ways of looking at things but other people's too. Some of the questions I was asked made me think 'of course I can do that, why didn't I think of that before?' The questioning techniques also encouraged me to challenge others and so help them find the answers they needed themselves."

## Do you have a budget for trustee development?

NCVO and the Governance and Workforce Hubs recently produced a resource to help organisations better understand the costing and funding implications of governance and workforce development. These costs are sometimes called organisational development.

By better understanding the costs of supporting and developing your trustee board, your organisation will be better able to plan, budget, cost and fundraise for development.

Please also see the section on full cost recovery (section 7.1)

**More information**
Funding and Costing Workforce and Governance Development (Ceri Hutton and Stephanie Sexton – Governance Hub, 2007) – available from NCVO.

The enthusiasm, desire and commitment for continuous learning is one of the key attributes a trustee can have. No one knows everything and everyone has something to learn to help them in their role. By being systematic in identifying the needs of the organisation, the skills of existing members and the training needs and recruitment priorities that will help fill any gaps you will improve your own, the boards and the organisation's performance.

## Checklist

Have you carried out an assessment of the skills, qualities, knowledge and perspectives trustees bring to the board?

Are all trustees offered the opportunity to develop their skills further via appropriate learning opportunities?

Do you have a budget for individual trustee development?

# 19

# Building the board

## 19.1

### Introduction

Did you know that over a third of charities experience difficulties in recruiting trustees and two thirds struggle to find trustees with the appropriate skills – but that over 80% rely on word of mouth or personal recommendations to find their new board members?[1]

Surveys have also found that trustee boards do not reflect the population, with less than 1% aged under 25[2] and black and minority ethnic groups under-represented.

The Charity Commission have recommended that poor recruitment and induction procedures for trustees can lead to problems such as:

- lack of clarity about duties and responsibilities
- failure to recognise where advice should be taken
- failure to manage conflicts of interest
- vesting control in an 'inner core' instead of the whole board.

Board recruitment, induction and support are not things to be left to chance. As Cyril O'Houle said in Governing Boards, *"A good board is a victory, not a gift."*

[1] Charity Commission publication *Start as you mean to go on: trustee recruitment and induction* (RS10) and .Charity Commission publication *Trustee recruitment, selection and induction* (RS1). Crown Copyright.

[2] *Latest Trends in Charity Governance and Trusteeship* (Chris Cornforth – NCVO, 2001).

# 19.2

This chapter outlines the methods your organisation could adopt to find new board members with the appropriate skills and to help ensure trustee opportunities reach a wide group of people.

Five questions for building a happy board:

1) Why are we recruiting new trustees?
2) Are we ready to bring in new people?
3) What we you looking for?
4) How do we attract and select people?
5) How do we keep trustees motivated once they have joined?

## Preparing the ground

### Decide who will lead your recruitment programme

Who will take forward your trustee recruitment activities? Decide on one individual or small group – perhaps the chair, vice-chair or small working group – who will take responsibility for sustaining the process. Your board may decide to call this group a nominating committee with a specific remit to recruit new trustees. Or, the group may be a governance committee with a wider remit to improve the organisation's governance, perhaps calling itself a 'governance committee'.

### Devise an action plan

The first step is to draw up an action plan setting out what you will do at each stage of the recruitment process. It is also helpful to have a timetable. Does the board and potential new trustees know how long it is likely to take between an individual expressing interest in a vacancy and their being formally appointed or elected as a trustee?

Use the headings in this chapter as the basis for your action plan. There is also a very useful pull out and keep action plan in the Trustee Recruitment Toolkit which you can download from the NCVO website (see resources section).

# 19.3

## Who are you looking for?

### Start with your governing document

Your governing document (which may be called a constitution, trust deed, memorandum and articles of association or another name – see chapter 2) is your rule book for the way your charity is governed. This should be the first place to look for terms of office, eligibility, procedures for election and so on. For example, some charities have powers to co-opt people on to the board, a useful way of complementing the skills and experience of your elected trustees.

### Why do you want to recruit?

Ask yourself what you need to make your board most effective. Does it have the right mix of skills or experience to oversee new areas of service delivery? Could it better reflect changes to the ethnic or age profile of the beneficiaries? Does it need an injection of 'new blood' in preparation for existing, more experienced trustees reaching the end of their term of service?

Nationally, surveys have shown that trustee boards do not reflect the population as a whole, with minority groups and young people in particular under-represented in trustee roles. The tendency for many charities to recruit only using word of mouth also inevitably limits the number and diversity of people who can access trustee opportunities. For this reason many organisations have looked at how their recruitment practices can help create a more inclusive and diverse trustee board.

# 19.4

## Creating an inclusive and diverse trustee board

### What do we mean when we talk about an inclusive and diverse trustee board?

An inclusive trustee board can have many characteristics:

- it can be more responsive to the community it serves, because trustees will have actively worked to see how board membership reflects the wider community
- it can bring fresh perspectives to the way the organisation is governed, by bringing together people from different backgrounds and with different perspectives
- it accesses a wider pool of talent and skill – if you openly promote your board vacancies to a wide group of people you are more likely to attract people with the skills your organisation needs
- it is more inclusive in the way its mission is fulfilled, by involving a range of people and interests
- it sets an example about inclusion 'from the top'. If your organisation has a commitment to diversity – typically, in a policy – then an inclusive and diverse board is an ideal way to demonstrate that your organisation is acting on its policy.
- it is inclusive and accessible in the way it operates – whether it is the venue for meetings, the format of papers or the culture in the boardroom

## Some misconceptions about board diversity

- **A diverse board is not one that simply looks diverse**
  Appointing a trustee on the basis of their age or ethnic background alone, without considering what they can offer by way of skills or knowledge or how they can contribute to the organisation's worth, can risk being a token gesture.

- **A diverse board is not one that automatically expects an individual to represent their entire community**
  Everyone has something to offer as a trustee, and it may not be what you expect. A finance expert brings other skills beyond financial expertise (and they may not want to simply carry on their day job!). A person who has a disability does not automatically 'represent' all people with disabilities. Have you considered what the board expects from its new trustees, and how the board is perceived by the new board member? Make sure expectations on both sides are matched.

- **A diverse board is not just about democratically representing all interests around a table**
  Creating a large board with a large number of different groups 'represented' risks creating an unwieldy decision making process, and, perhaps more seriously, can create a perception that trustees are appointed only to represent particular sectional interests. Better to think first about how you want to include diverse views in the decision making process and then look at how this can happen – through board membership? Through advisory or working groups? Through consultation?

## Questions to consider in creating an inclusive and diverse board

- Are you confident that the strategy and performance of the organisation which you are responsible for matches the charity's mission and is keeping up with a changing environment?
- Could your board better reflect more of society, your beneficiaries and stakeholders, and could it harness people's talents better?
- What skills and knowledge are missing from your board?
- What would be the ideal composition of your board?
- Have you already identified people who could join your board? Are there people already in the organisation who could become involved at board level?
- What will be the challenges and the benefits to the organisation of a diverse and inclusive board?
- Is trusteeship the best way to involve people in the decision-making process? Are there other forms of involvement (sub-committees, forums, advisory groups) which could involve people more effectively?
- Are you ready to involve more people on your board?
- Are potential trustees ready to be involved on the board?
- Why are you looking at the diversity of your board? Do you want to improve the work of your organisation and board – or do you, or does someone else, think it will 'look good'?

## Practical steps to creating an inclusive board

### Identify the obstacles to diversity

The following exercise, from the Governance Hub's Trustee Recruitment Toolkit, can be carried out by your board to examine the obstacles to diversity and some of the measures to overcome them.

| What prevents a broader range of people from joining our board? | What can we do to overcome these obstacles? |
| --- | --- |
| Lack of awareness of the organisation and its relevance | • Go on a publicity drive specifically with this group of people.<br>• Organise events, or attend events held by minority ethnic groups, young people or people with disabilities (depending on who it is you are trying to recruit). |
| Lack of interest in our organisation | • Build relationships with the underrepresented group to demonstrate that your organisation is relevant to them.<br>• Consider partnerships with organisations that do have good links already. |
| Time and place of meeting (inconvenient and inaccessible) | • Review the time and place of meetings and be willing to change. |
| Use of jargon | • Adopt a Plain English approach. |
| Lack of confidence among potential candidates | • Offer training, getting to know us sessions.<br>• Invite people to get involved in other activities first.<br>• Offer to provide a mentor. |
| Lack of appropriate support (e.g. information in large print, availability of interpretation, lack of Plain English in our documents) | • Seek advice from organisations like RNID, RNIB and People First on the services available.<br>• Remember however not to make assumptions about what any individual needs – ask them. |
| We don't know what prevents people | • Ask them.<br>• A well-considered consultation exercise with a community can be an excellent way to build relationships, provided you are committed to following through on the results. |

Review your board's profile

How does the membership of your board reflect the diverse communities your organisation serves – and does so in a way that helps your board do its job better?

Does the board contain the right mix of skills, knowledge, experience and perspectives that you need to govern effectively?

Do you involve users at board level? User involvement can help bring an important perspective to board decision making and create a more inclusive organisation. User involvement in governance is not just an issue of board recruitment but can take place in a number of ways (see chapter 12).

A skills audit is a useful way of identifying what board members bring and the gaps in skills and knowledge on the board – see chapter 17 for a sample skills audit.

Review board recruitment methods

An inclusive approach to board recruitment benefits everyone. Use the suggestions later in this and the next chapter to help you plan your recruitment, selection and induction programme to best meet the needs of your prospective and new trustees.

# 19.5

## Preparing the vacancy

Before promoting a trustee vacancy it's vital that the role is clearly agreed, set out, in writing, and understood by all. It would be a shame if keen prospective board members were put off because they didn't understand what they were being asked to do and what would be expected of them.

First, check that board members clearly understand the form duties and responsibilities of trusteeship and any specific roles attached to the particular vacancy.

Next, plan to put together a pack of information for potential trustees. This should provide the applicant with basic information about the role and the organisation – but not too much detail as more can be provided later on in the process. As a minimum you should include:

- role description, setting out the duties, responsibilities, expectations (especially time commitment and any additional duties), eligibility criteria and an expenses policy (see chapter 3)
- background to the organisation
- sufficient information to be able to apply – an application form or instructions on how to apply or be nominated

# 19.6

## How do you attract new trustees?

Over 80 per cent of trustees are recruited through word of mouth.[3] However, other methods of recruitment exist and can help widen your search and the pool of potential trustees.

Making the approach

Remember to sell trusteeship: emphasise the positive and rewarding contribution trustees make to society. But do be realistic about the time commitment and responsibilities. The last thing you should say is "well, it's only a few hours every three months"! The role of an honorary officer, in particular, may in practice be much more time-consuming than the formal business of meetings because of their additional duties.

Inform your members

If your trustees are drawn from membership, you could circulate information about the skills required in advance of elections and circulate biographies of candidates during the election process. Within the organisation advisory groups or similar bodies can be good "training ground" for potential trustees.

[3] Charity Commission publication *Start as you mean to go on: trustee recruitment and induction* (RS10). Crown Copyright.

### Promote to the wider public

Promoting your vacancy to the wider public helps you to be transparent and reach as wide a pool of potential trustees as possible. Methods can include:

**Advertising or news features**
Advertising (paid or free adverts) or features about your organisation in a newspaper (sometimes called advertorials) can help promote your message to the public and include reference to your trustee vacancy. Try advertising in newspapers (national or local), professional magazines, websites or, locally, in community centres, surgeries or other public places.

**Trustee brokerage services**
A number of agencies offer specialist trustee recruitment services. NCVO produces a brokerage directory, Trustee Bank. Each service promotes trustee vacancies to a particular group – for example professionals, retired people or black and minority ethnic people. Using a brokerage service can help your board access people with particular skills and from diverse backgrounds.

**Specialist recruitment agencies**
Recruitment agencies can find and select trustees, chairs and treasurers. While the costs involved may be high, it can be a useful way of recruiting to key positions.

## Case study

### Organisational perspective – Kids' Clubs Network

Historically, trustees at national childcare organisation Kids' Clubs Network have come from the childcare field. But in 2001 the charity decided that it wanted to widen the board's experience. It was also under-represented by black and minority ethnic members on the board, so was keen to encourage more diversity.

The following advert appeared in the Guardian (Wednesday and Saturday) and appeared on the newspaper's website. The ad was also placed in The Voice, the weekly newspaper covering black and minority ethnic issues.

*"Kids' Clubs Network is a leading national childcare organisation, spearheading the development of new opportunities for children and parents.*

*Help this innovative charity go places as a Trustee Board Member. Use your skills and experience to make an important contribution by joining this forward-looking,imaginative organisation at a time of rapid expansion and opportunity. As an elected or co-opted board member, you will be involved in developing strategy, marketing and business campaigns to support the growth of the organisation and its services. If you have the relevant skills we would like to hear from you.*

*The position is voluntary, but reasonable expenses will be paid. Contact details XXXX"*

# 19.7

## Selection and appointment of trustees

By now you should have one or more potential trustees. They may have applied through your advertising process, or they may have been formally nominated via your organisation's rules.

Check who is making the final decision on appointment or election. Is it a decision by members at an Annual General Meeting? Can the trustee board decide between themselves? Is the appointment made by an outside organisation (see chapter 1)?

### When trustees make the final decision

If trustees make the final decision, you may decide to go through a selection process to narrow down applicants and create a shortlist.

Start by agreeing the 'must have' qualities from the trustees' person specification. Then, agree how you will assess them. Make sure those conducting interviews and making the decision understand the role and the key qualities needed.

When you have made your decision or recommendation, remember to thank everyone who applied – not just the successful candidates. Think about how you can say no 'positively'. If you have followed a systematic process then make it clear to trustees that you are looking for specific skills and experience. When you turn people down are there other ways of involving them in the organisation?

### When members make the final decision

If members make the final decision, it is likely your governing document will specify the way in which trustees are elected. Make sure you carefully follow your procedures.

Some organisations, in addition, help members choose between the candidates – for example by asking candidates to produce a biography for circulation to members at the Annual General Meeting.

Some organisations go further, by involving the board in selecting candidates or identifying recommended candidates. For example:

- a sub-committee of the board shortlists candidate(s) who are then nominated by trustees and put to members. Members may have the right to put forward alternative candidates.
- A list of candidates is 'recommended' by the board – but other candidates may be entitled to stand for election too if they wish

Remember to ensure that any method is consistent with your governing document.

### Keep it legal

- Make sure you carefully follow the procedures for the appointment or election of trustees as set out in your organisation's governing document
- Have you checked that trustees are eligible to serve? Information about trustee eligibility should have been included in the application pack. Use the declaration below as a checklist for eligibility. There is also a useful Formality checklist in the Trustee Recruitment Toolkit (free to download – see resources section). You may also decide to take up references.
- Make sure you ask trustees to sign a declaration that they eligible and willing to serve (see box below)
- If your charity works with young or vulnerable people make sure the trustees seek any necessary disclosures from the Criminal Records Bureau.

## Example Trustee Declaration

I declare that I am not disqualified from acting as a charity trustee and that:

- I am aged 18 years or over at the date of this election or appointment (only relevant for unincorporated charities);
- I am capable of managing and administering my own affairs;
- I do not have an unspent conviction relating to any offence involving deception or dishonesty;
- I am not an undischarged bankrupt nor have I made a composition or arrangement with, or granted a trust deed for, my creditors (ignore if discharged from such an arrangement);
- I am not subject to a disqualification order under the Company Directors Disqualification Act 1986 or to an Order made under section 429(b) of the Insolvency Act 1986;
- I have not been removed from the office of charity trustee or trustee for a charity by an Order made by the Charity Commissioners or the High Court on the grounds of any misconduct or mismanagement nor am I subject to an Order under section 7 of the Law Reform (Miscellaneous Provisions) (Scotland) Act 1990, preventing me from being concerned in the management or control of any relevant organisation or body.

For charities that work with children:

- I am not subject to a disqualification Order under the Criminal Justice and Court Services Act 2000.

For charities that work with vulnerable adults:

- I am not disqualified under the Protection of Vulnerable Adults List.

Signed ________________________________ Date ______________

This declaration is an extract from the Charity Commission's *Declaration of Eligibility for Newly-Appointed Trustees* (CSD 1382) (Crown Copyright).

The case studies that follow illustrate different methods taken by boards to select candidates.

## **Case study** – Advocacy West Lancashire

### The organisation

Advocacy West Lancashire (AWL) was established in 1994 to provide a service of representation and support for any member of the community who experiences difficulties in getting their message across when communicating with health care, social, or other statutory services.

Following rapid growth to the organisation, the trustees identified significant skills gaps on the board, including in the area of human resources and financial expertise.

AWL tried to recruit new members through voluntary sector networks and organisations but this produced no new skilled members.

The Board then agreed to publicly advertise new vacancies in a similar way to recruiting staff. Drawing on ideas and methods from other organisations, an advertisement was placed in the local newspaper (the Liverpool Echo):

*"Up to eight (8) eligible persons with business experience to become members of our Board of Trustees. We are especially interested in those professionals who have human resource, financial management or fundraising skills and knowledge. Individuals with varying backgrounds in business who are interested in a volunteer leadership role in the community are encouraged to apply. Your experience may be varied, but a practical approach and the capability to contribute to strategic direction and financial management is essential."*

More than 20 people, all meeting the professional criteria, responded to the advert and 13 were elected to the board. Of these, nine remain (early 2007), with four having stood down after deciding trusteeship was not for them. The recruitment campaign in total cost approximately £ 1000.

AWL felt that the process had helped to recharge and regenerate its board, gaining enthusiasts with relevant skills. It has laid the ground work for sound development of the organisation's governance – subsequent activities included strategic planning and developing more robust financial procedures.

What advice can AWL give to other organisations?

*"Advertise. Well run organisations start with good governance. Good governance starts with the Board members. Board members must have the skills and commitment to actively work on behalf of the organisation. If you don't have the skills required, openly advertise for them"*

## **Case study** – SHARE Community

Share Community expanded their board with four new trustees appointed in groups of two.

### Identifying the need

A board review had made recommendations to broaden the range of skills and backgrounds on the board. Through a mixture of brokerage services and personal networks a number of candidates were identified.

### Information

A pack of information was sent out to prospective candidates with a request for CVs where application forms were not used by brokers.

### Selection

The chair and chief executive conducted informal discussions with a selection of candidates. This was not so much an 'interview' but an opportunity for the candidates to find out more about the organisation and the board – and for the board to find out more about the candidates and how they might fit in. Four candidates were recommended to the board for approval and references checked.

### Appointment and induction

Before appointment the new trustees signed a trustee declaration and were then sent an information pack on their roles and responsibilities and relevant training courses. As well as the more usual aspects of induction – meeting with senior staff, a site visit and so on – they felt it was important for new trustees to get a feel for the way the organisation runs. The charity runs regular events such as garden parties and trustees are invited to attend these to meet volunteers, donors and people from the local community.

Tips from SHARE

*"Be very clear about what you need and don't be hurried into appointing the wrong person; and use as many sources of potential trustees as possible to have the best chance of getting the mix of skills and personal characteristics you need."*

# 19.8

## Recruiting to specific roles (chair, treasurer etc.)

### Check the legals

Sometimes organisations have separate rules for the appointment or election of trustees with specific roles, so make sure you carefully check your governing document and other rules and incorporate them into your plan and timescale.

### Clarifying the role

Have you reviewed the role and specific duties of the post to which you are recruiting? It may be, for example, that the existing postholder has been in office for some years, during which time the role may have evolved to suit their particular skills and the organisation's life cycle.

Don't make assumptions about the duties of a postholder – check the section on 'who's who in the boardroom' (chapter 4) as a guide. If you don't have a role description or if it needs updating, check yours against the model role descriptions in chapter 4.

### Recruitment methods

Are there specific avenues that might help you attract a candidate with what may be specialist skills? For example, some trustee brokerage services advertise vacancies to people from particular professional backgrounds, like that operated by the Charity Finance Directors' Group – useful if you are looking for a treasurer.

### Selection and election / appointment

You may decided to have a different – perhaps more formal – process for selecting candidates for the role of an honorary officer. Remember to ensure that any process complies with your governing document.

# 19.9

## Planning the next recruitment campaign

Continuous improvement of the selection and recruitment process should make it easier for an organisation to find the right person for the role. Get feedback from trustees who have gone through the process; this can be collected after an initial period on the board or at exit interview stage. Find out what worked, what didn't and what else could have helped.

# 19.10

## Succession planning

The trustee cycle

Once a successful board mix has been achieved, it should be constantly reviewed and refreshed to ensure that the balance is maintained. Part of this is about creating a culture of trustees moving on: trusteeship is not necessarily permanent, but the needs of the organisation – and the needs of the board – change over time. And there are always people who really do need to move on!

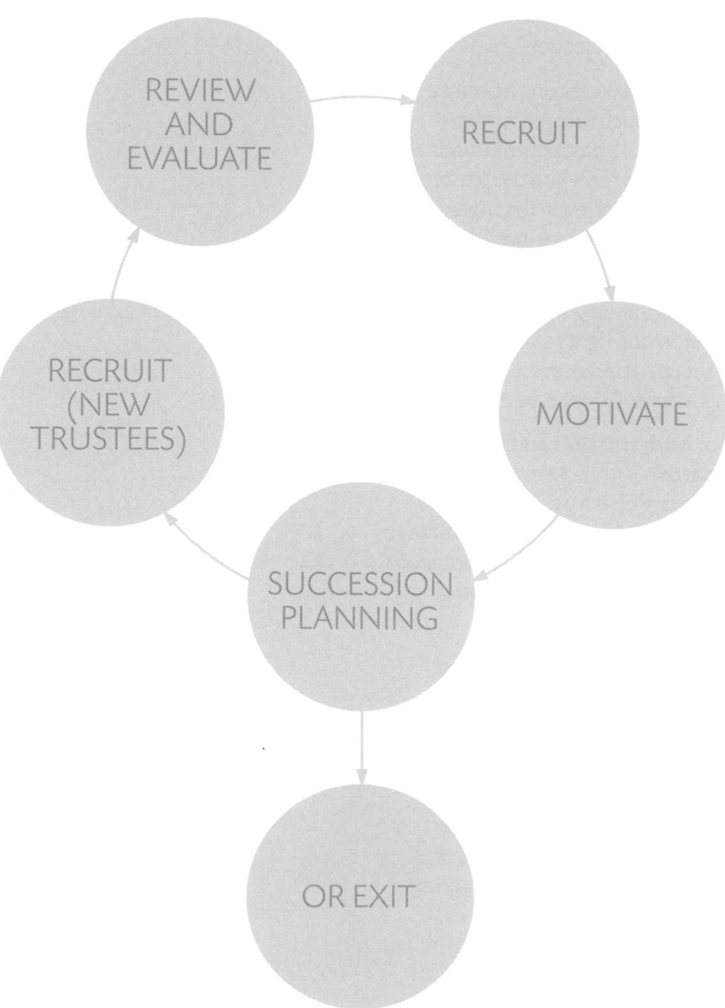

Succession planning – key issues

**For board development**

- how to convince people that they need to move on, both for themselves and for the organisation without giving rise to feelings of failure and rejection
- how to make leaving a positive event which recognises the individual's past contributions and successes (how can the trustee still remain involved in the organisation – as adviser, as vice-president?)

**For the individual trustee**

- understanding that there is not an automatic right to stay and be retained because you have given successfully in the past.

**For both trustees and trustee boards**

- moving on is a positive strategy – understand the positive advantages of the rolling board, of maintaining continuity and also encouraging new people to join
- create a culture of new blood within the organisation
- recognise that individual and organisation do not necessarily grow in parallel, or at the same pace, or in the same direction. What were valuable skills and approaches at one time may not be what the organisation and individual need right now or in the future.

## Checklist

Do you have a plan to recruit new board members that fits in with your board recruitment cycle?

Have trustees discussed the benefits and challenges of an inclusive and diverse board?

Do you need to review your board recruitment practices – and, if necessary, the provisions in your governing document?

Do you ensure opportunities to join the board are promoted as widely as possible, within the terms of your governing document?

Are new board members eligible to serve and properly elected or appointed?

# 20

# Induction

# 20.1

## Induction – getting it right from the start

Induction is a key part of making your trustee board effective. For trustees, it provides an opportunity to learn about their new role and about different aspects of their new charity. For existing board members, induction is a way of identifying the needs of the new trustee and finding ways to support them.

However, surveys have shown that induction is by no means standard practice. Did you know that only approximately one quarter of trustees receive induction and training?[4]. In a survey of trustee support in rural areas, two-thirds received no formal training[5]. The Charity Commission's recent survey of induction practices found that less than half of trustees received a copy of the charity's governing document[6].

Induction programmes need not be lengthy or expensive. If your organisation has a limited (or no) budget for induction there are many resources available, some in this guide and some online, which can be tailored to your own needs. These include model role descriptions, skills audits, hints and tips and induction checklists.

[4] *Recent trends in charity governance and trusteeship*

[5] (Chris Cornforth – NCVO, 2001) *Supporting Rural Voluntary Action* (Holly Yates – NCVO, 2001)

[6] Charity Commission publication *Start as you Mean to Go On: Trustee Recruitment and Induction* (RS10). Crown Copyright.

# 20.2

Charity Commission guidance

The Commission emphasise that new trustees are more likely to feel welcome to the charity, and start making a positive difference sooner, if they have immediate access to the charity's aims and objectives and are given a working knowledge of the way the charity operates from the outset.

The Charity Commission recommend that all trustees receive some form of induction, with the aim of ensuring new trustees have a clear understanding of their roles and responsibilities. All trustees should have access to the charity's governing document.

## Planning the induction programme

### Tailoring induction to the individual's needs

Every trustee brings their unique experiences to the board so each will require particular support or training. Some trustees may value personal development opportunities and have time to carry them out; others may feel that a lifetime's experience in the workplace equips them for their role. Some believe passionately in the cause but feel they lack skills or confidence. Sometimes trustee elected to specific roles have other needs – new chairs may need support if they lack previous chairing experience, or may find it useful to be mentored by an existing chair of another charity.

Yet, all trustees require certain skills and qualities to carry out their role, and all trustees certainly need information and clarity about their duties and responsibilities. Any induction programme should aim to cover the following four areas:

- The key responsibilities – the factual level involves ensuring the trustee has information about the essential duties and responsibilities and the role of a charity.
- Understanding the role – going beyond the role description or written induction pack and ensuring new trustees have a very clear understanding of their prospective role.
- Getting to know the organisation – learning about the history, culture, values, traditions and issues facing the organisation.
- The trustee's own development – ensuring the new trustee settles into their role and can access support and development opportunities.

To try and meet the needs of different organisations, The Good Trustee Guide has set out a range of suggested activities for a new trustee's induction, divided into 'essentials' and 'options'. When new trustees join the board, try discussing the range of suggested activities below with them and decide which will best meet your charity's and the trustee's needs.

# 20.3

## Inducting trustees into specific roles

Individuals taking on specific roles – honorary officers such as the chair, secretary, treasurer or other specific role on the board (see chapter 4) – will need an induction programme tailored to their needs.

To start planning an induction into a specific role, begin with the role description itself. What are the skills and qualities required in the role description or person specification? Next, how does the new postholder feel about the skills and qualities required? Are there gaps? How do they feel they can learn about their new role? Use the planning table below as a starting point (the example given is for the role of chair).

Planning the chair's induction

| Specific role | The skills required include | Possible induction activities |
|---|---|---|
| Responsibilities as a charity trustee | Objectivity<br>Working as a team | Observing the board<br>Attending training / briefing<br>Joining a trustee network |
| Chairing trustee board meetings | Listening<br>Timekeeping<br>Summarising issues | Observing the outgoing chair<br>Attending training<br>Being mentored by another chair |
| ... other roles (see role description)... | | |

Many of the suggested activities below can be adapted to the needs of an a board member in a specific role. For example, a new treasurer could arrange to be mentored from someone in a similar position in another charity, or they could shadow the outgoing postholder. They may need a longer or more in-depth induction into their role and more meetings with trustees and staff.

## Induction activities

Essential elements of a trustee's induction

**1) The induction pack**

As a minimum, all trustees should receive

- a written statement of their responsibilities (often called a role description – if you do not have one, see chapter 4 for an example) – and
- a pack of essential information (an induction pack)

The pack is the basic part of any induction: a trustee should be given one to keep. The pack should be reviewed every year (a good time to do this is before your Annual General Meeting if you hold one).

The pack may contain a lot of information and highlights how it can take time, and a variety of different activities, to get to grips with the role. Don't just rely on an induction pack!

The pack should include as a minimum:

- Governing document
- Standing orders
- Sets of recent board papers and minutes and dates of next meetings
- Terms of reference for committees, sub-committees, working groups
- Annual Reports and Accounts for the previous three years
- Policy documents including equal opportunities and financial controls
- A description of the duties of a trustee and a list of expected skills, qualities, knowledge and experience
- Profiles of trustees and contact details
- Chief executive / head of staff's job description if you employ one

You should also consider including:

- Guidance about the organisation:
  – Its history
  – Mission statement
  – Structure (committees, user groups, staff and volunteers)
  – Any offices or buildings
  – Newsletter / other marketing materials
- Formal documents about the organisation:
  – Details of how the organisation approaches staff appraisal
  – Business plans/strategic plans/ work programme
- Documents about the organisation's governance:
  – Task descriptions of other trustees and honorary officers
  – A manual giving guidance on trustee roles and responsibilities of trustees
  – Code of conduct for trustees and agreement – this might list the values trustees are expected to uphold (eg confidentiality) and practical things
  – Self-assessment form to indicate skills, experience, interests and support needs
- Other useful governance documents:
  – Charity Commission CC3 'The Essential Trustee' publication
  – The summary Code of Governance
  – The pocket version of the National Occupational Standards for Trustees and Management Committee Members

## Induction pack checklist

An induction pack should provide, as a minimum, enough information for a new trustee to be able to list the following:

- Who the trustees and honorary officers are and what they do
- How long trustees serve for
- Frequency, dates and length of trustee meetings
- Sub-committees
- Date of the next Annual General Meeting (if applicable)
- A brief background to the organisation (history, funders, staffing, achievements)
- The board's current priorities

### 2) Getting to know other trustees

New trustees should be made to feel welcome, valued and part of the team. At their first board meeting, the chair should formally welcome a new trustee and invite them to

- introduce themselves
- say why they wanted to become a trustee
- say something about how they feel they can contribute to the work of the trustee board

Some organisations ask new trustees to write a short CV or biography for circulation with the board papers.

Existing members of the committee should introduce themselves to the new person and describe briefly their involvement with the organisation.

**Tip:** New trustees could attend a first meeting in an observer role, before they are appointed or commit to the position.

## Options and ideas for trustee inductions

#### Use trustee inductions as a refresher for all trustees

When new trustees join a board, it's a good opportunity to refresh all trustees on governance and trusteeship essentials. This could be followed by a social event when trustees have an opportunity to get to know each other. The session may include:

- A briefing on the charity's history
- Review of important documents such as the governing document and other organisational policies
- Discussion of the duties and responsibilities of trustees
- Discussion of the skills involved in an effective board

#### Hold an induction workshop

For new trustees, it's vital they spend some time with the chair and, if applicable, key staff, to get a really good understanding of the Charity and what will be involved in the role.

You could offer this on a one to one basis over a drink or lunch; or, if your organisation is large or if you have an influx of several new trustees, this could form a group discussion and combine with a discussion about trustee roles and responsibilities (see above). Use the suggested topic areas below as prompts for the meeting:

- About the charity's structure or activities. This could include presentations from key staff if your organisation is large enough
- About the role of the board
- About the time-commitment involved in being a trustee
- Conduct and behaviour expected of a trustee (eg a discussion about conflicts of interest)
- Skills and interests new trustees could contribute to the organisation
- About the board's relationship with staff
- About any support or training opportunities available

### Mentoring or buddying a new trustee

It's useful to offer a new trustee the chance to learn informally about the role from somebody else in a similar position. You could team up each new trustee with an existing board member. Or, a new trustee may prefer to be mentored by a trustee from another charity.

### Accessing support, advice and information

Along with the Good Trustee Guide there are plenty of other materials and sources of support for board members.

Some useful websites for new trustees include:

- www.ncvo-vol.org.uk has a wide range of online factsheets and best practice guidance
- www.icsa.org.uk has a range of best practice guides
- www.charitycommission.gov.uk has guidance on the regulatory requirements of charities
- www.trusteenet.org.uk is an online network for trustees, run by Charity Trustee Networks

### Essential reading for trustees includes

- The Essential Trustee: What you Need to Know (CC3 – from the Charity Commission)
- Good Governance: The Code of Governance for the Voluntary and Community Sector
- National Occupational Standards for Trustees and Management Committee Members
- The Trustee Standards Toolkit

Local organisations should try contacting their local support agency (sometimes called a Council for Voluntary Service) to find out about support available close to home. For example, some areas organise a local trustee support network – see www.navca.org.uk for details of local support agencies and www.trusteenet.org.uk for details of local trustee networks.

### Reviewing or appraising the role of a trustee

A review meeting – often with the chair of the board – a couple of months after a new trustee has joined can help clarify any aspects of the new trustee's role that are unclear and find out whether further training, development or support (formal or informal) is required.

Some charities provide trustees with the opportunity for an 'appraisal' – a review of their role, usually every twelve months, where there is an opportunity to reflect on their role and performance as a trustee. You may consider setting this up for your organisation – if so, it is important to think about this at induction stage.

### Identifying learning and development opportunities

See chapter 17 for guidance on helping trustees identify their skills and development needs and chapter 18 for guidance and ideas on learning opportunities available for trustees.

## **Case study** – Advocacy West Lancashire

Advocacy West Lancashire recruited a number of new trustees with specific professional skills to its board in 2003. A very intensive induction programme was organised for the mostly new board members who all received trustee handbooks, the constitution, information about Advocacy West Lancashire and the Charity Commission booklet on trustee roles and responsibilities . A one day event on a Saturday involved briefings from the Chief Executive and the coordinators of each project.

AWL suggest: "Provide proper induction and support to harness the potential of your new trustees and develop their teamwork"

## **Case study** – Patrick McCurry, management committee, Mind Tower Hamlets

"All new trustees are given a pack describing their role and key policies in the organisation, such as the strategic plan. The first committee meeting following the AGM is an induction meeting. We split into small groups and were asked to divide a list of topics between operational and strategic responsibility. This is an important issue, as it's very easy for trustee boards to end up discussing operational matters when their job is to focus on the strategic questions."

## **Case study** – Nathalie Mununga – a young trustee at a local YMCA

"I realised I had something to give. I have experience working with children and young people, and am young myself. I think it's important to young people to have a voice, especially in organisations that are working on their behalf.

"I was approached by my local YMCA. They had seen the work I do with children and young people to promote inter-cultural integration and they wanted me to share my expertise with their Youth board."

**What I enjoy about being a trustee . . .and what I don't**
"There is a lot of responsibility, but I was given training on what's involved. I'm also able to ask other trustees who have experience that I don't. I've learnt a lot by being a trustee. I've been able to improve my English which is not my first language – actually it's my third! I now have experience of speaking in public and I feel more confident. "

**What's involved in being a trustee**
"I get involved in a wide range of issues from strategic planning and making policy for the organisation to taking decisions on personnel. I usually attend one meeting per month of three hours. I find it quite easy to fit around my working life. "

**What I bring to being a trustee**
"I bring my experience of working with young people, good financial skills and first-hand experience of being a young woman!"

**What tips would I give?**
"Be clear about what you can offer and what you want to get out of it. That way both you and the organisation benefit. It's easy to think you are too busy – but you can make the time for it. Finally don't be scared. Of course you can't know everything from the beginning. But you will learn, and people will help you – especially if you ask."

## Checklist for new trustees

Provide copies of the checklist below for new trustees: they can use it to record progress and ensure that their induction process covers all essential aspects of the role.

| Activity | ✓ | Comments |
|---|---|---|
| Have you received an induction pack including the organisation's governing document and annual report and accounts? | | |
| Have you been offered an induction programme? | | |
| Do you have a statement of your roles and responsibilities as a trustee and chair? | | |
| Have you identified what you can offer by way of skills, experiences and knowledge? | | |
| Do you have a copy of any trustee documents and policies (eg a code of practice)? | | |
| Do you know when the organisation was set up and its history? | | |
| Do you know the aims of the organisation? | | |
| Do you know about the activities of the organisation? | | |
| Do you know how your organisation is funded? | | |
| Do you know about the key issues facing the organisation? | | |
| Do you know about future projects or activities planned? | | |
| Do you know about other organisations or people your organisation has networks or special relationships with? | | |
| Do you understand the structure of the organisation and your role in it? | | |
| Do you understand the staff and volunteer structure and your relationship with staff and volunteers? | | |
| Do you understand your role and responsibilities and expected duties as a trustee? | | |
| Have you met with trustees and the chief executive (if there is one) and had a visit to premises or activities? | | |
| Have you met and got to know the other trustees and got their contact details? | | |
| Do you know how the work of the organisation relates to initiatives undertaken by other organisations? | | |
| Do you have support or training needs and are they being addressed? | | |
| Do you feel you are ready to take on your role? | | |
| Do you think the board needs to review its induction programme? | | |

# 21

# Effective meetings and decision-making

## 21.1

### Introduction

A board can only carry out its role effectively if it maintains strong decision-making processes and procedures. The 12 responsibilities of the board outlined in Part One require trustees to act collectively, with the board meeting as the main focus of discussion and decision-making.

# 21.2

## Board meeting basics

### Types of meetings

Trustees are typically involved in the following types of meetings:

- board meetings – formal meetings of the charity's trustee board as required by the charity's governing document, where trustees discuss business and take decisions
- general meetings – meetings of the charity's membership (if there is one) as required by the governing document, where members discuss issues, receive reports and take decisions
- sub-committee meetings – sub committees of the trustee board as set out in the governing document and/or as agreed by the board or membership
- advisory or working groups – other groups of trustees, staff, members, users or stakeholders, usually advisory, that provide information or advice for trustees or carry out detailed work
- other meetings – social, fundraising or other meetings for a particular purpose, that trustees typically attend but that are not directly related to the governance of the organisation

Remember that trustees may wear different 'hats' at different meetings. For example, at a trustee board meeting, trustees will be expected to act collectively and take formal decisions in their role as a charity trustee. At a sub-committee meeting, however, trustees that attend the meeting will be in a different role, expected to act within the terms of reference of the sub-committee: their duties and responsibilities as a member of the committee will be as set out in the terms of reference. For a discussion about the different role trustees can play or 'hats' they can wear in an organisation, see section 11.3.

### How many people should be present at a trustee board meeting?

The quorum is the minimum number of voting members who must be present for a meeting's decisions to be valid. This should be set out in your charity's governing document.

### Who should chair the meeting?

The chair of trustees is responsible for chairing the meetings of the trustee board. Your governing document may set out procedures governing what happens if the chair is not present. The chair should:

- understand their responsibilities in chairing the meeting and any formal procedures that govern the conduct of the meeting – these may be set out in the charity's governing document or other procedures
- understand the issues to be addressed in the meeting – such as the charity's financial position and any advice that is to be considered
- ensure that a proper agenda has been drawn up, in consultation with all relevant parties
- keep discussions focused, stimulate discussion and draw out quiet members
- be clear as to the status of participants at a board meeting – trustees, staff, advisors or observers
- recognise a potential decision when one arises
- ensure that decisions are clearly minuted

# 21.3

### Can our trustees meet by telephone or video conference?

Participants in a meeting must be able to see and hear each other for the decisions at the meeting to be valid – unless your governing document specifies otherwise. Video-conferencing is a valid form of meeting (unless prohibited by your governing document) but telephone conference is not (unless it is allowed by your governing document).

If you regularly conduct board meetings using video conference facilities, the Charity Commission recommend that all trustee boards hold at least one physical meeting of all trustees per year – further information in Charity Commission publication Charities and Meetings (CC48).

## Running a board meeting

### The Agenda

As a rule of thumb, efficient meeting agendas include two or three substantive items at most. These are the decision-making and monitoring issues that your trustee board must consider. Incidental information – which doesn't require discussion or a decision by the board – can be studied outside of meetings.

## A typical board agenda

1) Apologies, welcome and agenda review
2) Minutes of last meeting
3) Matters arising not covered elsewhere on the agenda
4) Internal committee matters (e.g., new members)
5) Financial report
6) Funding and fundraising
7) Staff matters (for larger organisations a report from the senior employee is usual)
8) Activities or issues specific to this meeting
9) Any other business
10) Date of future meetings

## Ideas for improving board agendas

### Strategic agendas

The strategic planning process (see chapter 6) may identify strategic priorities for the organisation which can then be used to structure meetings of the trustee board. For example, each board meeting could be planned around a central strategic issue.

### Consent agenda

One way of avoiding too much time on repetitive items is to run a 'consent agenda'. This is a component of the meeting where routine items and resolutions are grouped together and are voted on without discussion. If a member requests it beforehand an item can be removed from the consent agenda to be separated out for discussion.

### CIA

This technique has been used in a housing trust and stands for Control, Influence and Accept. Each agenda item is classified into one of three categories:

- Control – is the item a decision for the board to make or action to be taken?
- Influence – is the item one which the board/committee can influence or shape the scope of?
- Accept – is it a recommendation to be accepted or a proposal to be signed off by the board?

If there are too many 'A's then perhaps the board needs to rethink its role in the organisation – is it simply rubber-stamping other people's decisions?

### Board papers and information

John Carver, a management consultant, describes three types of board information:

- Decision information: used to make decisions, such as agreeing the organisation's strategic plan. This type of information looks to the future and is designed to measure performance.
- Monitoring information: enables the board to assess whether the organisation's plans are being met. It looks to the past and provides a specific survey of performance against criteria. An example is the annual review of an organisation's strategic plan.
- Incidental information: for the general information of the board and not related to board action. Committee reports may fall into this category.

The following is an example of a schedule for circulating information to board members:

**Two weeks before the board meeting**

- Agenda
- Information categorised as being either for discussion, information or decision
- Financial information

**At least two weeks before the board meeting at which it is discussed**

- Annual budget
- Audit report
- Strategic plan

# 21.4

**After each board meeting**

- Minutes
- Notice of next meeting.

**Monthly**

- Financial report
- Significant published articles about the organisation.

**Quarterly**

- Financial report

**Regularly, when appropriate**

- Memo from the chief executive or chair summarising current activities, accomplishments and needs
- Updated material for the trustee board handbook
- Advance copies of publications, brochures or promotional material
- Annual report

### Taking and using minutes

The minutes are a formal record of what has happened at a board meeting. Minutes are an invaluable source of information for those at the meeting as well as for those who could not make the meeting.

Taking minutes is not an easy skill so make sure your minute taker has support and training if necessary and has a general awareness of the topics to be discussed.

Good minutes are

- a true and accurate record of what happened at the meeting – including what was decided and who was actioned to carry it out
- clear and concise about the main points of discussion

Minutes should always be circulated as quickly as possible otherwise they can become out of date! Usually, the minutes of a meeting are formally agreed at the next meeting of trustees, signed by the chair and filed in a minute book as a formal record of decisions taken. The minute book should be kept in a safe place.

## Improving board meetings

### Participating in meetings

Whether you are a new trustee, or just want to learn more about an unfamiliar subject, remember the following:

- Learn about the issues which are going to be discussed
- Listen to others during the meeting
- Think before you speak
- Speak clearly and be brief
- Do not be afraid to speak
- Be reasonable and listen to other people's points of view
- Let go! Even if you disagree with a decision, in the end you may have to let go if there is a broader consensus of opinion.

### Essentials of good decision-making

Good decision-making is generally the result of a systematic process. The main stages of decision-making may be summarised as:

- clarification – gather the facts and be clear about the proposal. Decision may have to be deferred whilst further clarification is sought or advice sought
- debate – get a broad cross-section of view points. Allow all the alternatives to be aired
- decision – try to achieve consensus but do not delay unnecessarily. If necessary put it to a vote.

## Decision making checklist

Does your board receive adequate information on which to base its decisions?

Does it have the power to make the decisions?

Does the board take advice when not confident in making a decision?

Have a range of possible options, solutions or strategies been identified?

Are all decisions accurately recorded?

Is it clear who is responsible for implementing decisions?

Are your board's decisions reported to those affected by them?

Does your board review the implementation of its decisions?

### Electronic communication

Email, telephone conferencing and the internet have opened up many new possibilities for improving the information systems of boards. These include:

- circulating board agendas by email
- using web 'chat' facilities for informal discussions
- emailing draft funding applications for comment
- web pages containing latest information and updates about the organisation
- video conferencing, which reduces the costs of involving overseas participants.

Protocols are key and it's important to note the following:

- Know the legal restrictions over conducting virtual board meetings (see above)
- Email is convenient but beware of excluding trustees from discussions or information just because they don't have access to email
- Will trustees want to print out lengthy reports on their home computers?
- Does your expenses policy cover the cost of internet connections and the cost of paper and printing materials by trustees at home?
- Don't be tempted to shorten deadlines for sending out papers just because they are being emailed!

## Better meetings checklist

- Start and end meetings on time and assign time-limits to agenda items
- Schedule meetings for times when most participants can make it. Don't assume participants can take time off work or devote weekends to meetings. Remember school holidays and religious festivals
- Hold meetings in a place that is convenient, secure and accessible for all participants
- Provide transport and/or reimburse legitimate travel expenses
- Circulate the agenda at least a week in advance with papers
- Offer refreshments
- Schedule in breaks
- Prepare the meeting room in advance providing supplies such as name tags, flip charts, overhead projectors, pens, paper and video equipment
- Make sure that seating is comfortable and that all participants can see, hear and be seen by each other
- Appoint a secretary or individual who will 'service' the meeting by providing administrative support – preparing meeting rooms , circulating necessary papers and taking minutes (see below). This is sometimes carried out by more than one person.

# 21.5

## Other meetings

### General meetings

Membership organisations will hold general meetings of all members as required by the organisation's governing document. Such meetings are held in order that members can carry out their formal responsibilities as set out in the governing document. Annual General Meetings often include the election of trustees and these and other General Meetings may, for example, be called to approve changes to the governing document. The specific responsibilities of members, and the procedures for holding meetings, will vary depending on your organisation's legal structure and the content of your organisation's governing document.

## Companies Act 2006 – changes to general meetings

The Companies Act 2006 brought in a number of changes in company law governing the holding and conduct of general meetings. Some changes override the provisions in a Company's Memorandum and Articles of Association whereas other provisions require the documents to be changed.

An important new provision in the Companies Act is the right for a member to appoint a proxy to vote on their behalf. This right exists regardless of what the articles say, and all Companies must ensure they comply with this new right.

A number of provisions – the notice period for general meetings and the deadline circulating accounts to members, for example – have been changed to simplify company administration but usually require a change to the organisation's governing documents.

The changes are too detailed to set out in the Good Trustee Guide and it is recommended that companies check their governing documents and practices against the new Acts – a useful summary is available on Sandy Adirondack's website at www.sandy-a.co.uk

Sub-committee meetings

The rules governing sub-committees may be set out in your organisation's governing document or in associated standing orders, by laws or rules. You may also have agreed terms of reference for sub-committees. See below for more information.

Best practice

Much of the best practice concerning better board meetings can be adapted to other meetings, but remember to ensure any procedures you adopt are consistent with your governing document and with regulatory requirements.

# 21.6

## Effective governance structures

The size and composition of a trustee board, and the way it relates to other parts of the charity's governance structure (members, sub-committees, advisors and so on) can have a major impact on how efficient, and how effective, trustees are in carrying out their duties.

It has been increasingly common in recent years for charities to review governance structures, to ensure that the structure and composition of the board is effective and best meeting the charity's needs.

# 21.7

## Board size

A survey of governing boards in England and Wales by the Open University Business School found an average board size of 9.5[7]. However, the research also showed that the size of boards varied dramatically, between 4 and 150 members. The size of a board is often a result of several factors, including its legal framework, stage of development and its size and income.

Boards need to be large enough to bring in a range of skills, backgrounds and have enough people to carry out the work, but small enough to work effectively as a team. The consensus of opinion favours smaller rather than larger boards and suggests an optimum number of between 8 and 12.

Dangers of...

**...too large a board?**

- A dominant inner core and the marginalisation of some individual trustees
- Inefficient discussion and decision-making.

**...too small a board?**

- Overload of work on a small number of individuals
- May not bring enough skills and perspectives
- May not be 'legitimate' in representing stakeholder perspectives.

[7] *Recent Trends in Charity Governance and Trusteeship* (Chris Cornforth – NCVO, 2001)

# 21.8

## Board composition

### Trustees with specific roles

As organisations change and develop, so too do the roles of specific board members, particularly those usually known as 'honorary officers' (see chapter 4). For example:

- the duties of a chair may include responsibilities agreed as a matter of custom and practice or because of the skills a particular individual can bring.
- As an organisation grows in size, the duties of a treasurer are likely to change from a hands on individual involved in book-keeping, to a role more focused on financial oversight, providing advice and reports to the board.
- The role of secretary can change with an organisation's legal structure. For example, companies limited by guarantee were until recently required to appoint a Company Secretary. In larger organisations this role is often taken by a member of staff.
- The role of vice chair is one that can be useful either as a deputy for the chair, or as a position for an incoming or outgoing chair.

It is good practice to periodically review the role and contribution of honorary officers or other trustees with specific roles, to ensure that the range of positions and their duties best meet the needs of the charity. See chapter 4 for guidance on the duties and responsibilities of trustees with specific roles and chapters 19 and 20 for guidance on recruitment and induction.

### Trustees appointed by outside organisations

Some organisations give the power to appoint certain trustees to outside organisations (see chapter 1). It is good practice periodically to review the role of trustees appointed in this way:

- Do trustees appointed by outside organisations fully understand their role as a charity trustee?
- Do potential conflicts of interest between a trustee's role and their external role exist?
- If so, do trustees follow a conflicts of interest policy?
- If so, are any such conflicts manageable (this may be particularly significant if there is a funding relationship between the charity and the organisation making the appointment)?
- Does the inclusion of appointed trustees improve the governance of the charity?
- Would it be more appropriate for such appointments to be made to non-voting positions in an advisory capacity to the board?

### Questions to consider

How can your board attract the 'right' number of people with the right skills, knowledge, experience and perspectives to join the board? (Note: what is right for one organisation and its stage of development may not be right for another!)

Are there ways of utilising the skills and experience of individuals other than using them as members of the board? (For example, experts, co-opted non-voting individuals, advisory groups.)

If there is a "two-tier board" – for example, a large board of trustees and a smaller executive sub-committee – is it time to review the composition and effectiveness of the board and its committee, to avoid the risk of an "inner circle" dominating the trustee board?

In a large board (e.g. in excess of 19 members) how can effective governance and good teamworking be enhanced?

# 21.9

Remember that any changes you make must be consistent with your governing document and should involve consultation with the organisation that makes the appointment. It is quite likely that any change will require a change to your governing document.

NCVO is currently updating its guidance for local authority members who are appointed to the boards of charities. Please contact NCVO for more information.

## Board relationships

### Sub-committees

Sub-committees play an important role in the lives of boards. They can help the board save time by dealing with the detail of board issues separately from the main meeting and are a valuable training ground for new board members, future chairs and a mechanism for involving trustees and outside advisers.

However, too many committees can mean that the board loses overall oversight and that decision-making and delegation lines are not clear. Or committees may find themselves starved of any authority or resources by an over-controlling board.

**Advantages of sub-committees**

- an effective way of utilising board member expertise and external advisers
- helps to foster good working relations with staff
- potential trustees and advisers can be invited to join sub-committees
- chairing a sub-committee is a good training ground for a future chair.

**Disadvantages**

- board may lose their oversight of the charity
- confusion over the respective roles of the board, sub-committees and staff
- board may be unwilling to challenge the decisions of 'expert' sub-committees
- decision-making process can become lengthy
- overload of meetings
- indefinite lifespan.

**Key principles**

- Committees serve the board, not the other way round
- They should not take decisions on behalf of the board unless it has been explicitly authorised
- Where committees replicate internal management divisions there could be a confusion between board and management roles
- Take a flexible approach, which allows your board to create sub-committees when the need arises and to disband them when the need is fulfilled (try changing terminology and calling committees working groups or advisory groups and see how they are then perceived)
- Have a clear remit and set of guidelines ('terms of reference') setting out role and powers (see below). You may have a code which covers overall the role and remit of committees for your board and the expected membership of each by board members.
- Know which 'hat' you are wearing. Trustees who serve on a sub-committee should also be able to distinguish between their role as board member and their role as sub-committee member.

# 21.10

### Working parties

Working parties are an alternative to sub-committees and are typically task-oriented – focus on one particular topic – and time-limited – finish as soon as work is complete. An example of a working party is a group set up to oversee a governance review (see Part four).

### Advisory groups

An advisory group – council, committee or assembly – is often a representative grouping of users or stakeholders that provide advice and feedback to trustees. Such a council may be formally elected by members, and the council in turn may elect some or all of the trustee board, although the exact relationships vary. Some councils are purely advisory and are set up informally.

The creation of such councils has been increasingly popular in recent years, particularly for boards with a large, elected structure, as a way of involving users and stakeholders but without making the trustee board too large and unwieldy (see below).

### Terms of reference

All sub-committees , working parties and advisory groups need terms of reference which give a clear indication of what is expected and to whom the group is accountable. Terms of reference should include the following:

- name of the committee/group
- membership – including office where appropriate (e.g. the honorary treasurer and three trustees) and voting rights
- purpose – brief statement of why the committee exists
- delegated authority – whether it has decision-making powers or is purely advisory
- frequency – how often meetings are to be held
- duration – maximum length of meetings
- chair – the name or office of person acting as the chair
- serviced by – person acting as secretary or minute taker
- reporting procedure – the committee or board to whom it must report
- quorum – the minimum number of people who must be present at a meeting including any officer (e.g. five members of the sub-committee including at least three trustees and either the chair or vice-chair).

Remember: terms of reference must be consistent with your governing document.

## Some models of board size and composition

### The large representative board

One model that used to be common in large membership organisations is the large elected trustee board (say, with more than 30 members), where trustees are elected from membership, often from different sections of the membership based around geographical areas or other groupings. This model has become less popular in recent years, often because it is felt that such boards are too large to work effectively. A number of organisations have opted to move away from this type of model towards a small board / advisory council model (see 'mixed board' and 'advisory council' below).

### The small 'skills based' board

Another model of governance – often used by those without a large membership structure or where the only members are the current board members – comprises a small trustee board (say, less than 10 members), with trustees appointed by the board based on an assessment of the skills, experiences and perspectives required by the board.

### The mixed board

A trend in recent years, particularly for boards with a large, elected structure, has been to create a smaller trustee board which is partly elected by members (or representatives of members) and partly appointed by the other trustees (such appointments sometimes called co-options). This is sometimes backed up by a larger advisory group or council of members (see below). This model has the advantage of a democratic structure, but small enough to take effective decisions and with the option of the board being able to draw in additional skills and perspectives by appointing additional trustees themselves.

### The advisory council

Another trend in recent years, particularly for boards with a large, elected structure, has been to create a smaller trustee board (see above) backed by a larger, representative advisory council, group, committee or assembly. This development is often based on a recognition that effective governance needs a careful balance between the need to bring in the perspectives of users and stakeholders (which tends towards a larger decision making structure) and the need to ensure that trustees discharge their legal responsibilities via efficient and effective governance (which tends towards a smaller decision making structure).

In these cases, the responsibilities of the advisory group can vary: some are elected by members; some are partly appointed by outside agencies; some have the responsibility of electing some or all of the trustee board.

Further guidance on governance issues for membership organisations can be found in section 16.2 and in NCVO's Good Membership Guide.

## Checklist

Do you hold board meetings as required by the governing document?

If you hold 'virtual' meetings by telephone or video conferencing, do they comply with your governing document and regulatory guidance?

Do trustees receive information in advance of board meetings that is timely and in a format suitable to make decisions?

Do you need to review your current board and committee structure and composition to assess if it is currently serving the governance needs of your organisation?

Do all board members have a clear understanding of your organisation's committee structure and their involvement in it?

Do all your committees and working parties have written terms of reference?

Are all your committees and working parties clear about the extent of their delegated powers and who they report to?

Have you reviewed your board's size and composition to ensure it is fit for purpose?

# Part Four:

# Improving Governance

# 22

# Carrying out a governance review

## 22.1

### Introduction

The Code of Governance recommends that boards take time out periodically to review their own effectiveness and the effectiveness of the organisation. It is becoming increasingly common for charities to carry out governance reviews and there are now a number of different tools and approaches available.

A governance review is a systematic way of improving how your charity is governed and reviewing how effectively your board carries out its responsibilities.

A governance review can take place for many reasons and take many forms. A review may take place to explore how well the board works together, or may be part of a wider assessment of the way the charity is run. A governance review could be carried out as a self-assessment, via an informal discussion via a 1-1 appraisal of trustees, or via a quality system.

# 22.2

Why should organisations review their governance? What are the benefits of carrying out a review? The Governance Hub, in its publication Better Governance[1], listed six benefits that can arise from improving an organisation's governance:

1) strategic focus – better governance can help an organisation be healthier and make more robust long term decisions
2) risk focus – better governance can help trustees anticipate future risks and be better placed to make the most of new opportunities
3) mission focus – better governance can help ensure an organisation is using its resources to best meet its mission
4) reputation focus – better governance gives people confidence that your organisation is well run and effective
5) relationship focus – better governance helps ensure that the many voices in your organisation – users, staff, volunteers, funders and others – can input into decision making
6) learning focus – finally, better governance can help develop a more creative organisation that learns from experience and can respond to new challenges.

## Reviewing your governance – getting started

### Why do you want to carry out a governance review?

A good place to begin a governance review is to consider the motivation behind a desire to improve governance and to consider the practicalities of how you would like to take the process forward. Use the questions in the box below to help frame your approach. The answers should help you in choosing the most suitable approach to your governance review.

[1] *Better Governance: An Introduction to Measuring and Improving Board Effectiveness* (Mark Parker – Governance Hub, 2006)

## Governance review questionnaire

Use the questions below as a guide to help choose which approach to a governance review will best meet your charity's needs.

1) Why do you want to review and improve your governance? What changes do you want to make?
   - We want to look at the effectiveness of your board – its role, the way it works together as a team and how it makes decisions
   - We want to look at the effectiveness of individual trustees – their role and performance
   - We want to be sure our board and organisation is operating well with sound, up to date policies and procedures and sound governance arrangements
2) How do you want to carry out the review?
   - Using a comprehensive approach looking at governance within the context of the whole organisation
   - Using an approach that can be externally checked or accredited
   - By comparing our organisation with other similar organisations
   - By comparing our organisation to a sector-wide standard or set of principles
   - By using an off the shelf system that we can adapt to our needs
   - By using a self-assessment method
   - By using a questionnaire
   - Informally, perhaps via an 'away day' discussion with board members
3) How much do you want to commit in terms of time and resources?

   **Budget**
   - We have a reasonable budget to do this – we could engage a consultant or pay for an accredited system
   - We have little or no budget to do this – we prefer to do the work in house or choose an approach that is low cost or doesn't take a lot of time

   **Time**
   - We want to invest a considerable amount of time over a longer period
   - We want to invest a lot of time over a short period
   - We can only commit to a small amount of time, perhaps one or two meetings

## Governance review tools

### Specialist governance review tools

There are a number of toolkits or frameworks that can help a charity specifically review its governance arrangements and the effectiveness of its board.

**The Code of Governance** and accompanying Code of Governance Toolkit provide a systematic method of assessing how an organisation's governance compares to the principles set out in the Code. Since 2005 the Code has been widely used and promoted as a key good governance framework. The Code consists of seven principles of Good Governance (see chapter 5), each accompanied by a series of detailed principles.

The Toolkit can be used to carry out a systematic assessment of your charity's governance arrangements and the effectiveness of the board. The toolkit is designed so that a governance review can best meet the needs of your charity and the time and resources available. The toolkit is available to download free from the NCVO website (see resources section).

**The National Occupational Standards** for Trustees and Management Committee Members is also a framework for reviewing the effectiveness of an organisation's governance. The 'NOS' are particularly useful for reviewing the role and contribution (or 'appraisal') of individual trustees (see chapter 23).

There are also a range of other governance review tools developed by a variety of different organisations. For example, prior to the development of the Code, NCVO published **The Good Governance Action Plan**. This is designed as a quality system specifically for trustee boards, intended to help board members and staff evaluate the effectiveness of their board.

There are also more informal governance review methods that your board can adopt – for example checklists or questionnaires that can be used as a basis for discussion. See section 22.6 for examples and 22.5 for suggestions.

### Individual trustee reviews/appraisals

You may want to look specifically at the role, performance and support needs of individual trustees. These tools are sometimes called 'trustee appraisal' tools. An example of a framework that looks at the skills and competencies of individual trustees is the National Occupational Standards for Trustees and Management Committee Members. These approaches are explored further in Chapter 23.

### Benchmarking

Benchmarking is the process of comparing your organisation's performance with that of other organisations. You can benchmark governance in the same way that you can compare other aspects of your organisation's operations. An example of a benchmarking service that specifically looks at governance is BoardsCount. Benchmarking can also form part of a wider governance review.

### A governance review as part of a quality system

A quality assurance system is a systematic way of ensuring your organisation undertakes a continuous process of learning, developing and reviewing, usually by aiming to meet an agreed level of performance. Systems look at the quality of an organisation's governance alongside other areas of the organisation. An example of a quality assurance system that includes governance is PQASSO (Practical Quality Assurance System for Small Organisations) (see chapter 13).

Governance review comparison table

| Type of review | What is it? | Examples of tools | Useful when... | More information |
|---|---|---|---|---|
| Governance review | A periodic process of reflecting on the effectiveness of the board and the organisation's governance arrangements | Code of Governance Toolkit | You want to look specifically at the role and effectiveness of the board, and how the board is organised and supported | This chapter |
| Trustee appraisal | A process of reviewing the role, contribution and support needs of individual trustees | National Occupational Standards for Trustees and Management Committee Members | You want to look specifically at the individual trustee's role and needs | Chapter 23 |
| Benchmarking | A process of comparing an organisation's governance with other organisations | Boards Count | You want to compare your practices with another organisation | Chapter 13 (general information) |
| Quality system | A framework covering all aspects of an organisation's work, usually completed via self-assessment and often with an option of externally accreditation | PQASSO | You want to reach a consistent standard across the organisation (including its governance) | Chapter 13 |

# 22.3

## Governance reviews – meeting your needs

A governance review can be a large or a small piece of work depending on the needs of your board and the resources available. How much time can you commit to a governance review? Here are some ideas:

**... ten or twenty minutes?**
Reflection: your board may take a few minutes at the end of a meeting to consider:

- how well has this meeting gone?
- were there areas we lingered too long over?
- did we get too sidetracked at any point?
- do the decisions we reached seem to be the right ones?
- how could the meeting have been better?

If you only have a short space of time try dipping into the Code of Governance to discuss one or two principles or try one of the shorter exercises in the Code of Governance Toolkit. The Governance Hub has also published a pack of 26 cards, each including simple, illustrated explanations of some terms used in governance. The cards include questions or exercises aimed at helping you and your organisation reflect on how you operate as a board. Available from NCVO – see resources section.

**...one or two hours?**
In a longer discussion session, trustees could review their role against the summary Code of Governance (see exercise 1 in section 22.6, below). Or, one of the longer exercises in the Code of Governance Toolkit could be followed by an identification of action points. In this way, a short exercise can help provide a snapshot of the board's position, stimulate discussion and reflection and identify action points to be taken forward.

**... a longer period?**
The Code of Governance can be used over a longer period of time to carry out a comprehensive review of every aspect of your charity's governance.

See below for guidance on how to structure a bigger review.

# 22.4

## Organising the process and accessing support

Using working groups
A small working group could be established to oversee the governance review process.
The group's duties could involve: recommending an overall review process; carrying out detailed reviews of specific areas of the board's work; auditing documentation such as policies and procedures and the governing document; gathering evidence or administering a questionnaire; reporting back to the board with recommendations; or planning a board discussion or away day.

# 22.5

Accessing external support

Some organisations find it useful to hire an external consultant or facilitator for all or part of a governance review process. External input offers the advantage of providing outside expertise and an 'objective' perspective. It can be useful if the organisation's staff or trustees have limited time to invest in the more detailed aspects of the process. It also allows participants to be equally involved in discussions, because the management of the process or specific discussion sessions can be left to the facilitator. This can be particularly helpful for the chair who may otherwise take on, for example, the role of chairing an away day.

On the downside, your organisation may not be able to afford the cost of a consultant. And your board may not be happy or comfortable with a person from 'outside' involved in analysing what may be sensitive issues.

## Gathering information

A governance review involves building up a picture of how effectively your charity is governed. How, in practice, you create this picture will depend on the size and scope of your review and the information required

### Questionnaires

A common way of carrying out a governance review is to ask each board member to comment on the board's performance via a questionnaire or completion of a survey. The results are then collated into a report and discussed collectively. The advantage of this approach is that it can encourage trustees to be more open because of the confidential nature of the process. The disadvantage is that trustees may not want to fill out formal questionnaires and the process can be time-consuming if a large questionnaire is used or if you have a large trustee board. Where large questionnaires are used the process often takes place less frequently than once per year (e.g. every two years).

The Code of Governance can be used as the basis for a questionnaire survey. The full, or summary, versions of the Code have been adapted into survey form as part of the Code of Governance Toolkit and can be downloaded from the NCVO website.

### Audit of documents

A governance review will usually include a 'desk' review of documents and policies. Such a review can help you identify evidence of good practice (useful if you are adopting an approach like the Code of Governance Toolkit where you will be assessing your governance against a set of criteria) as well as being an opportunity to review the accuracy and consistency of policies and procedures. For example:

- Are key board policies and procedures in place? Can you find up to date role descriptions for trustees, a board conflicts of interest policy and a trustee induction pack? Have you compared the induction pack against the sample list of contents in chapter 19?
- Are there up to date and accurate terms of reference for sub-committees? Have you reviewed the governing document and compared it with terms of reference to ensure both are consistent?

### Group discussion

A group discussion can be a valuable way for the board to reflect on its role and performance. Collective discussion of responsibilities and relationships can help trustees gain a greater insight into their role and help achieve a consensus in identifying priorities and action points for a governance review.

Group discussions can take place in a variety of ways. For some organisations, their governance review might take place entirely within a short group discussion – for example, reviewing the twelve responsibilities (see exercises below) and agreeing action points. Other organisations may carry out an audit or questionnaire and use the findings as the basis for a carefully planned away day.

A slot at each board meeting could be used to discuss one or two aspects of good governance. Or, one longer board meeting each year could incorporate a board review. Some organisations take a few minutes at the end of each meeting to reflect on the board's performance.

An away day (see box) to review your board's performance can be productive. It has the advantage of taking board members out of the meeting room environment and allowing time for in-depth discussion of board progress.

The Code of Governance and associated Toolkit can be used as the basis for a group discussion. For example:

- the Toolkit contains a range of practical training exercises based on the Code (eg on roles and responsibilities or board/staff relationships)
- the seven Code principles can form the basis of a general discussion about how the board carries out its responsibilities
- the Toolkit provides guidance and example exercises on how to organise a group discussion as the introduction to a more comprehensive board review.

## Planning an away day

1) Prepare
Advance preparation helps set the agenda for the day and helps gain ownership by the board of the agenda. Individual questionnaires can be a way of identifying topics for discussion; or a discussion at a board meeting, perhaps using one of the shorter questionnaires (see exercise 3), could also help prioritise topics.

2) Plan
A small working group can meet to decide on the topics for the day, based on information gathered. The group can consider practicalities such as:

- do we need a facilitator?
- should we invite a guest speaker?
- should we break into small groups to discuss each topic?
- is the day for the board only or are staff invited?

A clear and agreed structure will avoid the day being bogged down in discussions that can't be resolved on the day. And remember the golden rule: don't try to cover too much in a day!

3) On the day
Make sure you leave space at the end of the day for agreeing next steps and closure.

Be realistic about what can be agreed in a single day – many issues will need further consideration at future meetings, so try not to make expectations too high

Your away day should:

- have clear and meaningful objectives
- enable all trustees to participate
- involve activities to encourage trustee input
- include a facility for feedback and further action
- be fun!

## Governance review case study – Diabetes UK

Diabetes UK benchmarked their annual board performance and strategy review against the Code of Good Governance.

The organisation's governance team reviewed compliance with the full Code of Governance, and trustees were asked to complete a questionnaire based on a summary of the Code.

The output from both of these exercises was considered at an 'away weekend' and recommendations to address areas of concern were put to their performance review subcommittee.

The organisation felt that the Code helps bring a source of authority to a governance review, and can give subsequent recommendations more legitimacy.

## Governance review case study – Allergy UK

Allergy UK developed a code of governance and a set of supporting procedures for their organisation, drawing on the national Code of Governance. The first step was to develop a draft Code relevant to their organisation. Part of the production of a draft included a review of the organisation's policies and procedures against the draft Code.

The draft Code was circulated to trustees by the chief executive, and comments were sought in order to refine the draft. The draft was also sent to staff who were able to explore how the Code affected them via a one day staff workshop.

A further two day workshop was held with trustees and key staff to review the work done and prepare final versions of the documents. These were then formally adopted at the next trustees meeting.

The final Code includes the organisation's mission statement, values, code of governance, governance procedures and policies and organisational procedures and policies. It is now reviewed by the entire staff team annually and forms a key part of staff induction.

As well as improving the way the organisation works, the process of developing the code has deepened relationships between trustees and staff.

Allergy UK's lessons and tips: "Design a process that allows staff and trustees to work together. Ensure you look not only at the code of governance but also how it links with other policies and procedures in the organisation. Allow enough time, including from the CEO and senior management. The process in Allergy UK took circa three months."

# 22.6

## Example governance review exercises

### Exercise 1

A governance review using the summary Code of Governance

The Code of Governance has seven principles, with a number of supporting principles and detailed principles under each heading. You can use the supporting or main principles to carry out a short assessment of your governance or the detailed principles to carry out a more in depth assessment.

The example exercise below reproduces one of the seven Code principles as an example of how the summary principles can be used as the basis for a short governance review or discussion.

The full survey template for both the summary and full Code of Governance is available to download from the NCVO website.

| Principle D – The High Performance Board | Satisfied | Quite satisfied | Not satisfied | Notes |
|---|---|---|---|---|
| Trustees should understand their duties and responsibilities and have a statement defining them | | | | |
| The board should organise its work to ensure that it makes the most effective use of the time, skills and knowledge of trustees | | | | |
| Trustees should ensure that they receive the advice and information the need in order to make good decisions | | | | |
| The trustees should have the diverse range of skills, experience and knowledge needed to run the organisation effectively | | | | |
| Trustees should ensure that they receive the necessary induction, training and ongoing support needed to discharge their duties | | | | |
| The Board should make proper arrangements for the supervision, support, appraisal and remuneration of its chief executive | | | | |

### Exercise 2

Short board assessment

The table below can be used as the basis for a quick board assessment. It is based on the 'twelve essential board responsibilities' – see pages 11-12 for a fuller description of each heading.

| Area of responsibility | We do this by: | We can improve this by: | Action points |
|---|---|---|---|
| Set and maintain vision, mission and values | | | |
| Develop strategy | | | |
| Establish and monitor policies | | | |
| Ensure compliance with the governing document | | | |
| Ensure accountability | | | |
| Ensure compliance with the law | | | |
| Maintain proper fiscal oversight | | | |
| Respect the role of staff / volunteers | | | |
| Maintain effective board performance | | | |
| Promote the organisation | | | |
| **Where staff are employed:** | | | |
| Set up employment procedures | | | |
| Select and support the chief executive | | | |

**Exercise 3**

Sample board self-assessment questionnaire

This short questionnaire can be completed by trustees or used as a basis for discussion:

- Does your board set clear objectives for the organisation?
- Does your board establish the organisation's priorities?
- Has your board got procedures for ensuring that assets are used effectively and efficiently?
- Does your board monitor the work of the organisation?
- Does your board monitor compliance with legislation, such as charity and company law?
- Does your board monitor that reporting to donors, staff, volunteers and other stakeholders is carried out?
- Does your board appraise the performance of the director and his/her management of the work of the staff?
- Do all members of your board attend meetings regularly and prepare thoroughly for them? Does your governing document give you powers to delegate to:
  – Sub-committees?
  – Staff?
- Are your powers of delegation adequate? If not, do they need revision?

## Checklist

Does your board periodically carry out a governance review, either formally or informally?

Do you act on the findings of the review?

# 23

# Trustee review or appraisal

## 23.1

### Introduction

Part Three highlighted the importance of reviewing with new trustees the contribution they are making and any support needs they have. This principle could be extended to all trustees.

An individual assessment is a way for trustees to evaluate their own personal contribution. It could highlight individual strengths and weaknesses, support needs and areas where trustees could use their own skills, experience and interests additionally to benefit the charity. Such an assessment can be carried out via an 'informal review' or a more formal 'appraisal'.

A sample list of questions is provided at the end of this chapter, designed to help individual trustees to reflect on how they perform as a trustee. Also important are a trustee's own development needs:

- What development needs do I have?
- What kind of support do I need from the board?
- What motivates me in the role?
- What would I like to be done differently?
- What enriches my experience as a trustee?
- How would I like to contribute to the board?

# 23.2

## National Occupational Standards for Trustees and Management Committee Members

The National Occupational Standards for Trustees and Management Committee members set out the functions and responsibilities of individual trustees. They provide a way of assessing the performance of individual trustees and the knowledge and understanding they need to carry out their role.

The NOS are a useful framework to help review and support an individual trustee's contribution.

The Trustee and Management Committee National Occupational Standards – Toolkit (Liza Ramrayka – NCVO, 2006) – available free to download from NCVO – contains some 15 different exercises that individual trustees, or the board, can use, to develop their skills and contribution.

## Ideas for carrying out individual trustee reviews

### Questionnaire

A simple questionnaire could be sent out to trustees once a year asking for each trustee's comments on their own performance (see exercise 1, below, for an example).

### Review meeting

A meeting with the chair once a year would allow a trustee to reflect on their experience as a board member. If a more formal appraisal system is to be used then this meeting could refer back to action points set the previous year or at the beginning of their term of office.

### Code of conduct

At the basic level all trustees should have a role description and many agree a code of conduct (see chapter 4). A review of a trustee's role and contribution can reference to these and provide an opportunity to highlight where issues may have occurred (for example, in conflicts of interest).

### Appraisal

Some charities now appraise the performance of board members and that of the chair. The approach taken varies. It can take the form of an informal discussion, often between the chair and each trustee. Alternatively, a pre-meeting questionnaire can be drawn up for the trustee to identify their strengths, areas of improvement, support needs and where they would like to develop in the future. It is important that whoever conducts the appraisal is skilled in giving feedback because of the sometimes sensitive nature of the topic.

Appraisal of the chair is more of a challenge because there is no 'manager' of the chair. One approach is for the deputy chair to speak informally to each trustee about the chair's performance and then feed this back in a session with the chair.

### Linking review or appraisal to learning and development

A review or 'appraisal' – of whatever format – is a good opportunity to explore individual trustees' learning and development needs. See chapter 18 for more information.

# 23.3

## Individual trustee review exercises

### Exercise 1

How do you contribute?

Ask each trustee to complete the questionnaire. Use it as the basis for a one to one with each trustee and the chair, or collate the results for a board discussion.

1) I understand the organisation's mission.
2) I support the mission.
3) I am knowledgeable about the organisation's major programmes and services.
4) I follow trends and important developments in areas related to the work of the organisation.
5) I read the organisation's financial statements.
6) I understand the organisation's financial statements.
7) I act knowledgeably and prudently when making recommendations about how the organisation's funds should be invested or spent.
8) I advise and assist the chief executive when asked.
9) I have a good working relationship with the chief executive.
10) I have a good working relationship with other board members.
11) I recommend qualified individuals with relevant skills and experience as possible nominees for the board.
12) I prepare for and participate in board and committee meetings as well as other activities of the organisation.
13) I willingly volunteer and use my special skills to further the organisation's mission.
14) I complete all assignments in a responsible and timely manner.
15) I keep an eye on the organisation's public image in the media and among members of the community.
16) I take advantage or opportunities to enhance the organisation's public image by speaking to individuals, business and community leaders about the organisation.
17) I speak for the organisation only when authorised to do so.
18) I respect the confidentiality of the board's executive sessions.
19) I suggest agenda items for future board and committee meetings.
20) I focus my attention on long-term and significant policy issues rather than short-term administrative matters.
21) I avoid burdening the staff with special requests for favours.
22) I see to it that my communications with staff below the chief executive never undermine the relationship between the chief executive and his or her staff.
23) I avoid in fact and in perception conflicts of interest that might embarrass the board or organisation and disclose to the board in a timely manner any possible conflicts.
24) My opinions are heard and considered in the boardroom.
25) I find serving on the board to be a satisfying experience.

Exercise 2

Quality checker

Individual trustees can complete this questionnaire to reflect on what they bring to the board by way of qualities and skills. Taken from the National Occupational Standards for Trustees and Management Committee Members Toolkit.

## Checklist

Do you provide an opportunity for individual trustees to reflect on their role, contribution and support needs as a board member?

| Quality | I can demonstrate this by: | I can learn more about this by: |
|---|---|---|
| be committed to the purpose, objects and values of the organisation | | |
| be constructive about other trustees' opinions in discussions, and in response to staff members' contributions at meetings | | |
| be able to act reasonably and responsibly when undertaking such duties and performing tasks | | |
| be able to maintain confidentiality on sensitive and confidential information | | |
| be supportive of the values (and ethics) of the organisation | | |
| understand the importance and purpose of meetings, and be committed to preparing for them adequately and attending them regularly | | |
| be able to analyse information and, when necessary, challenge constructively | | |
| be able to make collective decisions and stand by them | | |
| be able to respect boundaries between executive and governance functions | | |

Part Five:

# Further Information and Support

# 24

# Resources

The Good Trustee Guide aims to provide trustees with a comprehensive overview of their roles and responsibilities – but it is not exhaustive. There are a great many sources of information and support covering all aspects of the governance and management of voluntary organisations. Contact details can be found in the next chapter.

# Part one: The Essentials

### The Essentials

Charity Commission publication *The Essential Trustee* (CC3)

Charity Commission publication *Finding new trustees – What charities need to know* (CC30) and associated operational guidance on disqualification and waivers (OG41 & OG42)

Charity Commission *Statement from the Commission regarding young people under 18 years old as charity trustees,* (linked from Charity Commission publication CC30)

Charity Commission publication *Users on board* (CC24)

Charity Commission publication CC30 *Finding New Trustees: What charities need to know*

Companies House *Directors and Secretaries Guide* (GBA1)

*Good Governance: A Code for the Voluntary and Community Sector* available from the NCVO website.

*National Occupational Standards for Trustees and Management Committee Members* available from the UK Workforce Hub website.

*Guidence in the legal status of Charity Chief Executives* (acevo, 2006)

### Charitable status – general

Charity Commission publication *Registering as a Charity* (CC21)

*Charitable Status: A Practical Handbook* (Julian Blake – Directory of Social Change, 2008)

Charity Commission *Charities and Public Benefit statutory guidance* – available on the Charity Commission website under About Charities – Public Benefit.

### Charitable status and political activities

*Good Campaigns Guide: Campaigning for Impact* (Jim Coe and Tess Kingham – NCVO, 2005)

Charity Commission guidance *Speaking Out – Guidance on Campaigning and Political Activity by Charities* (Version March 2008)

*Tips on good practice in campaigning* (Jim Coe and Tess Kingham – NCVO, 2007)

*Campaigning for success: How to cope if you achieve your campaign goal* (Jonathan Ellis – NCVO, 2007)

*Campaigning in Collaboration* (Sarah Shimmin and Gareth Coles – NCVO, 2007)

*Challenges to effectiveness and impact* (Sarah Shimmin and Gareth Coles – NCVO, 2007)

### Charitable status and trading

HMRC *Charity trading and business activities* website page

Charity Commission publication *Trustees, trading and tax* (CC35)

*Charities, Trading and the Law* (Stephen Lloyd and Alice Faure Walker – Jordan Publishing, 2008)

Charity Commission publication *Charities and Fundraising* (CC20)

Companies House guidance booklet *Company Formation* (GBF1)

### Legal structures

Charity Commission publication *Choosing and Preparing a Governing Document* (CC22).

*Governance and Organisational Structures* (Governance Hub, 2007) – an on-line guide about the common organisational and legal structures, including newer forms outlined in the Charities Act 2006 including Community Interest Companies and Charitable Incorporated Organisations. Free to download from the NCVO website.

Charity Commission publication *Changing your Charity's Governing Document* (CC36)

Charity Commission web page *Setting up a company to replace an existing charity* (see About Charities).

*Being Who You Say You Are – A Guide for Faith-Based Organisations* (Faithworks – Governance Hub, 2007)

*The Voluntary Sector Legal Handbook* (Sandy Adirondack – Directory of Social Change, 2001) – planned to be updated in early 2009. A comprehensive guide to voluntary sector law.

*Voluntary But Not Amateur* (Jacki Reason & Ruth Hayes – Directory of Social Change – new edition Spring 2009)

### Duties of trustees

Charity Commission publication *The Essential Trustee: What you need to know* (CC3)

*Good Governance: A Code for the Voluntary and Community Sector* available from the NCVO website.

Charity Commission online guidance *A Guide To Conflicts of Interest For Charity Trustees* (linked from The Essential Trustee publication)

Charity Commission publication *Trustee expenses and payments* (CC11)

*Reducing the Risks: A Guide to trustee liabilities* (Governance Hub – 2007)

*Best Behaviour: Using trustee codes of conduct to improve governance practice* (Tesse Akpeki, edited by Marta Maretich, 2004)

### Board and committee structures

*Good Governance: the chair's role* (Dorothy Dalton – NCVO, 2006)

*A Chair's First 100 Days* (Tesse Akpeki – NCVO, 2005)

*Charity Treasurer's Handbook* (Gareth Morgan – Directory of Social Change, 2008)

*The Honorary Treasurer's Handbook* (Les Jones & Tesse Akpeki; Edited by Marta Maretich – NCVO, 2006)

*Matters Reserved for the Board of Trustees (England and Wales)* (ICSA Guidance Note 080307.2008) – available on their website (go to guidance, publications and policy – guidance notes and best practice guides)

## Part two: Good Governance

### Good Governance

*The Governance of Public and Non-profit Organisations: what do boards do?* (Chris Cornforth (ed.) – Routledge, 2003)

*The Good Governance Action Plan for Voluntary Organisations* (Adirondack, Sandy – NCVO, 2002)

*Good Governance: A Code for the Voluntary and Community Sector* available from the NCVO website.

Charity Commission publication *The Hallmarks of an Effective Charity* (CC10)

*Managing Without Profit* (Mike Hudson – Penguin, 1999)

*Just About Managing? A Guide to Effective Management for Voluntary Organisations and Community Groups* (Sandy Adirondack – London Voluntary Service Council, 4th edition 2006)

### Strategic planning

*Thinking Ahead: An introduction to strategic planning* (Jake Eliot – NCVO, 2008)

### Financial responsibilities

Charity Commission *Accounting and reporting by charities: statement of recommended practice* (revised 2005)

Charity Commission publication *Charity Reporting and Accounting: The essentials* (CC15)

*The Good Financial Management Guide for the Voluntary Sector* (Paul Palmer, Fiona Young and Neil Finlayson – NCVO, 2005)

HMRC webpages at www.hmrc.gov.uk/charities/index.htm

*Charity Finance Yearbook* (Plaza Publishing) – a reference source for charity professionals, published annually.

Charity Commission publication *Investment of Charitable Funds: Basic Principles* (CC14)

Charity Commission Operational Guidance *Endowed charities: a total return approach to investment* (OG83)

*Investing responsibly: a practical introduction for charity trustees* (EIRIS foundation, 2005). A short guide to ethical investment available free to download from the Sustainable Funding section of the NCVO website.

*The Good Investment Guide for the Voluntary Sector* (Catherine Wood – NCVO, 2007)

*Practical Guide to Financial Management* (Kate Sayer – Directory of Social Change, 2007)

*A Practical Guide to VAT for Charities* (Kate Sayer – Directory of Social Change, 3rd edition, 2008)

*Full Cost Recovery Toolkit* (acevo) – free to download from www.fullcostrecovery.org.uk

*Full Cost Recovery Business Planner* (acevo, 2008) – an advanced version of the full cost recovery template – details at www.fullcostrecovery.org.uk

Charity Commission publication *Charities' Reserves* (CC19)

Property

Charity Commission publication *The Official Custodian for Charities' Land Holding Service* (CC13)

Charity Commission publication *Disposing of Charity Land* (CC28)

Charity Commission guidance *Permanent Endowment: What is it and when can it be spent?* CSD-1347A

Fundraising

*Trustees Guide to Fundraising* (Institute of Fundraising, 2007)

*Introductory Pack on Funding and Finance* (Institute of Fundraising – Finance Hub, 2006) – available to download from the NCVO website at www.ncvo-vol.org.uk/sfp

*Making Giving Go Further* (Institute of Fundraising, 2008) – available to download from www.tax-effectivegiving.org.uk

Charity Commission publication *Charities and Commercial Partners* (RS2)

NCVO guide *Brief Guide to Loan Finance for Trustees* (NCVO) – available from the Sustainable Funding Project section of the NCVO website.

Public service delivery and contracting

Charity Commission publication *Charities and Public Service Delivery* – An Introduction and Overview (CC37)

*Before signing on the dotted line: All you need to know about procuring public sector contracts* (Richard Whiter, John Plumb, Mohamed Hans & Keith Morris – NCVO, 2006)

Policy

*Living policy: A complete guide to creating and implementing policy in voluntary organisations* (Becky Forrester, Tesse Akpeki and Marta Maretich – NCVO, 2004)

Charity Commission publication *Cause for complaint: how charities manage complaints about their service* (RS11)

Risk management

Charity Commission *Accounting and reporting by charities: statement of recommended practice* (revised 2005)

Charity Commission online guidance *Charities and Risk Management*

Health and safety

Health and Safety Executive website – 'businesses' section of their website setting out information about how organisations can manage health and safety.

*Charity and Voluntary Workers: a guide to Health and Safety at work* (HSE, 2006)

*Health & Safety Handbook* (Al Hinde & Charlie Kavanagh – Directory of Social Change, 2001)

ICT

*From Nightmare to Nirvana – an ICT Survival Guide for Trustees* (ICT Hub, 2008) – free to download from NCVO's ICT development services website (www.icthub.org.uk)

Data protection

Information Commissioner's Office *Data Protection Guide*, including *Good Practice Notes* (for example, a training checklist for small and medium sized organisations)

Employment

*The Good Guide to Employment: Managing and Developing People in Voluntary and Community Organisations* (NCVO)

*The Board's Responsibility for Appraising the Chief Executive – a guide for chairs and trustees* (Dorothy Dalton – NCVO, 2005)

*Recruiting a New Chief Executive: A guide for trustees and chairs* (Dorothy Dalton – NCVO, 2005)

Volunteer management

*Volunteering England Good Practice Bank*, available at www.volunteering.org.uk

Relations with staff and volunteers

*Good Governance: the chief executive's role* (Dorothy Dalton – NCVO, 2007)

*Lost in Translation: A complete guide to Chair/Chief Executive Partnerships* (Tesse Akpeki – NCVO, 2006)

*A CEO's Guide to Board Development* (Association of Chief Executives of Voluntary Organisations)

*Your Chair and Board – a survival guide and toolkit for CEOs* (acevo, 2008)

### Equality and diversity

*Making Diversity Happen: A Guide for Voluntary and Community Organisations* (NCVO, 2003)

*Are you looking at me? A practical guide to recruiting a diverse workforce* (NCVO, 2004)

*Managing Diversity in the Workplace* (NCVO, 2003)

*The Good Guide to Employment* (Wendy Blake Ranken – NCVO, 2008) contains useful guidance on equality and diversity in the workplace.

### User involvement

Charity Commission publication *Users on Board: Beneficiaries who become trustees* (CC24)

*Building Strategic Board Diversity* (NCVO, 2008)

*Users on Board* (NCVO, 2008)

### Making a difference

*True Colours: Uncovering the full value of your organisation* (Jake Eliot and Richard Piper – NCVO, 2008)

*Funding better performance* (Meg Abdy and Heather Mayall – Performance Hub, 2006)

*Is your campaign making a difference?* (Jim Coe and Ruth Mayne – NCVO, 2008)

### Examples of quality systems

PQASSO – the Practical Quality Assurance System for Small Organisations – Charities Evaluation Services (www.ces-vol.org.uk )

Investors in People – www.investorsinpeople.co.uk

EFQM Excellence Model – www.efqm.org

The Becoming VISIBLE Operating Standards for community organisations (Community Matters)

Investing in Volunteers – www.investinginvolunteers.org.uk

Charity Commission website *Meeting our requirements – Annual returns*

### Public relations

*Better Communication = Better Governance* (Tesse Akpeki and Tess Woodcraft – NCVO, 2005)

### Collaborative working

Charity Commission publication *Collaborative Working and Mergers: An introduction* (CC34 – 2006)

Charity Commission publication *Collaborative Working and Mergers* (RS4, 2003)

NCVO collaborative working guidance (details on the collaborative working section of the NCVO website):

- *Should you collaborate? Key questions*
- *Joint working agreements*
- *Staffing a collaborative project*
- *ICT tools to support collaborative working*
- *Working together to achieve your mission*
- *Joint working for public service delivery*
- *Sharing back office services*
- *Merger*
- *National organisations with local groups*
- *Collaborative working to make more effective use of ICT*

*Due diligence demystified: What it is and how you manage it* (NCVO, 2006)

*Campaigning in Collaboration* (Sarah Shimmin and Gareth Coles– NCVO, 2007)

Cripps, Alan & Carter, Mary (2006) *Mergers: A guide to literature on mergers for voluntary and community sector organisations* (London Housing Foundation)

*The Nonprofit Mergers Workbook Part 1: The Leader's Guide to Considering, Negotiating and Executing a Merger* (David La Piana – Board Source. USA, 2000)

### Managing change

*From Here to There: Managing change in third sector organisations* (Jake Eliot and Julie Pottinger – NCVO, 2008)

### Handling conflict

*You're not listening to me! Dealing with disputes: mediation and its benefits for voluntary organisations* (Linda Laurance and Anne Radford – NCVO, 2003)

Charity Commission guidance *Conflicts in your charity: a statement of approach by the Charity Commission* (June 2008 – under Meeting our Requirements on the Charity Commission website).

Charity Commission publication *Complaints about charities* (CC47)

## Part three: Developing the Board

### Effective trustees

*National Occupational Standards for Trustees and Management Committee Members* – available from the UK Workforce Hub website.

*Living Values: a pocket guide for trustees* (Geraldine Blake, David Robinson, Matthew Smeardon – Governance Hub and Community Links, 2006)

### Learning and development

Third Sector Leadership Centre – www.thirdsectorleadership.org.uk

Trustee networking – visit Charity Trustee Networks' website at www.trusteenet.org.uk

Information about accredited learning opportunities or qualifications for trustees – UK Workforce Hub – www.ukworkforcehub.org.uk

Trustee E-learning – http://trusteelearning.org/

*The Good Governance Action Plan Workbook* (Tesse Akpeki – NCVO, 2005) includes exercises and lesson plans for trustee boards.

*Code of Governance Toolkit* (Peter Dyer – Governance Hub, 2006) includes exercises and activities for trustee boards.

### Building the board

*Good Practice in Trustee Recruitment – Toolkit* (Ruth Lesirge, Rosalind Oakley and Joanie Spears – Governance Hub, 2006)

Charity Commission publication *Finding New Trustees: What Charities Need to Know* (CC30)

Charity Commission publication *Start as you mean to go on: trustee recruitment and induction* (RS10)

Charity Commission publication *Trustee recruitment, selection and induction* (RS1)

Charity Commission *Declaration of Eligibility for Newly-Appointed Trustees* (CSD 1382) – available via a link from publication CC30 (see above) or via the About Charities section of the website

*Latest Trends in Charity Governance and Trusteeship* (Chris Cornforth – NCVO, 2001)

NCVO Trustee Bank – www.ncvo-vol.org.uk

*Starting on the right track – a guide to recruiting and inducting a new chair* (Governance Hub – NCVO, 2007)

### Board diversity

*Building Strategic board diversity* (NCVO, 2008)

*Users on Board* (NCVO, 2008)

*Trust Youth* (Governance Hub, BYC (British Youth Council) and CRAE (Children's Rights Alliance for England) – Governance Hub, 2006) – a guide to what being a trustee means for children and young people.

*Involving Young People* (Tesse Akpeki – NCVO, 2001)

*Recruiting and Supporting Black and Minority Ethnic Trustees* (Tesse Akpeki – NCVO, 2001)

### Induction

*Good Practice in Trustee Recruitment – Toolkit* (Ruth Lesirge, Rosalind Oakley and Joanie Spears – Governance Hub, 2006)

Charity Commission publication *The Essential Trustee* (CC3)

*Good Governance: A Code for the Voluntary and Community Sector* including a summary version, available from the NCVO website.

*National Occupational Standards for Trustees and Management Committee Members* available from the UK workforce hub website.

*Trustee and Management Committee National Occupational Standards – Toolkit* (Liza Ramrayka – NCVO, 2006)

*Mentoring for Chairs* (Governance Hub) – a report based on a Governance Hub mentoring pilot programme – available from the NCVO website.

*Setting up a network for chairs* (Governance Hub, 2007) – an overview of how to set up and organise a chairs' network

*Enhancing Trusteeship through Mentoring* (Tesse Akpeki and Arthur Brown – NCVO, 2001)

*Developing Trustee Boards: A Manual for Trainers* (Tesse Akpeki and Marta Maretich (ed.) – NCVO, 2002)

*A-Z of Good Governance* (Governance Hub, 2006) – a set of 26 postcards each featuring a different aspect of good governance, ideal for using in board development sessions. Available from NCVO.

### Effective meetings and decision-making

Charity Commission publication *Charities and Meetings* (CC48)

*The Minute Takers Handbook* (Lee Comer & Paul Ticher – Directory of Social Change, 2002)

ICSA sample terms of reference for committees, available from the ICSA website – Guidance, publications and policy and then Guidance notes

*The Good Membership Guide for the Voluntary Sector* (Stephen Iliffe – NCVO, 2004)

## Part four: Improving Governance

### Governance reviews

*Better Governance: An Introduction to Measuring and Improving Board Effectiveness* (Mark Parker – Governance Hub, 2006) – available from NCVO.

*Benchmarking governance* – www.boardscount.com

*Good Governance: A Code for the Voluntary and Community Sector* – available from the NCVO website.

*Code of Governance Toolkit* (Peter Dyer – Governance Hub, 2006) – available from NCVO.

*National Occupational Standards for Trustees and Management Committee Members* – available from the UK Workforce Hub website.

*The Good Governance Action Plan for Voluntary Organisations* (Sandy Adirondack – NCVO, 2002)

*The Effective Retreat Planner: A Guide for Trustees and Planners* (Terrie Temkin and Tesse Akpeki – NCVO, 2003)

*Tending your Board: A seasonal guide to improving how your board works* (Governance Hub/bassac, 2006)

*A-Z of Good Governance* – available from NCVO

### Trustee appraisal

*Trustee and Management Committee National Occupational Standards – Toolkit* (Liza Ramrayka – NCVO, 2006)

*Trustee Standards in Practice – A Guide for Smaller Organisations* (Governance Hub) – available free to download from the NCVO website.

# 25

# Useful organisations

ACRE (Action with Communities in Rural England)
Tel: 01285 653477
www.acre.org.uk

Action with Communities in Rural England is the national umbrella of the Rural Community Action Network (RCAN), which operates at national, regional and local level in support of rural communities across the country. ACRE aim to promote a healthy, vibrant and sustainable rural community sector that is well connected to policy and decision-makers who play a part in delivering this aim.

ACAS
Tel. 0845 474747
www.acas.org.uk

Acas (Advisory, Conciliation and Arbitration Service) aim to improve organisations and working life through better employment relations. Acas supply information, independent advice and training.

Association of Charitable Foundations
Tel: 020 7255 4499
www.acf.org.uk

The Association of Charitable Foundations (ACF) is the UK wide support organisation for grant-making trusts and foundations of all types.

Association of Charity Independent Examiners
Tel: 01302 828338
www.acie.org.uk

ACIE was launched in 1999 as an association for people who carry out IE -to give support to independent examiners and to provide information relevant to their examination work.

BoardSource
www.boardsource.org

BoardSource is an organisation based in the USA, dedicated to increasing the effectiveness of nonprofit organisations by strengthening their boards of directors.

Charities Aid Foundation
Tel: 01732 520000
www.cafonline.org

The Charities Aid Foundation works to create greater value for charities and social enterprise by transforming the way donations are made and the way charitable funds are managed.

CEDR
Tel: 020 7536 6000
www.cedr.com
www.cedr-solve.com
(dispute resolution service)

CEDR work to cut the cost of conflict and create a world of choice and capability in conflict prevention and resolution.

The Charity Commission for England and Wales
Tel: 0845 3000 218
www.charitycommission.gov.uk

The Charity Commission for England and Wales is established by law as the regulator and registrar of charities in England and Wales. The Commission's aim is to provide the best possible regulation of these in order to increase charities' efficiency and effectiveness and public confidence and trust in them. The Charity Commission website contains a range of publications and online guidance.

Charities Evaluation Services (CES)
Tel: 020 7713 5722
www.ces-vol.org.uk

CES offer training, consultancy, external evaluations and publications to help voluntary and community organisations strengthen the quality of their work and achieve better outcomes for service users. CES also publish the PQASSO Practical Quality Assurance System for Small Organisations.

Charity Finance Directors' Group
www.cfdg.org.uk
Tel: 0845 345 3192

The Charity Finance Directors' Group is a membership organisation specialising in helping charities to manage their accounting, taxation, audit and other finance related functions. Services include a free advertising facility for organisations seeking a new trustee or treasurer.

Charity Trustee Networks
Tel: 01483 230280
www.trusteenet.org.uk

CTN provide opportunities for trustees to share knowledge and experience with each other, signpost to information and services and give trustees a voice to influence national policy.

Community Matters
Tel: 020 7837 7887
www.communitymatters.org.uk

Community Matters is the National Federation for Community Organisations. Community Matters publish the VISIBLE Operating Standards for community organisations.

The Community Network
Tel: 020 7923 5250
www.community-network.org

Community Network's telephone conference call service is tailored to meet the needs of charities and voluntary agencies.

The Compact
Commission for the Compact:
www.thecompact.org.uk
Tel: 0121 237 5900
Compact Voice (based at NCVO):
www.compactvoice.org.uk
Tel: 020 7520 2453

The Compact is an agreement between Government and the voluntary and community sector in England. It recognises shared values, principles and commitments and sets out guidelines for how both parties should work together.

### Companies House

Tel: 0303 1234 500
www.companieshouse.gov.uk

The main functions of Companies House are to incorporate and dissolve limited companies, examine and store company information delivered under the Companies Act and related legislation and make this information available to the public. The Companies House website includes useful guidance for companies, directors and company secretaries.

### Confederation of Indian Organisations (UK) (CIO)

Tel: 020 7928 9889
www.cio.org.uk

CIO works with South Asian organisations in the UK. The aim of CIO is to provide and develop high quality services that strengthen these organisations and be a strong voice on policy issues that affect the South Asian community.

### Co-operatives UK

Tel: 0161 246 2900
www.cooperatives-uk.coop

Co-operatives UK promote and develop co-operative enterprises for an increasingly successful and sustainable co-operative economy.

### Criminal Records Bureau

Tel: 0870 90 90 811
www.crb.gov.uk

The CRB is an Executive Agency of the Home Office set-up to help organisations make safer recruitment decisions. An important part of the CRB's role is to provide access to criminal record information through its Disclosure service. This service enables organisations in the public, private and voluntary sectors to make safer recruitment decisions by identifying candidates who may be unsuitable for certain work, especially that involve children or vulnerable adults.

### Directory of Social Change

Tel: 08450 77 77 07
www.dsc.org.uk

The Directory of Social Change provide information and training to voluntary and community organisations.

### FundRaising Standards Board

www.frsb.org.uk
Tel: 0845 402 5442

The Fundraising Standards Board (FRSB) runs a self-regulatory scheme for fundraising in the UK. Membership is voluntary and charities that join are asked to adhere to to the Codes of Fundraising Practice and the FRSB's Fundraising Promise. The FRSB aims to be a mark of reassurance for the public as regards fundraising. The FRSB handles complaints from donors about fundraising issues.

### Health and Safety Executive

Tel: 0845 345 0055
www.hse.gov.uk

HSE's job is to protect people against risks to health or safety arising out of work activities. HSE conduct and sponsor research, promote training, provide an information, and advisory service and submit proposals for new or revised regulations and approved codes of practice. The 'businesses' section of the HSE website is a useful source of information about how organisations can manage health and safety.

### HM Revenue and Customs

Tel: 0845 302 0203 (charities helpline)
www.hmrc.gov.uk/charities/index.htm (charities webpages)

HMRC is responsible for collecting the bulk of tax revenue.

### Industrial and Provident Societies (Financial Services Authority)

Tel: 0845 606 9966 (option 3) (Industrial and Provident Societies)
www.fsa.gov.uk (for IPSs go to 'doing business' – small firms – mutual societies)

The Financial Services Authority (FSA) is an independent non-governmental body, given statutory powers by the Financial Services and Markets Act 2000. The FSA is also the registering authority for societies which register under the Industrial and Provident Societies Act 1965 (I&P Act 1965).

### Information Commissioner's Office

Tel: 08456 30 60 60
www.ico.gov.uk

The Information Commissioner's Office is the UK's independent authority set up to promote access to official information and to protect personal information. The ICO website includes guides to data protection and good practice notes.

### Institute of Chartered Secretaries and Administrators

Tel: 020 7580 4741
www.icsa.org.uk

ICSA is the leading professional body for company secretaries and senior administrators across all sectors. ICSA's Charity Secretaries' Group provides a forum for those working in company secretarial or senior administrative roles in the not-for-profit sector. It is open to ICSA members, students and non-members. ICSA's website includes guidance, publications, good practice information and example and specimen documents.

### Institute of Fundraising

Tel: 020 7840 1000
Tax-Effective Giving Helpline:
0845 458 4586
www.institute-of-fundraising.org.uk
www.tax-effectivegiving.org.uk

The Institute of Fundraising is the professional membership body for UK fundraisers. Its aim is to promote the highest standard of fundraising practice.

### Investing in Volunteers

www.investinginvolunteers.org.uk

Investing in Volunteers is the UK quality standard for all organisations which involve volunteers in their work. IiV is delivered in England by Volunteering England.

### The Media Trust

Tel: 020 7217 3717
www.mediatrust.org

Media Trust works in partnership with the media industry to build effective communications for the charity and voluntary sectors. Services include Media and Communications training, Campaigns, Media Trust Productions, Community Newswire, Community Channel, Media Matching and Youth Media.

### National Association for Voluntary and Community Action

Tel: 0114 278 6636
www.navca.org.uk

NAVCA is the national voice of local third sector infrastructure in England. NAVCA members work with 164,000 local third sector groups and organisations that provide community services, regenerate neighbourhoods, promote volunteering and tackle discrimination in partnership with local public bodies. NAVCA's website lists contact details of member organisations.

### National Council for Voluntary Organisations (NCVO)

Tel: 0800 2 798 798 (helpdesk) or
020 7713 6161 (office)
www.ncvo-vol.org.uk

NCVO gives voice and support to civil society and is the largest umbrella body for the voluntary and community sector in England, with sister councils in Scotland, Wales and Northern Ireland. NCVO's helpdesk and website provide access to a range of support and information services. NCVO's services include:

- Governance and leadership – supporting good governance in the voluntary and community sector with resources, toolkits, information and advice.
- Sustainable Funding Project – The Sustainable Funding Project encourages and enables voluntary and community organisations to explore and exploit a full range of funding and financing options to develop a sustainable funding mix.
- Collaborative working team – offer good practice information and advice to help voluntary and community organisations make decisions about whether and how to work collaboratively.
- ICT development services – signposts voluntary and community organisations to resources that can help them make the most of technology. The work of the team builds on the legacy of work achieved by NCVO as accountable body of the ICT Hub (at www.icthub.org.uk).

- Campaigning and advocacy – a central resource for influencing, advocacy and campaigning in the voluntary and community sector. It supports organisations of all sizes that want to increase the impact of their campaigns, by communicating best practice principles and giving people the skills they need to put these into practice.

National Housing Federation
Tel: 020 7067 1010
www.housing.org.uk

The National Housing Federation represent 1,300 not-for-profit housing associations in England and campaign for better housing and neighbourhoods.

National Mediation Helpline – help in finding mediation services
Tel: 0845 6030809 (helpline)
www.nationalmediationhelpline.com

The Helpline's aim is to provide a simple, low cost method of resolving a wide range of disputes. The serviced will explain the basic principles of mediation, answer general enquiries relating to mediation and put you in contact with one of the Helpline's accredited mediation providers.

Northern Ireland Council for Voluntary Action (NICVA)
Tel: 028 9087 7777
www.nicva.org

NICVA is the Northern Ireland Council for Voluntary Action, the umbrella body for voluntary and community organisations in Northern Ireland.

Office of the Third Sector
Tel: 020 7276 6400
www.cabinetoffice.gov.uk/third_sector.aspx

As part of the Cabinet Office, the Office of the Third Sector leads work across government to support the environment for a thriving third sector (voluntary and community groups, social enterprises, charities, cooperatives and mutuals), enabling the sector to campaign for change, deliver public services, promote social enterprise and strengthen communities.

Sandy Adirondack legal update
www.sandy-a.co.uk/legal.htm

Sandy Adirondack's legal update for voluntary organisations provides information of a general nature for management committees/trustees and staff of voluntary organisations about legal changes over the past year, and forthcoming changes.

Scottish Council for Voluntary Organisations (SCVO)
Tel: 0131 556 3882
www.scvo.org.uk

The Scottish Council for Voluntary Organisations is the national body representing the voluntary sector. SCVO seeks to advance the values and shared interests of the voluntary sector.

Third Sector Leadership Centre
Tel: 01491 571 454 ext. 2184
www.thirdsectorleadership.org.uk

The Third Sector Leadership Centre is a catalyst to raise the profile of leadership and leadership development across the third sector.

The centre, a project within the UK Workforce Hub and based at the Henley Management College, has been set up to support leaders within the third sector, and to help them move forward.

UK Workforce Hub
Tel: 0800 2 798 798 (helpdesk)
www.ukworkforcehub.org.uk

The UK Workforce Hub helps third sector organisations make the best of their paid staff, volunteers and trustees through workforce development. In England, the Hub is hosted by NCVO.

The Hub's website is a useful source of information about learning and skills for trustees, including the National Occupational Standards for Trustees and Management Committee Members.

Volunteering England
Tel: 0845 305 6979
www.volunteering.org.uk

Volunteering England is England's volunteer development agency, working to support and increase the quality, quantity, impact and accessibility of volunteering throughout England. The Volunteering England website includes a Good Practice Bank of information and guidance on volunteer recruitment and management.

Wales Council for Voluntary Action (WCVA) Cyngor Gweithredu Gwirfoddol Cymru (CGGC)
Tel: 0800 2888329
www.wcva.org.uk

WCVA is the voice of the voluntary sector in Wales, representing and campaigning for voluntary organisations, volunteers and communities.

Working for a Charity
Tel: 020 7520 2512
www.wfac.org.uk

Working For A Charity exists to promote the voluntary sector as a positive career option for those seeking paid employment in the sector.

# 26

# Glossary

The entries include terms that trustees are likely to come across frequently.

**Accounting records**
Financial records (books, computerised accounting systes, invoices, receipts and other documentation) that are used to prepare annual accounts.

**Accounts**
Annual statements of the charity's financial position.

**Assets**
Items owned by a charity which have a monetary value. Fixed assets have a permanence normally exceeding one year (eg freehold property) and current assets are items that are expected to be changed or realised within one year (eg cash in the bank).

**Best practice**
In the context of the Good Trustee Guide, suggested guidance on how a particular area of trustee responsibility could be carried out, based on examples of the approach taken by other charities. This may take the form of case study examples or via reference to other guidance (for example, the Code of Governance).

**Board of trustees**
The group of people who govern the charity and have ultimate legal responsibility for all the charity's activities. Your charity might use a different term such as executive committee, management committee, council, governing body or steering committee.

### Breach of trust
A breach of trust occurs when a trustee or board acts outside its powers, as defined in the charity's governing document, or acts in breach of charity law. Examples include unlawful investments, unlawful trading or political activities, unlawful payments to trustees and using charity assets on activities not included in the charity's objects.

### Case study
In the context of the Good Trustee Guide, an example of how another charity has carried out an area of trustee responsibility. Case studies may be of named charities, or anonymous, or hypothetical.

### Charitable company limited by guarantee
A charity with the legal status of a private, non-profit-making company with members rather than shareholders. The liability of the members is limited to a nominal sum (usually £1 or £5) if the company does not have sufficient assets to pay a debt.

### Chief executive
The most senior member of the charity's paid staff. In your charity you may use a different name, such as the Director, general secretary, or director general.

In charitable companies, it is unlikely that this person will be a trustee of the charity so, even if called a director, he or she will not be a director as defined by company law.

### Code of conduct
A type of policy that sets standards for individual behaviour. Many organisations have codes of conduct for staff and the members of the trustee board.

### Code of Governance
In the Good Trustee Guide, Code of Governance refers to Good Governance: A Code for the Voluntary and Community Sector (see chapter 1). However, in a wider context, the term 'code of governance' refers to a set of principles outlining how an organisation should be governed.

### Code of practice
A type of policy that establishes standards for practice, providing guidelines for carrying out organisational activities.

### Company secretary
Many charitable companies appoint a company secretary whose duties are to ensure that the charity complies with the requirements of company law. This is no longer a legal requirement.

### Constitution
A term sometimes used to describe the governing document of a charity.

### Directors
Under company law, the group of people elected or nominated by the members of the company to run it. In a charitable company the company directors are also the charity trustees. In The Good Trustee Guide company directors are referred to as trustees.

### Fiduciary
This term is used where one person has rights and powers which he or she is bound to exercise for the benefit of another. The trustees of a charitable company, as company directors, stand in a fiduciary relationship with the company, so that they must act in the best interests of the company and not in their own interests.

### Funds
- Unrestricted funds – funds that are free to be spent by the trustees on anything that will further the charity's purposes.
- Designated funds – a form of unrestricted fund that trustees have allocated for special purposes (e.g. the construction of a new building).
- Restricted funds – subject to specific conditions imposed by the donor and binding on the trustees. Can only be spent on the purpose intended.
- Permanent endowment – Assets which have been given to the charity to keep in perpetuity but with the charity benefiting from the income that can be earned from the asset.

**Governing document/Governing instrument**
The documents setting out the objects, powers and rules of the charity.

**Governance**
"the systems and processes concerned with ensuring the overall direction, effectiveness, supervision and accountability of an organisation"[1]

**Guidance**
Suggestions, not necessarily prescriptive, about how the trustee board would like to see an issue implemented. Guidance often takes the form of examples of best practice in the sector.

**Honorary officers**
The chair, vice-chair, secretary and treasurer who undertake particular roles and carry out certain duties, but as 'first among equals'.

**Incorporated charity**
Has a separate legal identity (contracts can be signed in the name of the charity, and the charity can sue and be sued). An incorporated charity has limited liability for trading losses and under contracts (though not for some other liabilities). Charitable companies are normally incorporated as companies limited by guarantee, or more rarely by shares or under royal charter or by Act of Parliament.

**Investments**
Include shares, rental or lease of land, loans and units in collective invesment schemes. Investments do not include the process of purchasing items such as land for future sale which are usually described as trading.

**Liability**
A liability arises where a person or organisation is under an obligation to make a payment under contract or in respect of an unlawful act.

**Mission statement**
A statement setting out the purpose or aims of the charity.

**Objects**
A legal term for the main aims of a charity, as set out in the governing documents.

**Patron**
An honorary title given to a well-known person openly associated with the charity, but who takes neither the power nor the responsibility of trusteeship.

**Policy**
Written guidelines for the organisation created by the trustee board. Policies set standards and expectations for staff, volunteers and others. They establish the organisation's official position on questions of procedure and ethics. The trustee board also uses policy to regulate its own activity.

**Powers**
The actions which a charity can take, as set out in the governing documents and as defined in law.

**Protocol or Procedure**
A policy or part of a policy giving detailed guidance on how a certain activity will be carried out.

**Registered charity**
A charity registered with the Charity Commission. It has a charity number.

**Reserves**
Funds held by the charity that are freely available for use but not spent.

**Stakeholder**
People or organisations who have an interest, or stake, in the charity. Their interest may be formal (eg members) or less formal (eg the general public). See page XX.

**SORP**
The Statement of Recommended Practice (SORP) on Accounting by Charities. The SORP contains guidance on the production of charity annual reports and accounts based on the The Charities (Accounts and Reports) Regulations. See page 81.

[1] *The Governance of Public and Non-profit Organizations: what do boards do?* (Cornforth, CJ (ed.) – Routledge, 2003).

### Trustee
A voting member of the governing body responsible for the general control and management of a charity. In your charity the trustees might be known by a different term, such as a management committee member, director, council member, executive committee member or governor. In The Good Trustee Guide the term 'trustee' is used. Trustees are almost always unpaid for their role as a trustee.

### Unincorporated charity
Has no separate legal identity. Contracts, leases, property, etc. have to be held in the name of the trustees.